Class in Contemporary Britain

2nd Edition

Ken Roberts

palgrave
macmillan

First edition 2001 (previously entitled *Class in Modern Britain*)
Reprinted three times
Second edition 2011

First published 2011 by
PALGRAVE MACMILLAN

Palgrave Macmillan in the UK is an imprint of Macmillan Publishers Limited,
registered in England, company number 785998, of Houndmills, Basingstoke,
Hampshire RG21 6XS.

Palgrave Macmillan in the US is a division of St Martin's Press LLC,
175 Fifth Avenue, New York, NY 10010.

Palgrave Macmillan is the global academic imprint of the above companies
and has companies and representatives throughout the world.

Palgrave® and Macmillan® are registered trademarks in the United States,
the United Kingdom, Europe and other countries.

ISBN 978–0–230–23866–4

This book is printed on paper suitable for recycling and made from fully
managed and sustained forest sources. Logging, pulping and manufacturing
processes are expected to conform to the environmental regulations of the
country of origin.

A catalogue record for this book is available from the British Library.

A catalog record for this book is available from the Library of Congress.

10   9   8   7   6   5   4   3   2   1
20   19   18   17   16   15   14   13   12   11

Printed in China

Contents

List of Tables

List of Figures

List of Boxes

Introduction

1

Class inequalities today

Britain today is one of the most unequal countries in the western world, headed only by Portugal and the USA (Wilkinson and Pickett, 2009). Income inequality in Britain widened dramatically during the 1980s, due mainly to changes in the tax and welfare benefit regimes (which favoured the better-off). Inequalities stabilized during the early-1990s, then widened again after 1997 when New Labour was in government, due mainly to greater disparities in earnings from employment (National Equality Panel, 2010). In 2008 the median pay of full-time employees was £479 per week (£521 for men and £412 for women) (www.statistics.gov.uk). The top 10 per cent all had weekly earnings in excess of £956, while the lowest 10 per cent all earned less than £262. In 2006 the chief executives of the top 100 stock exchange listed companies earned an average of £53,846 per week (£2.8 million a year). Their pay had risen by 102 per cent since 2000, while average earnings rose by just 29 per cent (www.theregister. co.uk). Their *weekly* pay in 2006 was roughly twice the earnings of the average male in an entire year. Wealth in Britain is distributed even more unequally than income. The richest one per cent own over a third of all marketable assets (excluding housing). The bottom 50 per cent share just one per cent of the nation's total wealth (www.statistics.gov.uk). We need class analysis not just to describe, but to explain the causes and consequences of these inequalities.

There are serious consequences. Compared with children of top professionals and managers, the children of unskilled workers are 50 per cent more likely to die in infancy. As adults, the unskilled group are roughly twice as likely to die before reaching retirement age, and ten times more likely to have no natural teeth. Residents in Britain's most prosperous neighbourhoods can expect to live disability-free into their 70s, whereas in Britain's most deprived neighbourhoods disability-free life typically ends when people are in their 50s (Marmot Review, 2010). Children from the top group are six times more likely to go to university, and they are also six times more likely to stay in the top group than are those born at the bottom to rise to the top (Reid, 1998). Class is related to many other things – the ages at which people marry, how they vote, church attendance and risks of criminal conviction.

There are areas in which everyone loses in countries like Britain where inequalities are exceptionally wide. The most unequal western countries have the highest crime rates, the largest prison populations (relative to their total populations), more obese men and women, more teen pregnancies, lower educational attainments, and people die younger. It is not just poverty: inequality *per se* is a killer. There are areas in which even the richest people benefit from less inequality than exists in Britain: they live longest in the most equal western countries (Wilkinson and Pickett, 2009). There are no areas in which everyone appears to benefit from exceptionally wide inequalities. The most unequal countries are not necessarily the richest. So what are the obstacles to making Britain more equal? Class theory has answers.

Class inequalities and capitalism

The main reason why Britain has such wide economic inequalities is that the economy is capitalist, and capitalism has always generated much wider economic inequalities than any other kind of modern economy. We know this on account of 'natural experiments' that occurred during the twentieth century. In Yugoslavia there was a period between the 1950s and 1980s when work organizations were worker-managed, and the pay of all employees, including plant directors, was set by workers councils. These councils always voted to pay their directors more than rank and file employees, but the typical difference between top executive and average pay was around 2:1 (International Labour Office, 1962; Koyama, 1995). Plant directors under Soviet-style central economic planning were treated somewhat more generously. At different times and in different places the top:bottom pay ratio was between 2:1 and 13:1 (Ferge, 1979; Lane, 1982; Lane and O'Dell, 1978; Matthews, 1978; Yanowitch, 1977). In Britain today it is around 100:1.

Britain is one of the most unequal capitalist countries because its market economy is among the least regulated, meaning that pay levels (among other matters) do not have to be agreed between business leaders, trade unions and government. Put bluntly, owners and top managers pay themselves handsomely 'because they can'. However, Britain is simply one of the more extreme cases. All capitalist economies require vast economic inequalities: they need separate wealthy classes of capitalist owners in order to drive their market systems. We know this because of another set of 'natural experiments' that occurred towards the end of the twentieth century following the collapse of communism in Eastern Europe. Some initial privatizations of state industries were via vouchers which were sold cheaply (sometimes given away) to employees and the general public, thus turning them all into capitalists and, it was hoped, enthusiastic supporters of the change of system. What happened? Nothing! This was the problem. There were no changes in work practices in the plants. There was no new investment. A separate capitalist class is needed that is willing to dismiss employees, impose new work practices, and procure new investment (by borrowing, if necessary) in search of spectacular profits. Thus before long the new market economies had created new classes of capitalist 'oligarchs' (see, for example, Hoffman, 2002).

Markets are said to be more effective that any other coordinating mechanism for generating growth and thereby raising the incomes and living standards of all social classes. So everyone is supposed to benefit from the wide inequalities that a capitalist system requires. The proof is said to be that the world's oldest, most mature capitalist market economies (the western countries) enjoy the world's highest standards of living, and the convincing manner in which the west out-performed the communist bloc and won the Cold War. However, during the twenty-first century some long-standing strengths of capitalism may be regarded as serious liabilities. First, economic growth is no longer making people happier or more content with their lives (Layard, 2005). Once populations have been lifted well clear of poverty, further improvements in living standards cease to make them more satisfied. Second, growth now threatens to destabilize the natural environment on which human survival depends. Third, a shift in the class balance of power in favour of the very wealthy (the reasons are explained in chapter 7), means that nearly all the benefits of economic growth now go to those at the top while the bottom half or bottom third struggle to maintain their living standards.

Challenges for class theory and research

The job of class theory and research is to explain these patterns and trends in economic inequalities, and the consequences. Is class theory delivering?

Class has always been among sociology's strongest unifying concepts. Whatever their areas of specialization – economic life, the family, crime, education, politics etc – sociologists have also been interested in social class. This is because class positions have consequences in all parts of people's lives. Class analysis reveals links between the economic, the political, the social and the cultural. At any rate, this is the goal and promise of class analysis. However, in very recent times there has been a tendency for the study of class to become just another sociological specialism in which a coterie of class experts address one another and are ignored by the rest of their discipline. In so far as this is the case sociology as a whole is poorer. Class needs to remain a unifying concept. Latterly, class researchers have conceded that any diminished impact has been due, at least partly, to their own deficiencies.

In 1996 Harriett Bradley identified three challenges that class theory and research needed to address:

- Changes in the class structure.
- The increased importance, or at least awareness, of other social divisions, particularly gender and ethnic divisions.
- Postmodern thought.

Addressing change is a problem for class research partly on account of the limited available and readily comprehensible vocabulary. The standard language of class analysis – middle class and working class, sometimes prefixed by upper or lower – seems to set the scene in times past. Equally challenging, some of the big questions of the twentieth century are now dead and need to be replaced. For much of the last century an issue addressed repeatedly was whether the working class was likely to become the revolutionary force that Karl Marx (1818–1883) predicted. Clearly this is not happening, at least for the time being. Another issue that has been investigated to exhaustion is why working class children are out-performed in education. Either we now know the answers or the question needs replacing.

Divisions become an issue for sociology only when they are believed to be socially constructed, which has always been the case for class divisions. Race and gender have a different intellectual history. Until the Second World War, race was usually treated as a scientific category. Until second-wave feminism insisted otherwise in the 1960s, it was believed that women had been emancipated by first-wave feminism and that the remaining differences in the lives of men and women were expressions of their different biological natures. Ethnicity, race and gender are now all believed to be socially constructed categories, and in Britain these constructions changed radically during the second half of the twentieth century. Britain became a multi-ethnic, multi-cultural country. Women today play a much more prominent role than formerly in the labour market and in public life more generally. The different distributions of men and women, and different ethnic groups, between different occupation-based social classes is an obvious issue for class research to address, but the challenge is deeper than this. The experience of being middle class, or being working class, is likely to vary by both gender and ethnicity. Moreover, children are simultaneously socialized as boys and girls, into different social classes, and different ethnic groups, and these different identities must surely be fused together.

Modern thought was characterized by a faith in reason: confidence that rational beings who took account of all the evidence would discover the right answers, and would agree on these answers. The postmodern challenge is the claim that equally rational observers, confronting exactly the same evidence, may come to radically different conclusions. This challenge confronts all areas of sociological enquiry and, indeed, all disciplines (the natural sciences as well as the social sciences and humanities). In sociology in general, and in class analysis in particular, a response has been to treat lay 'theories' (everyday ideas) about class and other aspects of life with greater respect, and to cease treating expert views as the final word.

During the last ten years class researchers have accepted the need for renewal and have responded to Harriett Bradley's challenges (see Crompton and Scott, 2000; Devine and Savage, 2000), as will become evident throughout this book. However, class analysis has a heritage that must not be jettisoned wholesale.

In this opening chapter we next consider the meaning(s) of the word class. We see that different sociologists have defined class in rather different ways, but with important common denominators, and these do not need renewal. Class theory has a track record, a heritage on which to build. That said, this chapter and the entire book recognize that class theory and research currently face very serious challenges. The chapter concludes with a book plan – an explanation of the ground to be covered in each of the subsequent chapters.

What is class?

Anyone who is not entirely new to sociology knows that, although class is one of the most-used terms in the entire discipline, there is no agreed definition. All books on the subject must necessarily point out that Karl Marx and Max Weber, and functionalist sociologists, have defined class in different ways. Actually there are no longer any sociologists who stick faithfully to the original ideas of Marx or Weber, or full-strength functionalism, so the prefix 'neo' is often attached to present-day Marxists, Weberians and functionalists.

Karl Marx (1818–1883)

Marx was a German, a travelling scholar and would-be revolutionary, who settled in England from 1849 where he collaborated with Friedrich Engels who was also from Germany, from a family engaged in the textile industry. Engels became a socialist while a student, became Manchester-based while representing his family business, wrote a book about the industrial working class in that city, then began his association with Marx.

Everyone has heard of Karl Marx because he developed a theory that was to become the world's main change ideology of the twentieth century. He is the source of the most powerful critique of capitalism that has ever been produced. Marx argued that there were just two main classes in capitalist societies: first, the owners of the means of production, the bourgeoisie or capitalist class and second, the proletariat or working class. Phrases such as 'means of production' will be properly defined in due course. For present purposes Marx's meaning will be clear. Marx forecast that over time other classes would tend to disappear, that capitalist societies would be progressively polarized into their two main classes, and that conflict between these classes would lead eventually to the downfall of capitalism.

Present-day Marxists do not necessarily believe any of this. In sociology they are most likely to believe only that Marx's ideas are a good starting point. They recognize that capitalist societies have not become polarized, and that, in addition to the two main classes, there are additional classes in so-called ambiguous or contradictory locations. Again, these terms will be explained properly later on. Present-day Marxists acknowledge that the working class has not become a revolutionary force and seek to explain why. They are also most likely to accept that, while classes have an economic base, other factors – politics, ideology, race and gender divisions – can play important roles in class formation.

Indeed, so many modifications to the original theory have been introduced that it is sometimes difficult nowadays to distinguish the ideas of Marxists from those of other sociologists, except that the former always start by identifying classes in terms of their 'relationships to the means of production'.

Erik Olin Wright, an American sociologist, is probably the discipline's most prominent living, Marxist class theorist. His class schemes are discussed in detail in chapter 2, but to anticipate, in addition to the working class and owners (who can be sub-divided according to their numbers of employees, if any), there are managers who are salaried yet perform functions of capital (controlling workers and otherwise administering businesses in their employers' interests) and professionals with expert knowledge and skills who have to be trusted to use their skills and knowledge in their employers' interests. Managers and professionals are both said to receive exceptional rewards (compared with other employees) in exchange for their loyalty. The point to note is that these additional classes are derivative from the basic division and conflict of interests between capitalists and workers. Wright has also explained how Marxist class analysis can be rendered compatible with the perpetuation of the capitalist system. Compromises are said to be possible which serve the interests of the capitalist class while also satisfying the working class's short-term demands, and such compromises can be repeated again and again, thus maintaining the system (see Wright, 2000).

Max Weber (1864–1920)

Weber was another German, but unlike Marx, Max Weber spent his entire working life in his own country. Weber came a generation after Marx, and it is often said, with justification, that Weber's work is best understood as a debate with Marx, or probably more accurately, a debate with the ghost of Marx since it was the Marxist thinking of Weber's own lifetime with which he was engaged.

Whereas Marx said that classes were defined by their relationships to the means of production, Weber claimed that classes arose in market places, the labour market being the crucial market place in this context. So there was a class of people who hired, and another class who sold their labour power. These seem very much like Marx's two main classes. True, but whereas for Marx it was experiences at work (relationships to the means of production), for Weber it was the processes of gaining work (or hiring labour) and the rewards (life-chances) that arose from this, that were crucial. Also, Weber's conceptualization allows classes with different types of property, and selling different types of labour power, to be identified, and there is no assumption that over time other divisions will weaken and that we will be left with just two main classes. Any sociology that places people into classes according to the types of labour that they offer or the jobs that they do (manual or white-collar, for example) is liable to be categorized as neo-Weberian. Neo-Marxists who recognize managers and professionals as distinct classes thereby converge with Weberian thinking.

All told, Weber took the view that matters were much more complicated than Marx had suggested. Apart from offering a different definition of class, Weber also distinguished class from status. Scholars still argue over exactly what Weber meant by class and status, but for present purposes it is sufficient to understand how and why Weber is seen as having advocated a multidimensional view of stratification. He argued, as explained above, that classes were formed in market places, whereas, in Weber's view, status groups could be identified by the honour or prestige attached to their styles of life. Whereas Marx believed that other inequalities arose from an economic base of class divisions (though present-day Marxists acknowledge at least some limited autonomy for the cultural and political spheres), Weber argued that different inequalities had different sources, and that although in the real world the different types of stratification (into classes and status groups) interacted, neither was reducible to the other. Weber believed that political parties could be based on either classes or status groups, or factions of either, but that political success or failure was not governed entirely by the strength of parties' bases because much depended on the political skills of the movements' leaders.

Whether it is possible and, if so, whether it is useful to distinguish class from status is an issue that intrigues some specialists in class analysis but can be relied on to turn-off any wider potential audience. Tak Wing Chan and John Goldthorpe (2004) show that there is a status hierarchy in Britain, with people's positions indicated by the occupations of their closest friends, and that while this status hierarchy is related to class positions, there are variations of status within classes. Moreover, they show that status (as measured by themselves), is superior to their class measurements in predicting people's preferences as regards music to listen to and newspapers to read. Hence their case for keeping class and status separate. The contrary view is that, in everyday real life, class and status differences are fused together when people judge who are their equals, who is above and who is beneath them in the social hierarchy (see, for example, Bottero, 2005). This argument is an example of what Rosemary Crompton (1998) calls pseudo-debates in class theory, because it is possible for both sides to be correct in their own arguments.

Nowadays sociologists can qualify for the neo-Weberian tag in many different ways. It may be their interest in market processes and outcomes. It may be their identification of class divisions among workers. It may be because they do not prioritize any, but recognize many factors (jobs, education, and housing, for example) as helping to fix individuals' positions in the system of stratification (see Box 1.1). Or it may be because they focus on status, probably, in practice, the prestige attached to occupations (though this is not what Weber himself meant by status), when measuring class. Indeed, any non-Marxist, non-functionalist (see below) sociology is liable to be labelled as neo-Weberian.

Box 1.1   Social stratification and social divisions

Social stratification is the most all-embracing term used in sociology when analysing inequalities. There is a deliberate geological analogy (which should not be taken too literally) – strata of rock (people) lying on top of one another.

All known societies have been stratified, and sociologists have identified different types of stratification systems – slavery, estates, castes and the class systems of modern societies. Weber introduced a further distinction between class and status. Class systems are different from the types of stratification that existed in earlier societies.

- First, classes are relatively open, meaning that mobility is possible (and quite common).
- Second, classes have an economic base (how we earn our livings) rather than being based on law or religion. So mobility does not require legal verification, or a religious ceremony, or the permission of one's owner: people simply change their jobs.

Social division is an even more all-embracing term. Here the groups may exist in parallel rather than above and beneath each other. Stratification is just one possibility: one of many types of social division. Sociologists usually speak of gender and ethnicity as bases for social divisions. The extent to which one group (a sex or ethnic group) is above others, and how class, gender and ethnic divisions interact, then become matters for research and debate (as we shall see throughout the following chapters).

Functionalism

This theory was popular and influential in mid-twentieth century North American sociology. It explains social practices in terms of the functions that they perform for their wider societies. So functionalists have argued that social stratification is functional. They claim that inequalities motivate people with the required talent to compete to enter, then to perform as effectively as possible in, important positions. They also argue that inequalities help to integrate societies by affirming the importance of well-rewarded positions, and expressing the wider society's approval and gratitude to the incumbents.

Nowadays full-strength functionalism has few, if any, supporters in sociology. The criticisms have been devastating. Functionalism confuses effects with causes. As regards stratification, it has been counter-argued that, rather than integrating society, inequalities are just as likely to provoke conflict. Also, inequalities can obstruct the ascent of talent to important positions. However, functionalism still reigns in everyday commonsense and economic theory. It is said that the higher earners must remain so, or become even better paid, in order to keep them in their jobs, and that the rewards that they receive are necessary compensation for the effort, training or responsibility, and no more than commensurate with the value of their work to society. Market processes, if allowed to operate freely, are said to ensure that the rewards people receive match the value that they add to the goods and services that they help to produce and sell.

There is a softer version of functionalism in sociology which maintains simply that there are functional pre-requisites or imperatives for the survival of any society: that there must be procedures for rearing children and resolving disputes, for example. It is argued that all practices can be analysed to establish the ways and extent to which they are functional (and dysfunctional). Sociologists who have examined stratification in this way have claimed that some inequality is inevitable, for the reasons given by full strength functionalism, but they admit that this does not explain the particular types and degrees of inequality that are found in different societies.

Nowadays most sociologists concur that 'conflict theories' offer the more plausible and powerful explanations. Both Marx and Weber are regarded as conflict theorists for these purposes. They explained inequalities in terms of the relative power that different groups were able to mobilize, in Marx's case in the relationships of production, and for Weber in market places (in the case of classes). Conflict theorists argue that the rewards of very well-paid employee groups have far less to do with the value of their work to society-at-large than their value to their employers.

Functionalism lives on in sociological class analysis only in so far as some sociologists conceptualize class 'gradationally'. Positions or individuals are portrayed as positioned along a continuous scale on which there are no clear divisions. This is the view of class that functionalism fosters – a ladder up which the talented can climb, with people at every level admiring and emulating those above. The theory (functionalism) that accounts for the sliding scale outcome is usually pushed well into the background nowadays, but some sociologists still believe that its model of inequalities is the one that approximates most closely to social reality. Gradational class scales do not necessarily assume consensus. Whether people feel that their own and other peoples positions are fair or unfair can remain an issue for research (see Bottero and Prandy, 2003). However, functionalist, consensus theories of class necessarily lead to the class structure being conceptualized gradationally.

Making a living

Sociologists are not in total agreement, but neither are we hopelessly at loggerheads over how to define class. Whether they are Marxists, Weberians or functionalists, sociologists have been agreed that classes have an economic foundation: they are composed of people with common experiences of making their livings. So people are invariably 'classed' at least partly on the basis of their occupations. However, we shall see in the following chapters that some sociologists now take the view that class positions depend not only on how people earn, but also on how they spend their money. They argue that class identities today are signalled and constructed partly on the basis of the neighbourhoods where people live, the houses that they buy or rent, the types of cars that they drive, and so on.

Sociologists are also agreed that modern societies' class systems of stratification are very different from the estates, castes and master-slave relationships that have been present elsewhere (see also Box 1.1, p 8).

- Feudal estates were legally defined entities. The different estates of the realm (Lords, church and commoners) all had their own legally defined rights and responsibilities.
- Under a caste system people are born into and must remain in a particular caste. The system is legitimized by religion, and all the castes have prescribed total ways of life from which the members cannot escape.
- Under slavery one group actually owns another rather than just purchases their labour power.

None of the sociological theories of class confuse this system of stratification with estates, castes or slavery.

Why class matters

Another point of agreement among all class theorists is that class matters; that class makes a difference in most areas of people's lives. Some 20 years ago there were claims that class had become a zombie concept and had ceased to do useful work in sociology (Beck, 1992; Pahl, 1989). However, in any society with wide economic inequalities, class is unlikely ever to become a redundant concept. In the present, just as in the past, their class positions make a considerable difference to people's health and education. This is just the beginning of the list. Compared with unskilled workers, managers and professionals are twice as likely to have made a will, to regard religion as very important, to do voluntary work, to go to the cinema, to visit wine bars and to take holidays away from home. The unskilled are twice as likely to 'worry all the time about being a victim of crime'. Managers and professionals spend four times as much on leisure goods and services, and in this class mothers with children aged under five are 30 times more likely than unskilled working class mothers to have full-time jobs (Reid, 1998). Why are all these things class-related? The relationships are strong. Class differences are huge. There is usually no need to apply statistical tests to see if they are significant. Class theory seeks and delivers explanations. Without class theory the differences remain inexplicable.

The socio-psychological and cultural dimensions of class

Sociologists who study class have other things in common. We share what we all feel to be well-grounded assumptions. Marxists, Weberians and functionalists all agree that their class locations are liable to get into people's heads and make impressions on their minds, their consciousness and unconsciousness. It is impossible to explain all the things that are related to class unless there is such imprinting. Income and wealth are likely to be the mediating variables in some things that class predicts, like going to the cinema and wine bars, and on holidays. But class is also related to people's attitudes: the importance that they attach to religion, whether they believe that it is government's task to provide citizens with jobs if they want them, to provide decent housing if people cannot otherwise afford it, and to reduce income inequalities (Reid, 1998). Why should any of this be so if class did not somehow get into people's heads?

It would be remarkable if class had no such effects given that we spend so much time at work, women as well as men nowadays, all those hours per week, and all those years throughout our adult lives. People do not necessarily stick in the same jobs, but, as we shall see in later chapters, they tend to stick in the same classes of jobs. If not, they tend to follow characteristic trajectories, like from skilled worker to supervisor, or junior to senior manager. People tend to associate with others in the same classes – at work, in their neighbourhoods – and so they also tend to marry one another.

Among class researchers there has been a rough division of labour between, on the one hand, those who study the shape of the class structure, mobility flows and rates, and who typically conduct large-scale surveys with representative samples, then, on the other hand, those who study class consciousness and related behaviour, typically using case study methods (Crompton, 1996a). This is another pseudo-debate; these are not competing groups of class researchers. Neither set of investigators has tried to stake monopoly claims for its own speciality within class analysis. Everyone wants to 'put it all together'. It is simply difficult to handle everything simultaneously.

Valerie Walkerdine and her colleagues (2001) argue that class is not something that is simply produced economically: it is performed, marked, written on minds and bodies. It can be 'spotted a mile off' even in the midst of our wish for it no longer to be there. Their own study, of 33 girls growing up in London, provides vivid illustrations of class getting into pretty well every aspect of the girls' lives. The observation that class is not simply 'out there' is neither new nor controversial. Marx distinguished a 'class in itself' from a 'class for itself'. Classes may be defined initially (by Marxists) by their relationships to the means of production, but they become more than simple aggregates of people when the actors begin to develop common types of identities and outlooks. Class may have an economic base, but class formation always involves cultural and social-psychological processes.

We need to be cautious here. Present-day class analysts do not assume that the members of any class will develop a particular, easily predictable, type of consciousness, and certainly not necessarily the kind of solidaristic and revolutionary consciousness that Marx believed would develop in the working class. People may not identify themselves with any class. Most people will place themselves in a class (usually the middle class or the working class) when invited to do so by researchers, provided the researchers prompt their respondents with checklists of possible class names, but it does not follow that these same people will think in class terms at any other time. In their everyday lives, depending on the situation, people are as likely, probably more likely, to think of themselves as women, husbands, parents, neighbours and suchlike.

Class analysts do not assume that people will regard other classes as enemies of their own. As a matter of fact, in response to survey questions, most people, roughly the same proportion nowadays as in the 1960s, say that there is a class struggle (Abercrombie and Warde, 2000). They also say, again in surveys, that the government represents a particular class (the upper class and the middle class rather than the working class in the case of the New Labour governments in the late 1990s and subsequently). However, an extreme form of individualism, an outright refusal to think in class terms, an insistence that there is no such thing as society, only individuals (a phrase made famous by Margaret Thatcher), and a belief that all classes share common interests, can all qualify as characteristic forms of class consciousness. Class analysts do not assume, because they know full well that it is not the case, that most people are dedicated class warriors.

People are usually ambivalent and hesitant, when asked by researchers to place themselves in a class (see Surridge, 2007). This is despite their willingness to agree (and most instantly agree) that there are classes 'out there'. They say that, 'I suppose that people would call me middle class, but…', or 'My parents were working class, but…' (see Savage et al, 2001). People's ambivalence may be due to the moral, value-laden significance of class. People may be reluctant to claim superiority by describing themselves as 'upper-middle' or to accept the implied stigma of being 'lower' (see Sayer 2002, 2005). Alternatively, they may be confused and uncertain as to exactly where class boundaries lie, and therefore exactly where they are positioned (see Payne and Grew, 2005). This may or may not be a distinctive feature of class identities in the twenty-first century. We (in sociology and the wider society) have tended to assume that people had stronger and clearer class identities in the past, but this may not have been the case (see Phillips and Western, 2004; Savage, 2005). People have probably always been most likely to regard themselves as simply 'normal' or 'ordinary', and to have preferred to stress their individuality rather than submerge their identities in any class. This does not mean that class no longer matters, or never mattered. Feeling just 'normal', and being unsure of one's class location, are in fact forms of class awareness.

Class and politics

Another point of agreement which transcends Marxist, Weberian and functionalist theorists is that class and politics are most likely to be thoroughly interwoven. This is another mediated link. How people make their livings cannot directly cause them to take part in any political action. The mediator will be class's imprint on their minds and social networks. It is presumed throughout class analysis, or at least envisaged, that (class) structure will lead to (class) consciousness which in turn will lead to (political) action. Thus class analysis seeks to unravel the relationships between economy, society and politics. Causation can be multi-directional. The organization of economic life may determine class divisions from which particular kinds of consciousness and political action arise, but these may then feed back, via government policies, into the economy and society.

'Politics', as the term is being used here, is not confined to party politics. Voting for a political party, becoming a member and involved in its campaigns, are political, but so too is any other collective action that is intended to change or preserve the macro-structure of society. So trade unions, professional associations, tenants' organizations, women's groups, racial equality movements and all other pressure groups are equally political.

When people identify with a class, and vote for a party because it is seen as representing the class in question, the link between class and politics is clear-cut, but this is not the only possible way, and it is probably not the usual way, in which political action is class-related. There seems to be a general tendency for people to attribute stronger class solidarity and motivation to others than they do to themselves. Conservative and Labour politicians alike, especially when in government, have always claimed that their own parties represent all classes of people, and have accused the other side of being in hock to sectional interests. Conservatives have accused Labour of being dependent on (working class) trade unions. Labour has accused the Conservatives of being dominated by out-of-touch aristocrats and other extremely wealthy, privately-educated groups. Another Labour accusation has been about the Conservative's sleazy links with business. However, given changes over time in the social backgrounds of Labour parliamentarians and Labour's appetite for large donations from wealthy patrons (see chapter 9), its staple shots have become liable to back-fire. A constant has been that, when in office, the leaders of both parties have claimed to be creating a classless Britain. Harold Macmillan, a Conservative prime minister in the late-1950s and early-1960s, thought that he was destroying the proletariat by enabling its members to enjoy rising standards of living. John Major claimed to be creating a classless society in the 1990s. His successor as prime minister, Tony Blair, claimed to be creating ladders of opportunity which would open middle class positions (middle Britain) to all. In the run-up to the 2010 general election, both parties claimed to be on the side of Britain's aspiring classes. Political leaders have always realized that they stand any hope of office only if they can attract votes from more than one class.

For their part, members of all classes know from first-hand experience just how divided their people are. Those who live on council estates have always known that not everyone votes Labour. Trade union activists have always known how difficult it is to maintain appearances of solidarity during negotiations, and especially during industrial action. Viewed from a distance, all classes appear more united than from within. So workers have resented how the upper and middle classes keep them down. The upwardly mobile sometimes feel frustrated at being unable to penetrate 'old boy networks'. Meanwhile, the higher classes have felt threatened by an organized working class. All these are characteristic forms of class consciousness and they are all political, that is, likely to persuade those concerned to support a particular party and specific policies.

All macro-social patterns are clearer when viewed from a distance, including historical distance. Looking back in time, it is fairly easy to see that class schisms and struggles have been major determinants of the direction of historical change. It would be difficult to begin to explain the rise of industrial capitalism without referring to how an ascendant class, the bourgeoisie, pioneered new forms of enterprise, and with the wealth thereby generated, contested the position of the older, ruling, landed classes, and thereby reshaped society. Equally, it is impossible to explain the twentieth century without mentioning that, by its beginning, a working class had already been formed and was organizing itself into trade unions and creating the Labour Party. The politics of the twentieth century was largely about the achievements and failures of working class power. The politics of the twenty-first century will be different largely because the class structure is now very different than in twentieth century industrial Britain.

Book plan

Before beginning to explore the details of class in modern Britain an appropriate class scheme – a map of the territory is needed. Lay people subscribe to class schemes. When they identify themselves as working class or middle class they usually have some ideas about which, if any, classes are above and beneath their own. Lay schemes are often vague and incomplete. Sociology's class schemes are not based squarely on lay conceptions. One should expect sociology's class schemes not to mirror, but, at the end of the day, to explain lay people's conceptions of class.

All sociological schemes are based on theories about the genesis of classes, and as we have seen, there has never been theoretical unanimity in sociology. So it should be no surprise that there is no unanimously agreed class scheme. Even so, sociologists are not hopelessly divided over which class scheme to use. When, in the 1990s, British sociologists were invited to recommend a replacement for the Registrar General's older social classes, there was broad agreement on a slightly modified version of a class scheme originally developed by John Goldthorpe in the course of conducting a large-scale study of social mobility in Britain in 1972. Chapter 2 presents this class scheme, together with the alternatives. This chapter also tackles the vexed question of who should be classified – individuals or households/families. This turns out to be one of the questions to which it is currently impossible to propose an answer that is right for all cases.

The main classes identified in the Goldthorpe scheme are a service class, sometimes alternatively called the salariat, but which is referred to as the new middle class or simply as the middle class throughout this book, and a working class. There are also intermediate classes – lower-level non-manual workers and a petit bourgeoisie comprising self-employed non-professionals and proprietors of small businesses. To these, the new (1998) official classification adds a bottom stratum, in effect an underclass, and most sociologists will concur that although it is fruitless to try to capture its members in survey research, the scheme should really be topped by an upper, capitalist class or over-class.

Equipped with this class scheme, chapter 3 traces the class effects of recent economic changes. These have led to a numerical decline of the working class and an expansion of the new middle class. This is well-known, but we shall see that there have been at least equally important changes in the occupations within all social classes, and in their social composition. There have been implications for typical forms of social consciousness and political proclivities within all the main classes.

Chapters 4 through 7 consider successively all the main and intermediate classes. Chapter 4 deals with the working class. It is shrinking and no longer contains the majority of the population. Since the 1960s another change in the working class has been its disorganization. Despite its still considerable size, the working class has declined drastically as a cultural and political force. This has been due to the steep contraction in manufacturing employment, the shift of employment from large to small establishments, the destruction of working class communities by a combination of rehousing, television and the motor car, higher absolute rates of upward mobility, the spread of unemployment and precarious jobs, and manual workers becoming more mixed in gender and ethnicity. In the course of all these changes the working class has lost its former organizations – trade unions and the Labour Party. Chapter 4 also considers the likelihood, actually the probability, of the persistence of high unemployment, and the intensification and spread of poverty, creating an underclass or excluded groups beneath the employed working class.

The intermediate classes – lower-level non-manual workers and the petit bourgeoisie – are the subjects of chapter 5. These are smaller than both the working class and the new middle class and lack the demographic base for full class formation. Membership of these classes is unstable, but this does not make the classes inconsequential either socially or politically. If office and laboratory workers and technicians were assimilated into the working class, this would again be the majority of the population. The self-employed and proprietors of small businesses can play a major ideological role in (apparently) demonstrating that anyone with sufficient enterprise can make it, and they were among the most enthusiastic Thatcherites in the 1980s.

Business people and self-employed professionals were the core of the old middle class. Nowadays they are vastly outnumbered by salaried professionals and managers, the core members of the new middle class, the subjects of chapter 6. Their numbers grew steadily throughout the twentieth century. Sometime in the twenty-first century they are likely to become the largest class. As a demographic entity, the new middle class is still in formation. Its recent growth rate means that its current members inevitably include many who have been upwardly mobile. There are numerous divisions within the new middle class – by levels, between managers and professionals, according to whether they work in the public or the private sector, and by lifestyle. They are certainly not a solidaristic class. Nor are they particularly conservative any longer. The middle class is no longer a small minority, needing to defend itself in the face of working class power. The new middle class has various discontents – sometimes about the macro-economic and political orders, but mainly about its own career situations. The new middle class is politically important if only because it now provides a clear majority of the activists in all the main political parties.

The old upper class comprised the monarchy, aristocracy and related families. The new upper class, or over-class, examined in chapter 7, has money at its core. The central members are capitalists – very wealthy individuals. They fulfil the demographic criteria for being treated as a class due to their ability to retain and then transmit their private property down the generations. The upper class is in fact contemporary Britain's best example of a well-knit class, aware of its vital interests, and able to act in a concerted way when necessary to protect these interests. The very wealthy have access to political elites, and are able to associate with titled folk and other celebrities. This network constitutes the modern upper class. The individuals concerned amount to less than one per cent of the population but they are currently the most powerful of all the classes.

Chapter 8 deals with social mobility. Most interest in this topic is about the extent to which people have equal opportunities, but in class analysis an at least equally important issue is the extent to which classes are demographic entities with critical masses of lifelong members and/or distinctive life-chances. The presumption is that unless a class is demographically distinct it is unlikely to develop a characteristic consciousness and all that follows. We shall see that the working class has met this test for many, many decades. The new middle class is on the way to becoming a stable demographic entity but will become properly formed only several decades into this twenty-first century. Class formation is a long-term process. It is still much too early to give a final answer as regards the consciousness and politics of the new middle class.

The long-term and ongoing trends are towards people born into the working class enjoying improved chances of social ascent, and the new middle class becoming self-recruiting. There have been major changes over time in absolute rates of social mobility. Relative rates, in contrast – the relative chances of people who start at different levels reaching a specific class destination – have remained remarkably stable. And these rates are similar, though not absolutely identical, in all modern societies. There are several explanations for the stability and the similarities, but none are totally convincing. This is one of the twenty-first century's unresolved sociological puzzles.

Chapter 9 is on contemporary politics. In a sense, this is the crunch chapter. A promise of class analysis has always been to unravel the links between the economy, society and politics. It will be argued that politics has been de-aligned from older class divisions, but that only a class explanation can account for how politics has changed. Contemporary politics reflects the new balance of class forces: a disorganized and disarmed working class, an ascendant upper class, and a new middle class that is more likely to address its discontents through career strategies and lifestyle choices than through politics.

The new middle class supplies nearly all our current members of parliament, but these may be better treated as one among many middle class career groups (professional politicians) rather than as class representatives. Except in places where nationalism has filled the void, politics is now substantially divorced from the people. This is the result of a particular balance of class forces. What will the outcome be? What can be said with confidence is that, just like previous balances, the current state of the class struggle is unlikely to last for long.

Summary

This chapter has explained that Britain is now one of the world's most unequal countries as a result of widening inequalities since the 1970s. It has laid-out the big challenge facing class theory and research: to identify the causes and consequences of these inequalities. The chapter then proceeded to consider how class is defined by Marxist, Weberian and functionalist sociologists, and noted common features. All regard class as having an economic base. All concepts of class group together people with similar ways of making their livings, that is, people in similar occupations. All sociologists who study class have additional common interests. We are all interested in how the class divisions that arise in economic life are liable to spill-over into people's minds and wider social relationships, and the implications for their political activities and preferences through which there may be feedback loops with politics impacting back on economic life, the class structure and the rest of society.

The next chapter will introduce the main sociological class schemes that correspond broadly with Weberian, Marxist and functionalist views of class. It will discuss which scheme gives the best results, and thereby lay-out a framework for the later chapters' detailed examination of the main classes in present-day Britain, how these are changing in some ways, and remaining much as ever in others.

Class Schemes and Scales

2

Introduction

The previous chapter has established that class remains very much alive and still plays a major part in our lives. In order to explore the contemporary class structure in detail we need an outline map. In other words, we need a class scheme or scale. This chapter describes the Registrar General's social class scheme that was first used to analyse the 1911 census. It then considers the main alternatives developed by sociologists:

- The Goldthorpe (Nuffield or Oxford) scheme;
- The schemes developed by the American sociologist, Erik Olin Wright;
- The Cambridge scale and other gradational scales.

The strengths and limitations of each are discussed. The chapter then considers who should be classified – individuals or households – and, if the latter, whose occupations should be taken into account. Related issues of how to incorporate gender and race/ethnicity into class analysis are also considered.

Recently the so-called 'employment aggregates' approach has been criticized for leading class analysis into an impasse (Crompton, 1998; Crompton and Scott, 2000; Devine, 1998). The criticisms are that employment aggregates overlook other factors that play a role in class formation (education, housing, gender and ethnicity, for example) and that the cultural dimension of class is omitted (people's beliefs, values and attitudes).

This book's position is that the criticisms are wrong. No-one claims that employment, job or occupation = class. The claim is simply that type of employment, indicated by occupation, is the best single indicator of class position and that, in the first instance, this best indicator is best used singularly. This is because:

- Occupation correlates (either as cause or effect) with other factors that may be implicated in class formation (education, income, housing etc).
- The social significance of occupations has remained relatively constant across time and place, whereas this is not the case with any other indicators.

For example, in Britain the significance of being a social housing tenant is different today than when families moved 'up' from inner-city slums and were rehoused on suburban council estates in the 1940s and 50s (see Lupton et al, 2009). Attending a secondary school is now universal and has an entirely different significance than before 1944 in Britain when most children received elementary schooling only.

■ Constructing social class scales by totalling points awarded for different indicators (occupation, housing, education etc) involves assigning arbitrary weights to the different factors, and allows individuals or households to achieve common total scores in many different ways. Thus people placed in similar class positions may not share any experiences in common. The procedure also obliterates any class 'divisions', and positions units (individuals or households) along a continuous scale, thereby preventing classes being identified relationally.

■ Occupations are what people do for substantial amounts of time every working day, every working week, every year throughout their working lives. Continuous experience is necessary to create classes as demographic entities, which is a pre-condition for the social, cultural and political dimensions of class formation to operate.

Thus the employment aggregates approach is just that, an approach, a start-point, and it is a necessary facilitator rather than an impediment to exploring all other aspects of class formation and relationships.

The (pre-1998) Registar General's social classes

Even today, the best known British social class scheme is probably the Registrar General's that was first used in the 1911 census, and remained the UK's official (government) class scheme up to 1998. The scheme had a long life, and its replacement is not very different. This is despite the new scheme having an entirely different theoretical rationale. Whatever their theoretical bases, class schemes usually identify much the same main divisions. The schemes may therefore be said to corroborate one another, which they should do, since they are trying to represent the same social reality.

We fully appreciate the value of having a class scheme only when we realize how much more difficult it was to explain things before such schemes existed. In earlier censuses (before 1911) Britain's working population had been grouped according to whether their jobs were in agriculture, mining, manufacturing or the armed forces etc, that is, in what we would now call different economic or businesses sectors. A major concern in 1911 was to map variations in mortality rates. The assumption was that if the sections of the population that were most vulnerable could be identified more precisely, this would provide clues to the causes, thus leading to preventative measures. Needless to say, the Registrar General's Class Scheme did predict variations in mortality rates (and has continued to do so ever since). It also predicted most other things that could be measured, which is why the scheme remained in use for the remainder of the twentieth century.

The scheme had six classes (class III was sub-divided into IIIa and IIIb in 1921). Classes I and II were higher and lower-level professionals, managers and administrative employees. Class IIIa comprised lower-level white-collar workers, while classes IIIb, IV and V were the skilled, semi-skilled and unskilled manual grades. The self-employed were classed according to their underlying occupations (electricians in the skilled working class etc). It was claimed (until 1981) that the classes grouped together occupations of similar social standing. Then in 1981 it was decided (by the government and the Registrar General's office) that the classes in fact represented skill levels. There was no wholesale re-assignment of occupations despite this major change in the alleged theoretical base.

Skill is rather difficult to measure. The length of time required to learn a job, and the level of qualification needed to enter, may not be technically necessary. There is always a huge judgemental factor in assessments of skill. How do you compare objectively two entirely different jobs? Is it to be in terms of the intrinsic difficulty or the severity of the consequences when mistakes are made? Is the surgeon's job technically more difficult than the butcher's?

Sociologists were never really satisfied with the Registrar General's original classes, firstly because of the absence of a plausible theoretical justification. Few sociologists believe that either social standing or skill are the principal bases on which classes are formed. Second, there had never been thorough large-scale research to justify the placement of occupations. From time-to-time occupations were re-classified on the basis of new evidence and expert opinion. For example, air pilots (who were originally classed with other drivers) were promoted into the professional grades, and postal delivery workers (who were originally placed with other public officials) were demoted into the semi-skilled manual class. New occupations such as computer programmer had to be newly classified in the same way – on the basis of any hard evidence that was available plus expert opinion. It was all rather messy and unsatisfactory. Despite this, sociologists were normally happy to use the scheme. Its longevity made it widely understood, and its widespread use, especially in analysing government information, meant that new data that was classified in the same way was comparable with many existing sources.

The NS-SEC class scheme

Nevertheless, when the research community was invited in the 1990s to propose a replacement class scheme, it responded willingly, and its proposal (Rose and O'Reilly, 1997), adopted in 1998 by the Office for National Statistics (by the then responsible government department) is a slightly modified version of a class scheme originally developed in the early-1970s by John Goldthorpe. The new official scheme is titled NS-SEC (National Statistics, Socio-Economic

NS-SEC		Goldthorpe names	Book's names
1.1	Employers (large organizations) and senior managers		
1.2	Higher professionals	Service class	Middle class
2	Lower managerial and professional		
3	Intermediate (eg. clerks, secretaries, computer operators)	Intermediate classes	Intermediate classes
4	Small employers and own-account non-professional		
5	Supervisors, craft and related		
6	Semi-routine (eg. cooks, bus drivers, hairdressers, shop assistants)	Working class	Working class
7	Routine (eg. waiters, cleaners, couriers)		
8	Never worked, long-term unemployed	–	Underclass

Figure 2.1 The 1998 official class scheme
National Statistics Socio-Economic Classification (NS-SEC)

Classification). In 2007 another slightly modified version of the Goldthorpe scheme was adopted by the European Union for collecting harmonized data from all member countries (see Rose and Harrision, 2007). The new UK official classification is presented in Figure 2.1 along with the original Goldthorpe class labels, and the labels used throughout this book.

Market and work situations

Since this has become the UK official classification the scheme has often been read as a linear scale (which in fact it is not), and as representing social standing or skill (whereas in fact neither is a principal consideration in placing occupations). Another misuse is to try to replicate the old white-blue collar dichotomy by combining classes 1–3 and classes 4–7, whereas the intention of the Goldthorpe scheme is to separate class 3 (intermediate) from middle class occupations proper, and to separate the self-employed (class 4) from all the other classes. The scheme purports to group together occupations which share common 'employment relations', that is, occupations which have common market situations (see Box 2.1 overleaf) and work situations.

The strength of an occupation's market position is reflected in the rewards from work that practitioners can expect. These rewards include, of course, the level of pay, and any fringe benefits such as health insurance and the use of a company vehicle, but future expectations (career prospects) can be at least as important as current earnings, and job security also needs to be taken into account.

Box 2.1   Markets

Markets exist when large numbers of buyers and sellers interact, and when prices are fixed by the interplay between supply and demand. There can be markets for anything – capital, goods, services and labour.

Markets have existed since ancient times, but played a relatively minor role when much production was by families and local communities for their own use, and/or when people were required to make their labour or goods available to a specific land-owner or governor.

Markets are never completely free. What we regard as free markets are in fact regulated by law, which allows buyers and sellers to interact 'freely', safeguards everyone from coercion, and enables bargains (contracts) to be enforced. Markets can be regulated in additional ways – by governments, cartels of firms, professional associations and trade unions. The object may be to set a floor or ceiling for prices, or to drive prices (for labour or goods) above what would otherwise be the market level.

Under communism, state and party regulation largely replaced market mechanisms. The outcome was a distinctive kind of modern society, and a rather different class structure to those that have arisen in countries with market economies.

Max Weber (see chapter 1, pp 9–12) was the founding father of modern sociology who highlighted the role of markets in the formation of classes.

Nowadays, markets have been globalized, and market forces (regulated in different ways and to varying extents) play a pivotal role in class formation throughout the entire world.

An occupation's work situation is its typical position in the system of authority and control, and the degree of autonomy that incumbents possess when performing their jobs. How closely are they supervised? How much discretion do they exercise? Are they responsible for, and do they have control over, the work of others? There are in fact just four basic work situations. One can be an employer, self-employed, a manager (performing ownership functions – see Box 2.2 overleaf), or a worker.

The Goldthorpe class scheme is widely regarded (within sociology) as neo-Weberian because it classifies occupations according to their market situations as well as their work situations (relationships to the means of production in Marxist terminology). As explained in chapter 1 (see pp 9–12), Max Weber himself believed that classes were formed in markets, in labour markets in the cases of people who needed to sell their labour. Weber recognized employers and workers as two major classes, but he also identified other class divisions depending on the assets (skills and qualifications) that individuals could offer in the labour market. Goldthorpe is entitled to insist that his scheme is really just as Marxist as Weberian because it pays equal regard to work situations.

Box 2.2   Ownership functions or functions of capital

One way of identifying these is to ask what the owner would do in a small enterprise where he or she was in sole command of the entire workforce. Among other things, he or she would hire staff, fix rates of pay, allocate tasks, make investment decisions, fix prices, maybe personally sell the products, and keep the books. As enterprises grow in size it becomes necessary to employ managers and professionals to perform many of these tasks.

Marxists (see chapter 1, pp 7–9) have sometimes argued that in a society where the means of production are collectively owned, all such 'unproductive' or 'socially unnecessary' functions of capital will be eliminated and the associated jobs will disappear. Others argue that it will always be necessary to have managers to co-ordinate workforces, accountants to keep the books, and so forth, though the managers and professionals might work differently, according to different priorities. In other words, the occupations and their functions are not necessarily unique to capitalist societies, though in such societies the relevant staff must necessarily be capitalism's functionaries.

However, Marxist sociologists prefer to classify occupations or jobs solely on the basis of their relationships to the means of production (see below).

As we shall see later (pp 49–58), Goldthorpe's scheme (like Marxist schemes) is relational (not gradational) in that it regards classes as formed largely through their relationships with one another – employing one another, and controlling or being controlled by one another at work, for example.

Now it is claimed (by the Goldthorpe scheme's supporters) that when occupations are grouped simultaneously according to their market and work situations, we find that they cluster into a limited number of classes. When the Goldthorpe scheme was first used (in Goldthorpe's 1972 social mobility survey, see chapter 8), it was not entirely clear how all the occupations had been placed, but the clustering has subsequently been confirmed in the analysis of large data sets which contain all the necessary information about work and market situations (see Evans and Mills, 1998).

The Goldthorpe/NS-SEC classes

There are just two main classes in the Goldthorpe scheme. One is composed of managers and professionals (classes 1 and 2 in the NS-SEC scheme). These occupations are characterized by their high and secure incomes that rise progressively as individuals' careers develop, by the authority that incumbents exercise in their work organizations, and by the discretion that they enjoy. Goldthorpe has placed great emphasis on the 'trust' or 'service' relationship with their employers. Managers and professionals do not normally have fixed hours of work, and their work is not monitored closely. They are trusted to act responsibly and to use their skills in their employers' interests. In exchange they are given relatively secure jobs, high incomes and progressive careers. Goldthorpe labels this class the 'service class' to stress its distinctive 'service' terms and conditions of employment, but this label is always liable to be misunderstood as referring to people who work in services as opposed to manufacturing, or servant-like occupations. It is doubtful whether anyone, outside sociology, identifies with the service class. New middle class, or just plain middle class, is just as good a label: it is the self-description used by most of the people in the class, and throughout the remainder of this book.

The second main Goldthorpe class is the working class, sub-divided by skill levels (classes 5, 6 and 7 in the NS-SEC scheme). These occupations are the polar opposites of the middle class. People are paid by the number of hours that they work, or according to how much they produce, and they are usually paid far less than people in management or professional jobs. On average, male white-collar workers earn half as much again as male manual employees, and female white-collar staff have a similar earnings advantage vis-a-vis their female manual counterparts. There is little trust in the working class employment relationship. Terms and conditions of work are strictly contractual. The jobs are generally less secure than those of managers and professionals so risks of unemployment are greater. Career prospects and fringe benefits are usually distinctly inferior, or non-existent, and most manual employees are not responsible for the work of any other staff. They do not exercise, but are expected to submit to authority. Table 2.1 presents some of the findings from a nationally representative sample that was questioned about their jobs and labour market experiences in the 1990s. The table illustrates the contrasts between middle class and working class jobs. The chances are that a middle class employee will initiate and decide his or her own daily tasks, and supervise someone. The chances are that a working class employee will do none of these things.

We can see in Table 2.1 that not all middle class jobs are reported (by the incumbents) to possess all the definitive middle class features. Conversely, some working class jobs are reported to possess some middle class features. There are different ways of responding to these exceptions. One is to argue that people should be classed according to the characteristics of their own jobs rather

Table 2.1 Automony, responsibility and social class

Autonomy/responsibility	Prof/Man %	Skilled %	Non-skilled %
Decides daily tasks	75	33	37
Initiates new tasks	75	45	38
Has supervisory responsibilities	68	35	21

Based on data in Gallie et al, 1998

than according to features deemed to be typical of their occupational groups (titles may be misleading). This is the course adopted by Erik Olin Wright (see below). The contrary arguments for classifying according to typical features of occupations' work and market situations are:

- The classes are clusters, which have cores and peripheries. There will be many jobs in all classes that do not possess all the definitive features.
- Exceptional cases may be individuals who occupy the relevant jobs for small spans of time in their working lives. For example, a beginning trainee manager will not have the security or authority that he or she can eventually expect.
- With other exceptional cases there may be compensating advantages or disadvantages, For example, a professional engineer may work for a small firm that can offer neither security nor fringe benefits in the hope of exceptional rewards should the firm thrive.
- In some cases, for whatever reasons, individuals may mis-report the relevant job features.

It is sometimes claimed that the staff-works, middle class/working class, distinction is a thing of the past, but this would be untrue even if everyone used the same canteens and addressed each other using forenames (which in practice is still the exception rather than the rule). Occupations at all levels have changed over time. These changes are discussed at length in the next chapter. In certain technical aspects, the old blue/white-collar divide has crumbled. For example, mechanization has taken much of the brute labour out of manual jobs. Meanwhile, offices have become stocked with technology. Nowadays manual workers and managers may both be required to work with computers. However, in terms of career prospects and other basic features of the market and work situations, there has been no collapse, or even a weakening, of this long-standing class division (Gallie, 1996; Whelan and Maitre, 2008).

The Goldthorpe/NS-SEC classification identifies two intermediate classes. One consists of lower-level office and some sales and laboratory staff. These jobs usually possess some middle class features. For example, there are often short career ladders. The jobs are thereby set above manual occupations but remain very inferior in all respects to occupations that are in the middle class proper. The intermediate position of these occupations is reflected in the occupants' collective uncertainty about their class locations. The majority of manual workers who identify with any class describe themselves as working class, while the majority of managers and professionals identify with the middle class. People in lower-level office jobs divide roughly 50:50 into middle class and working class identifiers.

The second intermediate class is the petit bourgeoisie – people who work for themselves or who own and run small businesses, except professionals who are placed, alongside other members of their occupations, in the service/middle class. Members of the petit bourgeoisie differ enormously in market success but they have such a distinctive work situation – working for themselves and being the boss – that they are grouped together on this basis.

The NS-SEC also has an 'underclass' (class 8) which was not in the original Goldthorpe scheme. This class is for people who have never worked, the long-term unemployed, and others who depend long-term on state social security. The case for recognizing such a class has strengthened since the 1970s due to the level of unemployment, and the extent to which social security benefits have dropped further and further behind average earnings. However, whether the people concerned really are a class apart is considered carefully in chapter 4.

An objection to the Goldthorpe scheme is that it does not recognize an upper or capitalist class. One reason why there is no such class in the NS-SEC version is simply that the scheme classifies people by their occupations rather than by their wealth, and company directors are placed in the top class. The original Goldthorpe scheme was intended to be used in survey research where, as we shall see later (in chapter 7), it is probably pointless to try to identify an upper class (most people who are so classified in large-scale surveys turn out to be neither very wealthy nor very powerful). However, if anyone wishes, for whatever reasons, to distinguish an upper class (as this book certainly does for reasons that will become clear in later chapters), this class can simply be placed on top of the ONS scheme.

A point to note is that the Goldthorpe scheme is not consistently hierarchical. The middle class is certainly above the working class, class 1 is above class 2, and classes 5, 6, 7 and 8 are in rank order, but lower-level office workers are not believed to be above the petit bourgeoisie, and it is not implied that all of the latter are beneath all members of the middle class, or above all members of the working class. The intermediate classes are simply distinct classes most of whose members occupy the intermediate space between the two main classes – the middle class and the working class. Goldthorpe has always insisted that we can speak unequivocally of someone having been socially mobile only if the person has moved from the middle class into the working class, or vice-versa. Movements into and out of the intermediate classes do not necessarily indicate that those concerned have risen or fallen. In its NS-SEC guise, the scheme is often treated as a fully linear scale, but sociologists should know better.

Strengths of the scheme

The original Goldthorpe scheme was received sometimes critically, but generally enthusiastically, in British sociology, as being superior to both its predecessors and contemporary rivals. The Goldthorpe scheme has several distinctive advantages. First, there is an explicit theoretical rationale. One can see why each occupation has been placed in its particular class, and if anyone suspects that an occupation has been misplaced, there are ground-rules for resolving the dispute. This also applies whenever new occupations are created. Second, the scheme sidesteps arguments about whether occupations should be classified according to their work or market situations by employing both criteria simultaneously.

One no longer has to be either a Marx or a Weber supporter. Third, in separating lower-level white-collar occupations from the middle class proper the Goldthorpe scheme disarms critics of class analysis who query whether there really is a major division between the middle and working classes, meaning all white-collar and all blue-collar workers respectively. The crucial contrast in the Goldthorpe scheme is between a middle class proper of managers and professionals on the one side, and the working class on the other. The fact that some occupations are intermediate need not mean that there are no clear class divisions.

The Goldthorpe scheme predicts things that one would expect a class scheme to predict (self-assigned class identities and political partisanship, for example, and much else besides), but, of course, virtually any class scheme will do this. It must be said that after all the careful conceptualization and dedicated research, the new class scheme is not all that different from the Registrar General's older social classes with a petit bourgeoisie and an underclass added. However, the Goldthorpe scheme has a much stronger theoretical justification.

Marxist schemes

Objections to other schemes

The Goldthorpe scheme has faced criticism from two flanks. First, from Marxists: their class schemes are rarely used in present-day Western or post-communist East European sociology, but the arguments never die. As in politics so in sociology: Marxism is a perpetual opposition.

Marxists object, of course, that the Goldthorpe scheme does not identify a separate capitalist class, but, as we have seen, this absence is easily corrected, if desired. More fundamentally, Marxists object to people being classed according to technical features of their jobs (whether they work mainly with their hands or with their heads, for example), and according to how well they are rewarded. Marxists insist that people should be classed solely by their social relationships to the means of production (see Box 2.3). They object to people being separated from the working class for what, to Marxists, are inadequate reasons, like being highly-paid.

Box 2.3   Forces, means, relationships and modes of production

These terms are associated with Marxism, but they can be detached from this body of theory.

The forces or means of production are the raw materials upon which people work, and the equipment that they use.

Relationships of production refers to the social (rather than the technical) division of labour, and, therefore, the social relationships into which people enter in order to use the forces/means of production. Marx, of course, regarded the employer-worker relationship as the principal, definitive relationship of production in capitalist societies.

A mode of production encompasses the forces/means, and the corresponding relationships of production. Marx identified the feudal mode, the capitalist mode, and so on. It was Marx's view that throughout history, under successive modes of production, the forces of production had been developed progressively, as far as the existing relationships of production would allow. However, he believed that points were reached when 'contradictions' arose between what the prevailing relationships of production would permit, and the potential of the forces of production. Thus under capitalism there was said to be an unfolding contradiction between the possibility of new technology releasing everyone from want, and capitalist relationships of production which condemned the working class to a subsistence existence, the persistent threat of unemployment and the severe deprivations involved. The inevitable (in the long-term) outcome of such a glaring contradiction was said to be revolutionary change (the advent of a new mode of production), with the momentum supplied by a formerly exploited class, or a faction of it. The working class was expected to develop a revolutionary consciousness as it became aware of the contradiction between its treatment under capitalism, and what the forces of production with which they worked were capable of delivering.

Contradictory class situations

For a long time Marxists have acknowledged that capitalist societies are not being progressively polarized into just two main classes. All their class schemes distinguish employers from workers, but for over a century Marxists have recognized additional class divisions and situations, as did Marx himself. Since the 1960s, Marxists have responded to the need to solve the middle class problem – how to classify them – and their solutions have involved the identification of various so-called contradictory or ambiguous class situations. Even if employers and workers are not the only classes, Marxists have continued to insist that class situations are defined essentially by workers' relationships to either or both of these two main classes.

Marxists have always expected that, once classes are correctly identified, we will see exploitation, domination, struggle and consciousness formation more clearly than through schemes that mis-locate the proper class boundaries.

The Wright schemes

The best-known, and most widely used, Marxist class schemes have been constructed by Erik Olin Wright (1979, 1985, 1994, 1996), an American sociologist. His ideas have not been dismissed out of hand. They have been treated very seriously. Indeed, his class schemes have been used in an international comparative research project to which the British contribution was *Social Class in Modern Britain,* a study conducted by Gordon Marshall and his colleagues (1988), all then at Essex University.

Wright himself has always been open-minded and willing to revise his ideas in response to criticism. In fact he undertook a major overhaul of his class scheme in the 1980s. His earlier scheme (see Figure 2.2a, p 30) had recognized a (grand) bourgeoisie, small employers, a petit bourgeoisie, managers (in the contradictory position of being employees yet performing functions of capital – see Box 2.2, p 23), semi-autonomous employees, a category that was meant to capture professionals but in practice became something of a rag-bag since cooks and caretakers, for instance, were sometimes placed there, and a working class.

Wright decided that his first attempt at a class scheme was too simple and that in practice there were more contradictory locations than he had identified. So he attempted to rectify these faults by making his scheme more consistently Marxist (so he said). His revised scheme (see Figure 2.2b, p 30) removes people from the working class depending on whether they own the businesses in which they work, or whether they control organizational assets (perform management functions), or whether they hold any credentialled skill assets (useful qualifications). One might wonder what place credentials have in a Marxist scheme. Other Marxists (for example, Gubbay, 1997) have queried the revised Wright scheme's Marxist pedigree. Wright appears to be trying to keep people such as university professors, who may have no management responsibilities, out of the working class. In his original scheme the semi-autonomous employee category was designed for this purpose but in practice the category had a wider embrace. The Marxist reasoning behind classifying people partly on the basis of their credentials, or lack of any, provided that the qualifications are relevant to and used in their jobs, is that those concerned have acquired special skills that are useful to their employers in exchange for which they receive a share of the surplus value (see Box 2.4) that other workers produce.

Box 2.4   Surplus value

Most present-day economists (and sociologists) have no use for this concept. However, the concept occupied a central place in Marx's theory about the operation and development of capitalist societies. Some (though not all) present-day Marxist sociologists continue to use the term.

We need to begin with the labour theory of value which asserts that the basic value of any commodity depends on the amount of labour required for its production. So the relative value of commodities depends primarily on how long it takes a worker, or workers, to produce them.

Labour itself has a basic value depending on its costs of production and reproduction. Workers need to be fed, clothed, housed, and so on, and they also need to be born, reared, educated and trained. So there can be variations in the basic value of different kinds of labour power. In market situations, commodities (including labour power) may be bought and sold at prices in excess of their basic value. The difference between the two is said to be surplus value which may be appropriated by an employer. It is also possible for workers themselves to acquire surplus value from the sale of their labour power on the basis of the particular skills and experience that they can offer, but this always depends on the employer being able to recoup the costs in the surplus value (profit) gained from the sale of the workers' output. It is only when the forces of production (the tools and machinery with which people work) have been developed to a level that enables workers to produce in excess of their own subsistence needs, that some people can engage in 'unproductive labour' or work that is not 'socially necessary' (to produce the relevant goods or services and to reproduce the worker). Examples include artists of various kinds and religious functionaries, plus a separate class of owners and the people who they employ (managers, for example) whose principal function (so Marxists claim) is not to create value but to extract surplus value from the real producers (see Box 2.2, p 23).

1. Bourgeoisie
2. Small employers
3. Petit bourgeoisie (self-employed, no employees)
4. Managers and supervisors
5. Semi-autonomous employees
6. Workers

Figure 2.2a Wright's original class scheme

Assets in the means of production

Owners	Non-owners Skill/credential assets				
	Experts	Skilled employees	Non-skilled		
1 Bourgeoisie	4 Expert managers	7 Semi-credentialled managers	10 Uncredentialled managers	**Managers**	
2 Small employers	5 Expert supervisors	8 Semi-credentialled supervisors	11 Uncredentialled supervisors	**Supervisors**	**Organization assets**
3 Petit bourgeoisie	6 Expert non-managers	9 Semi-credentialled workers	12 Proletarians	**Non-management**	

Figure 2.2b Wright's revised class scheme

Wright's scheme is not trying to persuade us that there are 12 distinct classes – three classes of employers and nine classes of employees. The cells are meant to be collapsed. Classes 4, 5 and 6 (the experts or full professionals), plus classes 7 and 10 (other senior managers) may be combined into a middle class. Class 12 is the pure proletariat. This leaves classes 8, 9 and 11 in intermediate positions.

A noteworthy feature of Wright's scheme or, more strictly, its use, is that individuals are classified not according to their occupations but by their jobs. Wright criticizes procedures (see Box 2.5) that assume that everyone with a common occupational title will be doing broadly similar jobs. Classifying people according to the character of their particular jobs is expected to lead to the discovery of stronger relationships between social class and most other things than occupation-based classifications. Wright has always suspected that many jobs with middle class occupational titles are really proletarian. When constructing his original scheme he was influenced by the ideas of Harry Braverman (1974) who had claimed that the development of capitalism led to a progressive degradation of labour as, in the search for profit under competitive conditions, employers subjected labour to forever tighter control. As this happened, both manual and white-collar jobs were said to be vulnerable to deskilling. Wright argues that classifying according to job characteristics enables everyone, whatever their occupational titles, to be classified correctly.

Box 2.5   Classifying people

Wright's scheme is the exception here. With virtually all other class schemes and scales this is a multi-stage process. First, individuals' jobs must be assigned to 'occupational unit groups'. Around 25,000 different occupations are currently recognized in official (government) registers: too many for all but the most common to be present in useful numbers even in large samples. So occupations are allocated to one or another of the 353 groups in SOC2000, the latest version of the UK government's standard occupational classification. Each group of occupations (SOC) is supposed to perform similar work, which requires similar experience, skills and qualifications. Neither the list of separate occupations, nor the standard groups (SOCs) are stable. New occupations are being created constantly. Likewise, entire new categories of occupations can be brought into existence – para-medical occupations, public relations experts, call-centre occupations more recently, and, even more recently still, occupations connected with electronic commerce. The standard occupational classification is being revised constantly.

Most countries today have their own SOCs. The SOC currently in use in the USA recognizes 822 types of occupations.

All the country-SOCs can be converted into ISCO-08 (the latest version of the International Standard Classification of Occupations) that is managed by the Geneva-based International Labour Office. Cross-national harmonization is necessary in order to permit cross-country comparisons.

It is only at the next stage in classifying people that most sociological class schemes and scales begin to do their original work. The schemes classify SOCs, not separate occupations. So SOCs can be allocated (using computer programmes nowadays) to the Registrar General's (pre-1998) social classes, or into the Goldthorpe (NS-SEC) scheme. The Cambridge class scale (see below) is also based on occupational unit groups (the SOCs nowadays). So once occupations have been allocated to SOCs, it is fairly straight-forward for sociologists to experiment, and to compare the results obtained with different class schemes. This is how Gordon Marshall and his colleagues (1988) were able to compare Goldthorpe's with other class schemes.

There are never-ending debates about the classes into which particular SOCs should be placed, especially when the occupations are completely new or when the character of the work has changed radically. It has been argued (successfully) that supermarket check-out staff should be placed in the working class rather than in the intermediate class where they would accompany people who sell motor cars and insurance policies, and who work in more traditional department stores. There is still a debate about where to place call-centre staff (intermediate at present in the official classification). Technical and supervisory jobs are another group of occupations whose location is currently controversial. Should they all be grouped together in an intermediate class (as in the original Goldthorpe class scheme)? Or, as in the new official classification, should most of them be either downgraded into the working class or upgraded into the middle class?

However, Wright's insistence on ignoring occupational titles leads to some peculiar-looking placements (see Marshall et al, 1988). For example, investment brokers, purchasing officers and suchlike can appear in the working class because, according to the answers that they give to interviewers, they are non-owners, do not have management responsibilities, and possess no job-relevant credentials. This does not necessarily mean that the scheme must be wrong. However, neither Wright himself nor anyone else has ever found any of the non-owner classes, except the workers, displaying a distinctive type of consciousness or political proclivities. No matter how the Wright scheme is collapsed, it fails to yield as strong predictions (correlations) as other class schemes with measurements that are expected to be class-related (see Marshall et al, 1988).

Wright's problem could be his application of Marxism. Other Marxists have distanced themselves from Wright. For example, Jonathan Gubbay (1997) has criticized the Weberian elements (like credentials) in Wright's revised scheme and has called for a more rigorous application of Marxist thinking. Gubbay would like classes to be recognized by examining flows of surplus value (see Box 2.4, pp 29–30) – who generates it and who receives it. Surplus value, according to Gubbay, is everything that is produced in excess of what is needed to reproduce labour power in the prevailing social and cultural contexts. So everyone who is paid above the minimum on which individuals are able to

continue to work is declared to be receiving surplus value. It is possible to establish who receives more than this minimum income (nearly everyone nowadays,
though to very different extents) but identifying where surplus value is created
is far more difficult. Within any firm it is always difficult to measure how much
of the collective output is due to each particular worker.

The fundamental problems in the Wright scheme, and other Marxist
attempts, are probably not the applications, but Marxism itself. The theory
discourages scheme constructors from classifying workers according to how
much they are paid, their job security, career prospects and other rewards
from work – the market situation part of the Goldthorpe rationale. Even John
Westergaard (1994), whose sociology has always been basically Marxist, has
protested against the futility of trying to exclude 'who gets what' from class
analysis.

Gradational scales

Over the last 30 years the challenge of Marxism has faded. This applies in
both sociology and international politics. Nowadays the main challenge to
neo-Weberian class schemes is from sociologists who prefer to conceptualize
class gradationally. The Weberians and gradationalists have always been the
main class camps in North American sociology and Europe has now fallen
into line.

Marxist and Weberian concepts of class have an important feature in common:
they are both relational. Each class is defined by its relationships with others –
employing or being employed by them, or controlling or being controlled by
them, for example. Classes are conceived as being formed by these relationships.
Gradational concepts, in contrast, identify classes in terms of how much they have
of whatever is considered valuable – power, income, status or whatever. These
schemes identify class differences rather than clear divisions. The class hierarchy
is conceived as a series of steps rather than distinct groups. American sociologists
have normally been comfortable with gradational class concepts. Functionalism
(see chapter 1, pp 8–9), the best-known theoretical under-pinning of this view
of class, was always most influential on the west of the Atlantic. European sociology has always been more hospitable to conflict theories and their relational
class concepts. However, we should note that gradational class schemes do not
necessarily embody functionalist thinking. This is so even when the scheme constructors claim public consensus over, for example, the prestige of different occupations. People in all types of occupations may agree on their ranking while some
or all consider the rankings unfair (see Bottero and Prandy, 2003). Conversely,
relational class schemes do not necessarily assume or imply a conflict of interests,
latent or conscious, between different classes. In principle, their interdependence
could bind members of different classes into Durkheimian-type organic solidarity
(Durkheim, 1893).

Occupational prestige scales

The first American occupational prestige scale, known as the North-Hatt scale, was based on research in 1947 into public estimations of the prestige of just 90 selected occupations. From this evidence base Otis Dudley Duncan developed a Socio-Economic Index (SEI). He regressed the prestige scores for 45 of the North-Hatt occupations onto education and income to produce an algorithm which was used to calculate SEI scores for all occupational categories used in the 1950 USA census (see Reiss, 1961). Basically the same procedure has been used to construct all subsequent American occupational prestige scales except that larger samples have been used than in the original North-Hatt research, and sub-samples of the general public have ranked different subsets of occupations, thereby creating large primary data bases. For example, rankings of 740 different occupations in the USA were used to create the National Opinion Research Center (NORC)/Government Social Survey (GSS) Occupational Prestige Scale (see Nakao and Treas, 1992).

In Britain the only occupational prestige scale to be developed as an alternative to the Registrar General's is the Hall-Jones scale (see Hall and Jones, 1950). They asked a sample to rank just 30 occupations according to their social standing. This limited evidence was used to create a seven class scheme into which all occupations could be placed, and the scale was used in the first large-scale study of social mobility in Britain in 1949 (see Glass, 1954). Subsequently the data from this fieldwork was recoded and analysed using the Goldthorpe class scheme.

The main gradational class scheme currently in use in Britain has been developed by a Cambridge group of sociologists (Robert Blackburn, Ken Prandy and Sandy Stewart). They began to develop their class scheme at the same time when the Goldthorpe (Oxford) scheme was being conceived for the 1972 social mobility survey. At that time the Cambridge group believed that Goldthorpe was leading the sociological study of class down a false trail.

Criticisms of 'box' schemes

The Cambridge group have four basic objections to Goldthorpe's and other box schemes. The first objection, of course, is that class is in fact gradational, not relational. The Cambridge group point out that all the alleged determinants of class position are distributed gradationally: that in reality the situation is not that some people's jobs are totally secure and others the exact opposite, and likewise with job autonomy, career prospects, pay and everything else. 'Putting people into boxes' is said to be a misleading, and unnecessary, sociological habit. The Cambridge group argue that sociology was on the right lines with the old Registrar General's social classes – six groups of occupations, each believed to be of broadly similar social standing. They believe that sociology took a false turn by trying to define the boundaries between classes more accurately instead of working towards positioning every occupation more precisely along a continuum.

The second objection to the Goldthorpe methodology is that it is pointless to try to define class precisely, in terms of market situation, work situation or anything else, and, in particular, to try to follow Weber in separating class from status. In practice, the Cambridge group argue, everything is merged into general stratification arrangements with actors located at various levels. Social distance (who people associate with as equals) is the Cambridge group's preferred way of locating people and their occupations within the country's general stratification arrangements.

Third, the Cambridge group take exception to identifying classes objectively, in terms of market or work situations, which are said to create class positions which actors then fill. The Cambridge view is that social classes, if they deserve the label, can only be formed in the course of actors evaluating their own and other people's positions.

Fourth, the Cambridge group believe that, ideally at any rate, class analysis should always incorporate a longitudinal, biographical dimension. They argue that how people respond in given positions will always depend, at least in part, on where they are coming from, and where they believe they are heading. They have argued, for example, that if the positions are occupied only temporarily, lower-level office jobs may have proletarian characteristics without the actors themselves being proletarianized. As we shall see in chapter 8, there is in fact a great deal of intra-career social mobility, which, according to the Cambridge group, makes it unrealistic to portray the population as occupying fixed 'boxes'.

The Cambridge alternative

The Cambridge group have not been armchair critics of the Goldthorpe classification. They have gathered their own data, and built an alternative Cambridge class scale. This is constructed by asking people to think of four friends and their occupations, as well as naming their own. The same information, about the subjects' and their partners' occupations, has also been collected about pairs at the time of their marriages. These questions have been asked of roughly 10,000 individuals, yielding approximately 70,000 pairs of occupations (chosen by each other). Occupations (SOCs in practice, see Box 2.5, pp 31–32) that are paired frequently are said to be socially close (near equals). Frequency of pairing is used as a measure of social proximity and distance. The more frequently occupations choose each other, the closer they are said to be.

When this information is analysed it is found that people in different occupations give symmetrical answers. Things do not simply have to turn out this way. Plumbers could name accountants as friends more frequently than accountants named plumbers, or vice-versa, but in practice there are no major inconsistencies of this type. It is also found that when all occupations are placed in relation to each other, as described above, they spread out along a single axis. Again, this does not simply have to be the case. In theory there could be several circles or networks of occupations that tended to choose one another. In practice, this is not what happens – occupations are spread out along a more or less straight line. Common-sense is used to tilt the line: the end with the accountants and doctors is set at the top, and the end with the road sweepers and labourers is set at the base. The axis is then calibrated at equal intervals and each occupation can be given a numerical score depending on its typical position. The scale is said to be measuring social class by grouping together occupations whose members associate with one another as equals, and, it is suggested, share similar lifestyles, and occupy the same levels of advantage and disadvantage in society's general stratification arrangements.

The first version of the Cambridge scale was developed on the basis of surveys of manual workers in Peterborough and white-collar workers in East Anglia in the 1960s and 70s, and was presented in the 1980 book, *Social Stratification and Occupations* (Stewart et al, 1980). Instead of being gratefully adopted the Cambridge scale was virtually ignored by British sociology whereas at that time the Goldthorpe scheme was receiving a generally favourable reception. So the Cambridge group persisted. They revised and consolidated their scale on the basis of additional research (Prandy, 1990; Prandy and Lambert, 2003), and have proceeded to show that it gives superior results to any of its rivals. The results are said to be superior in that the correlations are stronger with everything that social class is supposed to predict – children's education and the subjects' own voting intentions, for example. If the Cambridge scale is divided arbitrarily into the same number of classes, the relationships with dependent variables are shown to remain stronger than those obtained with the old Registrar General's and the new official (Goldthorpe) classification (Blackburn, 1998; Prandy, 1998a, 1998b; Prandy and Blackburn, 1997).

Wendy Bottero (2004, 2005) has proposed taking a step beyond the Cambridge scale in making social distance the unit in terms of which to place people in their society's general stratification arrangements. She suggests adopting stratification, rather than the class variant of stratification, as the core concept, and using social distance as the unit for measuring social inequality. Distance is to be assessed (as in the Cambridge scale) in terms of who people choose as close friends, as sexual partners, and to marry, but in Bottero's proposal economic differences (occupations, income, wealth) would be treated as just one set of personal attributes (others may be political position, gender, age and ethnicity) which play a part in fixing people's distance from one another. She argues that in practice all these contributors are fused together in fixing individuals' positions, and that priority should not be accorded *a priori* to economic differences. Bottero argues that inequalities (distances) are maintained and reproduced over time, and inter-generationally, not as a structure that is external to individuals but through everyday routine social interaction.

However, there is an overwhelming case for keeping class separate rather than, first, establishing social distance, then trying to identify the contribution of the economic. Class is different in that it is necessarily hierarchical, unlike gender and ethnic divisions which may or may not position one group above others. Social distance can be multi-dimensional. It is class, and only class, that necessarily introduces a hierarchical dimension to social distance. Interactions and intersections with gender and ethnic divisions (which are dealt with later in this chapter and then throughout the book) are best explored after class positions and relationships have been identified independently.

The Cambridge scale is a class scale which measures social distances between people with different occupations. Is this approach superior to that of relational class schemes?

Objections

One objection to the Cambridge scale is that it is not based on research with a nationally representative sample, but the Cambridge group have an adequate reply here. Since people at all levels appear to rank occupations in basically the same order, and since there appear to be no major differences by region or anything else, there are no reasons to suspect that the scale would be any different if derived from a random sample of the entire UK population.

A second objection is that the predictive power of the Cambridge scale is simply irrelevant. The scale yields stronger correlations with, for example, children's educational achievements, than the Goldthorpe scheme. Does this mean that the Cambridge group have a superior measurement of class? Critics say that this is not necessarily so: that the true relationships between social class and the dependent variables may be weaker than the Cambridge scale suggests, and that the strength of its relationships with dependent variables cannot be accepted as a test of whether an independent variable is being measured accurately (Evans, 1998; Rose, 1998). This argument would carry more weight had not the Goldthorpe scheme's supporters been willing to cite its own superior predictive power as a reason for preferring their scheme to Wright's (Marshall et al, 1988). Maybe this kind of evidence is less than decisive, but the ability to predict what any theory of class would lead one to expect cannot be dismissed as neither here nor there.

Third, and getting closer to the heart of this matter, it can be objected that, contrary to the Cambridge group's view, classes are not aggregates of people (in specified occupations) who associate as equals: that these social relationships may be *consequences* of class but they are not what class actually *is*.

Fourth, and related to this, the Cambridge group accept, alongside nearly all other class theorists, that actors should be classified according to their occupations, but the Cambridge scale is not based on a theory which offers possible explanations, which can then be tested, of why occupations are ranked as they are. The Cambridge scale may measure occupational rank accurately, but the scheme has no rationale comparable to market and work situations that might explain each occupation's class position.

Fifth, the Cambridge scale's critics argue that occupations are in fact grouped in clusters: they are not spread evenly in social space (Evans and Mills, 1998). It may be true that all the separate indicators of market situation – pay, job security and career prospects for example – are distributed gradationally, and likewise the pertinent features of work situations. But when occupations are grouped taking into account all these variables simultaneously, we see that some occupations consistently achieve positive scores, others negative, and other groups, like the petit bourgeoisie, have distinctive packages – employing oneself, and maybe other people, in combination with either a strong or weak market position. The justification for 'putting people into boxes' is not that there are clear boundaries (akin to ditches or fences) between classes which might act as barriers to mobility or friendships, but that the members of each class are scattered around concentrations or 'clumps' of occupations, each clump having a qualitatively distinctive class profile.

Sixth, the Cambridge scale does not lead to any theoretically based predictions about the kinds of consciousness and related political action that are most likely to develop at a given social level. The scheme has no underlying theory to explain, for example, the rise of the working class as a political force earlier in history, or to predict equivalent future developments. In short, the Cambridge scale (just like all occupational prestige scales) does not offer enough. It gives precise measurements which lead to strong predictions of some of the short-term consequences of class, but it is weak on explanations, especially explanations of class formation and the likely longer-term political consequences.

Readers who are new to these debates, who have no history of partisanship in the arguments, may wonder why supporters of the Goldthorpe/Oxford and Cambridge schemes cannot reconcile their differences. Why not treat the Cambridge scale as a ruler which gives precise measurements of the hierarchical positions of occupations within classes, and the distances between classes, while the Oxford scheme is allowed to identify the main divisions? The answer is that this type of harmonization would require both sides to compromise their positions, which neither is willing to do. The Cambridge group wish to define class gradationally and argue that introducing any divisions or 'boxes' misrepresents reality. The Goldthorpe scheme is not consistently hierarchical and its supporters have no wish to make it so, since, in their view, this would misrepresent class realities.

Who to classify?

Whatever the class scheme, we have to decide who to classify. In practice the choice is between individuals and household/families, and then, if the latter, whether to take account of everyone's occupations or just one member's job.

The conventional approach

The conventional practice in sociology has been to classify households according to the (usually male) head of household's occupation. There are persuasive reasons for treating the household as a unit that is stratified. Until the 1980s the persuasiveness of this practice was usually considered overwhelming and was rarely challenged. Members of a household were regarded as sharing common standards and styles of living. Children were, and usually still are, regarded as having singular family class backgrounds. The idea that members of a family might have different, even antagonistic, class interests, used to be considered ludicrous. It was argued that class conflict had to be kept out of the home otherwise the family would be unable to perform its own vital functions.

A related conventional practice has been to classify each household according to the occupation of the (usually male) head. Women living singly have been classified according to their own occupations. In the case of couples, it used to be nearly always, and it is still usually, the male who has the most continuous employment, who works the longest hours, who earns the most, and thereby, it is said, governs the entire household's standard of living and general social standing. Hence the justification of conventional practice.

John Goldthorpe has been a consistent defender of conventional practice subject to the qualification that the occupation of the household member with the dominant attachment to the labour market (not necessarily, but in practice still usually, a male) should be used to classify the family (see Goldthorpe, 1983; Erikson and Goldthorpe, 1988). An assumption or implication in conventional practice is that one member's employment (usually the employment of a male member) is normally more important than any employment of other household members in determining not only a household's class position, but in casting the shape of the entire class structure. Hence the justification for studying social mobility and class structure with male-only samples. All 10,000 respondents in Goldthorpe's 1972 social mobility survey were men (Goldthorpe et al, 1980). We should note here that surveys of representative samples of main household earners cannot be treated as if the samples' occupations represented those of the entire workforce, since 'secondary' earners' occupations are likely to be different to those of main earners because the secondaries tend to be a different sex, or younger.

During the last 30 years this conventional practice has come under fierce, broad-based attack. Indeed, virtually the only British defenders (in print) have been John Goldthorpe himself and his Oxford-based colleagues. Second-wave feminism in sociology has chosen the conventional way of doing class analysis as one of the bastions of patriarchal assumptions that must be overturned. The criticisms of the conventional approach now look just as persuasive as the latter once did.

First, the view that the members of a household share the same standard of living, style of life and class position has been challenged. Marriages are not always equal partnerships. There is not necessarily financial equality. The status and public recognition attached to the male's occupation are not necessarily passed on to his marital partner.

Second, nowadays women comprise nearly a half of the workforce (see chapter 3, pp 75–76). It was more realistic in the past to treat the male as the family's main link with the macro-social structure, mainly via the labour market, and the woman's main role as domestic. Nowadays single women are just as likely

Table 2.2   Economic activity rates, 2004/05 (in percentages)

Economic Activity	Males, 16–65	Females, 16–63
Employed	78	67
Unemployed	4	3
Inactive	19	31

Based on data in Li et al (2008)

to have paid employment as men, and around two-thirds of all women hold paid jobs (see Table 2.2). Career breaks following child-birth have become shorter. More and more women have been taking maternity leave rather than terminating their employment. Men are still more likely than women to be in paid employment (just under fourth-fifths compared with around two-thirds of women), but this gap has been closing. Less than a third of adult women are now economically inactive, and they include students, the long-term sick, and any who have retired ahead of the state retirement age, as well as housewives, and the latter are not necessarily long-term housewives. Given these trends, it has become difficult to justify ignoring women's employment in class analysis. There are more households where deciding which member's labour market attachment is dominant is anything but straight-forward. Moreover, it is impossible to explain the distribution of men between the different occupation-based class groups, and their mobility chances, without referring to the fact that some types of jobs are done mainly by women (see Hayes and Miller, 1993).

Third, more women (and men) are living singly or cohabiting outside marriage as a result of the rise in the typical ages of first marriages and mothers on first giving birth (now 29 on average), and the rise in rates of divorce and separation. People are living longer into old age and, as men tend to die younger, there are far more widows than widowers, and the former do not usually inherit their partners' full occupational pensions. Given these trends, one would expect more and more women to regard their own life-chances as depending more upon their own education and occupations rather than who they first marry, or with whom they are currently cohabiting. The foundations in the real world on which conventional practice once rested have weakened.

Individual classification

An alternative to conventional practice is to classify individuals, not households, so that everyone, males and females, can be classed according to their own occupations. Individual classification now has a wide body of supporters who have been able to show that women's own occupations make a difference (after controlling for the influence of their partners' occupations) to women's subjective class identities and political partisanship (Abbott, 1987). They have even been able to show that women's occupations have some influence on their husbands' politics (Hayes and Jones, 1992a, 1992b). In Britain young women have been shown to base their perceptions of their class positions on their own education and occupations, and to view their life-chances, including the resources that will be available to them following marriage, as being determined mainly by their own backgrounds and education (Stanworth, 1984; Charles 1990).

However, there are two big problems with individual classification. First, women in similar occupations are all placed in exactly the same class whether their partners are company directors, doctors or manual workers, with all that this entails for the women's standards and styles of living. Needless to say, this applies equally to men who may be partnered by cleaners or company directors.

Second, all the investigations that have conducted multivariate analysis with large data sets have discovered that the husband's occupation is still, even today, a better predictor of the wife's politics and class identity than her own job (Mills, 1994; Roberts and Marshall, 1995; Zipp and Plutzer, 1996). Husband's employment is the best predictor of a woman's lifestyle and her chances of avoiding poverty (Breen and Whelan, 1995). Why should their own occupations make a greater impression on men's own standards of living, class identities and politics, than women's own occupations make on theirs? Why should women be more responsive to their husbands' occupations than men are to their wives'? The only plausible answer is that, despite the protests of feminist thought, many women still see the domestic role as their primary role, and place themselves in society, and judge their interests, according to their male partners' occupations. And it is still usually the male who has the highest and least interrupted earnings (even though the number of exceptions has increased), and whose occupation, therefore, has the most influence on the household's standard of living and the lifestyles that all its members can afford.

There are powerful arguments both for and against conventional practice, and at present neither side can win because society is changing, the pace of change is uneven between social groups and among households within social groups, and no single method of classification is going to be right for everyone. In the USA Davis and Robinson (1988) have documented a trend over time towards women basing their class identities on both their own and their husbands' occupations rather than the latter's alone. They have also shown that in the USA males have not changed: they have always assessed, and continue to assess, their own class positions entirely on the basis of their own achievements. The chances are that the trends over time, and the sex difference, are basically the same in Britain. In so far as sociology's class schemes need to take popular conceptions into account, the change and dissensus currently found in society are bound to be reflected, some way or another, within sociology.

A different class scheme for women?

If men and women are to be classified individually, each according to their own occupations, the question arises as to whether the same class scheme is going

Table 2.3 Occupations of employed men and women, 2004/05 (in percentages)

Occupation	Men	Women
Middle class	40	37
Intermediate non-manual	6	20
Self-employed	13	5
Working class	41	38

Based on data in Li et al (2008)

to be equally appropriate for both sexes. The Goldthorpe scheme was initially developed from information about men's occupations. All well and good, if only men's occupations are to be taken into account when classifying the entire population. Can the scheme cope with women's jobs?

This question arises because even three decades and more following Britain's equal pay and equal opportunities legislation, men and women still tend to do different jobs. Labour markets remain segmented by gender. There are still many occupations that are done mainly by women. The inclusion of women's occupations in class analysis certainly alters the apparent shape of the class structure (see Table 2.3). Women are more likely than men to be in lower-level non-manual jobs, while men are more likely to be self-employed. Nowadays, however, there is little difference between the chances of male and female employees being in management and professional jobs on the one hand, and working class jobs on the other.

Advocates of the Goldthorpe scheme argue that it is gender neutral: that women's manual jobs, professional jobs and lower-level office jobs possess much the same market and work situation features as men's (Evans, 1996). Others are sceptical. Within broad categories such as professional, management, office and manual occupations, men and women still tend to choose, or are channelled into, different kinds of jobs. For example, routine non-manual women are more likely than men to do typing/word processing. The men are more likely to do administrative tasks that place them on career ladders. So would we be trying to place women (and men) in the same social class categories if women's occupations had been included when constructing the schemes? Or would we have identified rather different social class groups?

Angela Dale and her colleagues (1985) have shown that cluster analysis using features of just women's occupations produces groups that resemble, but are not exactly the same as, the Goldthorpe classes. They found that women's occupations formed the five main clusters in Figure 2.3. It can be argued additionally that, among women, class analysis really ought to take into account the inequalities between full-time and part-time jobs. Part-time jobs, that are filled

i. Professional and administrative
ii. Technical and supervisory
iii. Clerical, cooks, postwomen and bus conductors
iv. Service and production workers
v. Other manual employees in manufacturing

Figure 2.3 Women's occupational classes
Source: Dale at al (1985)

mainly by women, tend to be inferior to their full-time equivalents in most respects – pay per hour, job security, fringe benefits and promotion prospects. This applies at all levels, in retailing, and from junior office jobs to university lecturing. All the class schemes, developed by studying, and in order to study, mainly men, ignore the full-time/part-time dichotomy. It can also be argued that housewives would be recognized (given a class of their own) in a truly woman-friendly scheme. Critics argue that ignoring the domestic division of labour is masculinist: that it marginalizes women and conceals much of their work and their contributions to society (Crompton, 1996b).

Class analysis is threatened with grotesque complications, like using two entirely different class schemes and dispensing with the view that there is just one national class structure, and crediting children with dual social origins according to their mothers' and fathers' occupations. Maybe this latter complication will not be a distortion for the many children who nowadays have two sets of parents/step-parents.

Joint classification

A way of avoiding some of the above complications without returning to the conventional approach is to classify households using all adult members' (usually the husbands' and wives') occupations. One argument for doing this is basically the same as the case for the Cambridge scale – it gives the best predictions, the strongest correlations, with everything that class analysis is expected to predict like standards of living, political partisanship, and children's educational attainments (see Britten and Heath, 1983; Lampard, 1995; Leiulfsrud and Woodward, 1987). But as with all the other answers to 'Who to classify and how?' there are serious problems.

The basic problem with joint classification is that households can gain identical scores from various combinations of husbands' and wives' occupations. So the classes that are identified are not composed of people with common experiences. In other words, the measurement does not distinguish classes in the ordinary meaning of the term (within and outside sociology). As with the Cambridge scale, joint classification is fine if the objective is to develop the best possible predictors of children's educational attainments, standards of living and so on, but this is not exactly the same as identifying class groups.

Social change, gender and the class structure

As already indicated, at present there can be no single, unambiguously correct choice of method. The best choice will depend on the purpose. Individual classification has the edge when seeking the shape of the occupational class structure – the proportions of positions in different classes. On balance, at present, joint classification or the conventional practice are better when seeking class predictions – of the types of consciousness and political action that are most likely to be produced.

Changes in gender roles – both in the home and in the labour market – make it more difficult than formerly to classify the population whatever class scheme is used, and the changes in gender roles themselves are altering the shape of the class structure in ways that are discussed in greater detail in later chapters, but deserve an introduction here. Class and gender are entwined in one another. They are different social divisions. Neither can be reduced to the other. But they interact, as when gender influences people's jobs opportunities. More subtlely, each division becomes implicated in the other. So occupations can be gendered – considered most suitable for, and in practice entered by, mainly men or women. In some way or another, gender infiltrates all classes and class processes. This is why it is impossible to treat gender adequately in a separate chapter in a book on social class: gender must be treated throughout. For the time being, we can note just two (there are many other) ways in which changes in gender roles are affecting the shape of the class structure.

First, increased labour market participation by women has increased the proportion of cross-class households with adults in occupations in different classes. This is despite there being a strong tendency for like to marry like. Middle class men are more likely than working class males to marry middle class females, but there are many males in both classes who marry women whose own occupations are intermediate (office work mainly). This tends to blur class divisions. The blurring occurs in standards of living: gross income and spending levels are less clearly class-divided than would be the case if only males were employed. Dual-earning working class households may have higher gross incomes than single-earner middle class households.

Second, and simultaneously, women's increased labour market participation is tending to push the ends of the social class structure further apart. Like does tend to marry like. So there are now more households than in the past with two adults in well-paid middle class jobs. At the other extreme, there are more households containing adults of working age in which no-one is employed (see Bonney, 2007).

Class and ethnic divisions

Ethnic divisions pose similar challenges to gender for class analysis, but in the case of ethnicity the challenges are far more complicated because there are more than two ethnic groups in present-day Britain. There is a white British majority (which could be sub-divided into English, Scots etc) then numerous minorities. Data are collected routinely nowadays (for ethnic monitoring purposes) only for non-white minorities, but we see instantly that the differences are not pure white and black, advantaged versus disadvantaged.

All the statistics need to be treated with huge caution. First, the ethnic categories are imposed (by those who collect and analyse the data) and may not reflect real ethnic identities and differences accurately. Africans are not a single ethnic group, though over time those in Britain may become such a group. Second, the different minorities may differ in numerous ways – by length of time in Britain, age profiles, and educational backgrounds – and the numbers in sample surveys are rarely large enough to permit complicated breakdowns. All that said, the basic ethnic differences are presented in Tables 2.4 and 2.5.

Table 2.4 gives economic activity rates for males and females separately. We can note that some of the male groups have unusually high unemployment rates. This applies to the Black Caribbeans, Black Africans, Pakistanis and Bangladeshis, but not to the Indians or Chinese. There are high inactivity rates among Pakistani, Bangladeshi and Chinese males, which could be due to some or all of these groups containing unusually high proportions of students. Among women, the Pakistanis and Bangladeshis have a very low employment rate, and a very high inactivity rate, most likely due to the cultures of these minority groups. However, all the minorities, except Black Caribbeans, have higher inactivity rates than white women.

Table 2.4 Ethnic groups and economic activity, 2004/05 (in percentages)

Economic Activity	White	Black Caribbean	Black African	Indian	Pakistani/ Bangladeshi	Chinese
Men						
Employed	79	68	66	74	61	58
Unemployed	4	12	10	5	8	5
Inactive	18	21	25	21	31	38
Women						
Employed	69	65	48	58	23	56
Unemployed	3	5	6	3	4	3
Inactive	29	30	46	39	73	40

Source: Li et al (2008)

Table 2.5 Ethnic groups and occupations of employed members, 2004/05 (in percentages)

			Men			
Occupation	White	Black Caribbean	Black African	Indian	Pakistani/ Bangladeshi	Chinese
Middle class	40	28	39	47	23	45
Intermediate non-manual	6	8	5	8	7	3
Self-employed	13	12	6	13	22	20
Working class	41	52	49	32	48	32
			Women			
Middle class	37	43	37	42	23	41
Intermediate non-manual	20	20	13	17	20	13
Self-employed	5	2	2	5	7	11
Working class	38	35	47	36	50	36

Based on data in Li et al (2008)

In terms of the occupations of the members of the different ethnic groups who are in employment, Pakistanis, Bangladeshis and Chinese males have usually high proportions who are self-employed, whereas few Black Africans are in this category. Indian and Chinese males are over-represented in the middle class, while all the other minorities are over-represented in the working class vis-a-vis the white British. Among women there are fewer ethnic differences, but Pakistanis and Bangladeshis are very much under-represented in the middle class and (alongside Black African women) over-represented in the working class.

These figures are just the start-point for analysing interactions and intersections between class and ethnicity. Even when they are in the same class, members of different ethnic groups may be concentrated in different occupations, and the experience of being middle class, self-employed or working class is very likely to vary by ethnicity.

Summary

This chapter has appraised the main class schemes developed and used by British sociologists: the Registrar General's original class scheme, the Goldthorpe scheme, the Wright schemes, and the Cambridge scale. We have seen that the Goldthorpe scheme has special strengths, which is why it has become the scheme most widely used by present-day British sociologists, and increasingly in other countries also, and why, in a slightly modified form, it has been adopted as the official classification, first in the UK, and more recently by the EU. Over time the Goldthorpe scheme is bound to become more widely known, but not necessarily better understood.

This chapter has also considered whether individuals or households should be the units that are classified, and, if the latter, whose occupations are to be taken into account. The related issue of whether the same class scheme can be equally suitable for males and females, and all ethnic groups, has also been considered. We have seen that there are problems with all the solutions to these issues that have been proposed (when any have been sought – in practice when handling gender). This means that the issues cannot be considered settled and set aside: we must remain sensitive to the problems throughout all the following chapters.

Economic Change

3

Introduction

If class depends on a person's occupation (see chapter 1), then economic changes that alter the kinds of jobs that people are able to enter are bound to reshape the class structure. Here the Goldthorpe scheme (see chapter 2) is used as a background 'map' for revealing some broad class effects (details are added in later chapters) of recent economic and occupational changes, and developments in the UK's labour markets.

The first section examines the new (economic) times in which we are now said to live: how globalization and new technologies have undermined Fordism, increased labour market flexibility, expanded precarious, non-standard forms of employment (part-time, temporary and self-employment), broken up linear careers, contributed to the spread of unemployment and greater insecurity for people still in jobs who are generally expected to do more than in the past in some way or another, all amid wider income inequalities.

The second section focuses on changes in the occupational structure: the shift from manufacturing to service sector jobs, and from manual to non-manual occupations, and the implications for class demographics and social mobility.

The third section discusses the dispersal of the workforce that has occurred as a result of large firms introducing labour saving technology and work practices, and doing more sub-contracting, the rise in self-employment and in the proportion of jobs in small businesses, the decline of public sector employment, and in trade union membership, and the separation of places of work from places of residence.

The final section deals with ongoing changes in the age, gender and ethnic composition of the workforce, and the interaction between these trends and the above developments in the economy and labour markets.

New times

It is doubtful whether we really do live in an era where either the pace or the immensity of economic change is more dramatic than ever before. After all, there was an industrial revolution. During the twentieth century there were two world wars. All generations seem to believe that they are experiencing especially momentous changes. After the Second World War the survivors were impressed by the contrast between the pre-war depression on the one side, and the full employment and steady economic growth of the new era. In 1932 the unemployment rate had peaked at 22 per cent (claimant count, see below), over twice as high as the post-war peak that was recorded in the 1980s (Lindsay, 2003). Since the 1970s commentators have contrasted their own new era with the '30 glorious (post-war) years'. Change is endemic in modern industrial societies. They are inherently dynamic. A stable state is not an option. So there is nothing really new about our present age having novel features. In the early- to mid-twentieth century the future options appeared to be between fascism, free market capitalism, and various versions of socialism – state ownership and control (communism), syndicalism (worker cooperatives), consumer cooperatives, and social democracy (mixed economies with strong welfare states). Today we are offered an entirely different set of future scenarios (see Box 3.1).

Box 3.1   The future of work

There are wildly contrasting views.

i. Optimists say that new technology will eliminate most routine jobs while creating just as many if not more new jobs which require high level skills and qualifications. Simultaneously, new technology makes these jobs mobile – they can be located wherever the most suitable labour is available. Hence countries and their people will prosper if, but only if, they upgrade their workforces' skill and qualification levels. This was the thinking behind the European Union's Lisbon Strategy which was adopted in 2000, and was intended to make Europe the world's most competitive, dynamic, knowledge-driven economy. The UK government has subscribed to this vision (in public). 'In the longer term, the world economy is expected to double in size within the next 20 years, creating up to one billion new skilled jobs and industries and spreading global prosperity' (Cabinet Office, 2009, p 3). Virtually all governments all over the world now subscribe (or say that they subscribe) to this vision. Obviously, they cannot all become the most competitive, the most dynamic etc.

See also Reich, 1991.

ii. A jobless future. Here the claim is that new technology is destroying swathes of jobs and deskilling many of those that remain. We are said to have entered an era of jobless growth. Currently the predicament is said to be concealed by the spread of part-time jobs, and low paid, low productivity, menial jobs. The solution is said to lie in decoupling work and income, paying everyone a citizen's wage, and valuing all useful (often currently unpaid) work.

See Aronowitz and Di Fazio, 1994; Dunkerley, 1996; Forrester, 1999; Gorz, 1999.

iii. A precarious future. New technology, globalization and intensified competition are said to be destroying not jobs themselves so much as employment security. Brazilianization for all (or for most, or for many of us) is said to be the future. Rather

than less-developed countries catching-up, their labour conditions are expected to spread globally.
See Beck, 2000.

iv. A divided future. The claim here is that change is creating more 'lovely jobs' and more 'lousy jobs', thereby widening the division between elites in relatively secure, well-paid jobs, who can travel the world for work and for leisure, and underclasses who are poor, stuck in local communities (prisons for vagabonds), in which they are flawed consumers.
See Bauman, 1998a, 1998b; Goos and Manning, 2003.

Every generation has been able to comment on something new, and two phrases that occur again and again in accounts of recent and current changes are globalization and information technology. Both have profound direct and indirect implications for employment and the class structures in Britain and all other countries.

Globalization and new technology

In some respects globalization (see Box 3.2) is ironing out inter-country differences. It has become impossible to escape McDonalds. Wherever we go we encounter the same news (probably from CNN), music, international cuisine and consumer goods. Yet in other respects globalization sharpens inter-country differences. Tourists travel in order to see something different. Local populations may accentuate local customs as a way of resisting global forces. So everywhere globalization results in a unique mixture of the global and the local. A new word, *glocalization,* has been coined to describe this process.

Here we are concerned primarily with the economic aspects of globalization, which is certainly not ironing out inequalities in standards of living. Indeed, the gap between rich and poor countries widened in the closing decades of the twentieth century. Every country has to establish, or finds itself driven into, a particular niche in the global economy. The key globalizing developments in the world economy have been the creation of trans-national companies, hauling down trade barriers (tariffs), the globalization of financial markets, and the growth in the proportion of all output that is traded internationally. One result of all this is fiercer competition. A related consequence is that national governments are less able to manage their national economies according to their own priorities, oblivious to global trends. They can be helpless in the face of international flows of capital. Global markets, not national governments, appear to make the big decisions. If national governments try to control the export of capital they can be sure that little will flow in. Virtually all kinds of businesses – banking, motor cars, clothing and so on – have lost their former holds over domestic markets. This is despite the fact that in the UK most of the goods and services that we buy are still produced locally. The proportion of exports

---

Box 3.2 Globalization

This is not completely new. There have been world religions for several centuries. Nevertheless, it is only during the last 30 years that the term 'globalization' has been used extensively. It refers to a large number of interacting trends, some completely new, and others that have intensified.

■ The growth of trans-national companies that plan their activities on a global scale.
■ The growth of international trade.
■ Satellite communications and the internet.
■ The creation of world-wide (television) audiences for world sports events such as the Olympics and football's World Cup.
■ The same music, fashions and consumer goods now being available in all parts of the world.
■ The growth of international tourism.
■ Sensitivity to the global scale of, and the need for global solutions to, problems such as environmental sustainability and AIDS.
■ The global scope of new social movements such as Marxism (at one time), and, more recently, the peace and green movements.
■ The development of world political and judicial institutions such as the United Nations and the various international courts.

It can be useful to distinguish between internationalization and globalization. Businesses that operate internationally are not new. Nor is the international marketing of all kinds of goods and services. Today's globalization can be regarded as rather different. There are now businesses (trans-national companies) which do not belong to any particular country, and trans-national institutions such as the European Union, the World Trade Organization, the World Bank and the International Monetary Fund that owe no allegiance to particular states. A truly global trans-national labour movement would not be based on cooperation between national labour organizations, but rather would have national cells as subordinate branches.

---

in the UK's GNP was just 19 per cent in 2006. For the entire European Union (treated as a single entity) it was 12 per cent. However, the global average was 37 per cent. Some small countries, energy exporting countries, and top tourist destinations, are thoroughly bound into the global economy. Singapore's exports amount to 219 per cent of its GDP (a lot of imports are immediately exported). In Hong Kong it is 167 per cent. It is 76 per cent in Slovakia, 72 per cent in Belgium and 65 per cent in Azerbaijan (www.nationmaster.com). Globalization is a trend, certainly not an absolute state, though the trend itself is unmistakable. Maybe at some point the trend will be arrested. The street protests that regularly surround meetings of the G7, the G8 and G20, and the World Trade Organization (whose remit is to promote trade) perhaps indicate the development of a grassroots reaction against the global environment, and the economies of developed and less-developed countries alike, becoming matters that elected (or any other) national governments are unable to control.

Technological change is not new, but the latest generation (which with satellite communication, computers and the Internet, has helped to promote globalization) has several novel features. First, micro-computing affects virtually all products, industries and occupations in some way or another. Its applications are neither industry nor occupation specific. There can be few people whose working lives have been completely unaffected by the micro-chip. Second, the new technology is micro, and cheap. It can be installed virtually anywhere – inside washing machines and even wrist watches, and in study bedrooms. It is unnecessary nowadays to be a giant firm in order to take advantage of state-of-the art technology.

Globalization and technological change are the forces behind a variety of recent and ongoing shifts in the workforce which are examined in greater detail below: shifts between business sectors, especially from manufacturing to services, and from larger to smaller establishments. There have been equally important implications in the world's labour markets. In Europe, levels of unemployment have been higher since the 1970s than during the preceding 30 years. Related to this, more jobs are precarious. More jobs are part-time or officially temporary and permanent jobs are felt to be less secure than formerly. People in employment are having to work harder. Income inequalities have widened. New technologies and globalization have played a part in all these changes. They have not been the cause of, but the above trends have interacted with the UK workforce becoming more compressed in terms of age, more balanced in terms of gender, and more mixed in terms of ethnicity. We shall see that the effects of all these interacting changes have not been exactly the same – in fact they have often been completely different – in different sections of the workforce.

Flexible labour markets and workers

The hard data does not always suggest that there have been major changes. The shift from full-time to part-time jobs is the exception here: from 17 per cent to 26 per cent of all jobs in Britain between 1979 and 2009. Here there is a big difference between men's and women's jobs: 42 per cent of women's jobs are part-time compared with just 12 per cent of men's jobs.

A problem when measuring the shift from permanent to temporary posts is that until the 1980s government statistics did not make the distinction. Previously this was not an issue. Clearly, therefore, something has changed. However, in 2009 94.5 per cent of all UK jobs were still permanent, that is, with open-ended contracts. Here there is little difference between the sexes; 5.0 per cent of men's and 6.1 per cent of women's jobs were temporary (of finite duration). We need to bear in mind here that in the UK it is relatively easy (compared with other European Union countries) for employers to dismiss or declare permanent staff redundant. Permanent does not necessarily mean secure.

One view is that the much proclaimed end of 'jobs for life' and the advent of unprecedented workforce flexibility are myths, and that feelings of insecurity are largely the result of press scares and hype-books. Since 1990 the average time spent in a job has actually lengthened (see Taylor, 2002). Most job movements are still voluntary. Three-quarters of all employees say that they are not worried about losing their own jobs, and in this respect there has been little change since the 1970s (Denny, 1999).

However, labour turnover figures may be unsatisfactory as indicators of job security and insecurity. Employees may cling on because they are uncertain of finding new jobs. Voluntary departures may be prompted because the alternative is demotion or geographical relocation. Workers often jump before being pushed. Brendan Burchell and his colleagues (1999) interviewed 340 employees and managers in 20 work establishments in various parts of Britain. All the businesses had faced pressure to become more flexible as a result of tougher market competition, customers who wanted everything just in time, right first time every time, and at lower prices. There had been additional pressures from shareholders who wanted higher dividends and share values. All the businesses were achieving the necessary flexibility by some combination of redundancies, contracting-out, and changed work practices which could include multi-skilling, teamwork, delayering, changing hours of work (upwards, downwards or towards greater flexibility), and the relocation of jobs. Only 23 per cent of the employees said that there was 'any chance' of losing their own jobs during the next 12 months, but many still felt insecure. This was not because they regarded job loss as likely, but through fear of the consequences should this occur. Social security benefits have become less generous, and the chances of finding a new job without loss of status have diminished. Also, Burchell and his colleagues found that workers felt that their managers could not be trusted. The workers knew that managements' guarantees would become worthless if customers so decided (by taking their business elsewhere) or if the shareholders decided to sell the company (see also Doherty, 2009; Doogan, 2001). Under 30 year olds experience far more changes of status today than in the 1950s and 60s, sometimes in and out of government schemes, or educational courses, rather than straight from job to job (Pollock, 1997). They now take longer to 'settle', and some may never settle-down.

There are contrasting views on the implications of this new insecurity. One view is that it inflicts huge personal damage on workers and their lives outside the workplace. Richard Sennett (1999) claims that employees suffer from their inability to feel in control of their own lives; that they may even find it impossible to make sense of their lives. They know that their employers do not regard staff as indispensable, which makes it difficult for workers to maintain self-respect. Perceived lack of long-term commitment on the part of employers leads to an erosion of trust on the part of employees. Work commitment (the importance attached to having a job) may remain high, but job commitment is undermined. The types of family and housing careers that employees have come to expect have depended on employment security. Take this away, and so much else becomes shaky.

The opposite view is that employees can benefit from their release from earlier career constraints. They can treat jobs as projects in which they add to their human capital, record this on their CVs, then move on to further 'projects'. Thus apprenticeships become self-designed and careers become personal projects rather than laid-out by employing organizations (see Arthur et al, 1999; Beck, 1992; Bridges, 1995). This can sound splendid, but in their 1992 survey of a nationally representative sample of the British workforce, Gallie et al (1998) found that 47 per cent said that they had little or no choice when looking for their present or most recent jobs. We shall see in later chapters that the effects of and responses to the new labour market conditions vary tremendously between different age and occupational groups.

Labelling the era

A new vocabulary has been coined as an aid to understanding all these changes. We have already encountered globalization and labour market flexibility. It is also said that we have become a *post-industrial society*, meaning that there are fewer jobs in manufacturing (well under a fifth of all jobs today – see below), and that most employment is now in services. We are said to have become an *information society*, recognizing here the extent to which change is information technology driven. We are said to have become a *learning society* in two senses: there are more high-level jobs that demand qualifications (see below), and the pace of change requires education and training to be recurrent and lifelong. *Knowledge economy* is an alternative descriptor.

Box 3.3   Fordism

This term was coined by Antonio Gramsci (1891–1937), an Italian Marxist, a theorist, but also a leader of Italy's communist party, and a prisoner in Mussolini's gaols from 1926 until 1937. As often happens, the word Fordism has become widely used only since the system began to decline.

The name Ford is used because the firm pioneered what, at the time (in the 1920s), was a novel way of organizing industrial production. Ford introduced the mechanized assembly line, and pioneered the mass production of a standardized product, which enabled costs and prices to be hauled down to a level that stimulated mass consumption. The key features of Fordist production are:

- Capital intensive.
- Inflexible production processes.
- Hierarchical and bureaucratic management.
- Extensive use of semi-skilled labour performing routine tasks.
- Strong trade unions.

Prior to and following the Second World War, Fordist methods were adopted in the manufacture of a wide range of consumer goods.

Post-Fordism (see Box 3.3.) refers to how everything has become more flexible – enterprises, labour markets, occupations and workers. The name Ford is used because this firm led and typified the earlier era. Ford created a mass market for its cars through the mass production of standardized products, which enabled unit costs to be hauled down, thereby bringing private motoring within the average American family's means. Its success enabled Ford to employ thousands of workers in highly specialized and fairly secure jobs (for life if they could stand the pace). Firms like Ford, their products and their jobs, were among the most secure fixtures on the socio-economic landscape. They were affected by recessions, inevitably, but could be relied on to survive. We are now in new, post-Fordist times.

Non-standard employment

This term has been coined in recent years to acknowledge the spread of jobs with different terms and conditions to those that became standard, meaning full-time and permanent, early on, under Fordism. The largest segment of Britain's non-standard sector consists of part-time jobs. As we have seen, over two-fifths of all Britain's female employees are on part-time schedules (defined in government statistics as under 30 hours a week), and the proportion of males with part-time jobs (now 12 per cent) has been rising. It has also become common for students aged 14–15 and upwards to take part-time jobs. Most nominally full-time university students in Britain now take such jobs, largely from financial necessity as most students' grants have been wholly or partly replaced by loans, and fees have been introduced. However, another crucial fact of this situation is that there are more opportunities to work part-time nowadays, mainly in consumer services.

It is only fair to point out that many women (and some men) prefer part-time to full-time schedules (see Hakim, 1996). Women often find part-time employment more easily reconciled with their domestic roles. Something very similar can be said of students. But it must also be said that the arrangement is equally convenient for the employers. Nowadays part-time jobs are less likely to be created because the employers are unable to fill full-time posts than to fine-tune the number of staff at work to fluctuations in workflows, and to ensure that labour costs are no higher than absolutely necessary. So office staff may be hired for just 30, 25 or 20 hours a week if, in the employer's view, that is all that is required. Retail and other consumer services which need to be provided so as to coincide with consumers' life rhythms use part-time staff so that the workforces can be strengthened, often doubled or tripled in size, in the evenings and/or at weekends. The use of part-time staff is one way in which firms can achieve numerical flexibility. A rather controversial employer strategy is to guarantee no specific hours of work but to require staff to be on call whenever required. In the 1990s one fast food outlet gained notoriety by requiring staff to sign-off and sign-on when customers left and entered the premises.

Another form of non-standard employment is temporary. We have seen that the proportion of UK employees on officially temporary contracts – with specified end-dates – is in fact quite small, around five per cent. But to this we need to add workers who are on government 'training' schemes. The use of temps (who may have indefinite contracts with their agencies) is another way in which employers can achieve numerical flexibility and avoid carrying excess labour. Rather than staffing-up so as to be able to accommodate staff holidays and illnesses, employers have increasingly opted for lean and mean profiles, and have brought in temporary staff as and when necessary. Another advantage of using such staff, from the employer's point of view, is that they are usually not eligible for any union-agreed terms and conditions applicable to directly employed staff. And any temps who prove less than satisfactory can be dispensed with very quickly. Within the European Union, staff employed by a business in, say, Latvia, can be 'posted' to work on a contract in Britain, say on a construction site. The workers retain their Latvian terms and conditions of employment except that while in the UK statutory requirements must be observed (minimum pay law, health and safety regulations etc).

A third type of non-standard employment is self-employment which has become more widespread since the 1970s, and is discussed in greater detail below (p 71). Add together all the types of non-standard employment and they amount to over a third of all jobs. As explained above, the workers concerned would not all prefer standard, full-time, permanent contracts. The point remains that all non-standard forms of employment are more precarious than the mainline jobs of the Fordist era.

The spread of non-standard employment is sometimes applauded as evidence of businesses making themselves flexible so as to cope with post-Fordist conditions – rapid technological change and shifts in consumer preferences. As always, however, this is just one side of the story. In conditions of high unemployment it is possible to recruit to low quality jobs because workers have no choice. Non-standard employment is often a way in which employers transfer risks away from themselves and onto their workforces, and the least-skilled, lowest-paid workers have been the most vulnerable (Purcell et al, 1999).

Unemployment

Some would say that this has been the really big and crucial change in the labour market since the 1960s: the result of certain other trends like the collapse of manufacturing and the decline in manual employment (see below), and the cause of others such as the spread of poor quality, non-standard jobs. As ever, levels of unemployment rise and fall alongside business cycles, but around a much higher centre-point than from 1945 up to the mid-1970s.

There are different ways in which unemployment can be measured. The longest running time series in the UK is the claimant count (see Table 3.1). This gives the number of people claiming state benefits on account of their unemployment. The total is the primary figure. The unemployment rate is calculated

Table 3.1   Claimant count

Year	000s	%	Year	000s	%
1971	649	2.4	1991	2268	7.6
1972	719	2.7	1992	2742	9.2
1973	511	1.9	1993	2877	9.7
1974	514	1.9	1994	2599	8.8
1975	790	2.9	1995	2290	7.6
1976	1082	3.9	1996	2088	7.0
1977	1150	4.2	1997	1585	5.3
1978	1133	4.1	1998	1347	4.5
1979	1064	3.8	1999	1248	4.1
1980	1351	4.8	2000	1088	3.6
1981	2152	7.6	2001	970	3.2
1982	2521	9.0	2002	947	3.1
1983	2762	9.9	2003	933	3.0
1984	2888	10.1	2004	854	2.7
1985	2997	10.3	2005	862	2.7
1986	3067	10.5	2006	945	2.9
1987	2780	9.4	2007	863	2.7
1988	2253	7.6	2008	908	2.8
1989	1768	5.9	2009	1391	4.3
1990	1648	5.5			

Source: Office for National Statistics

by expressing the total of claimants as a fraction of the (estimated) size of the workforce. During the 1950s and 60s the claimant count remained under half a million. These were the decades of a kind of full employment that may never return to Britain. The level rose, and broke through the million threshold, in the mid-1970s, and then remained at over a million until the twenty-first century. During the 1980s the total of claimants peaked at just over three million in 1986, and remained above two million until 1997 when unemployment was in a long period of decline which lasted until 2004. However, by 2009 the total had passed a million again, 4.3 per cent of the workforce. The highest percentage in Table 3.1 is 10.5 per cent in 1986.

A second way of measuring unemployment is from the Labour Force Survey (see Table 3.2), which has been conducted on a continuous basis in the UK since the beginning of the 1990s. It is a random sample survey of adults from

Table 3.2 Unemployment rates UK, Labour Force Survey

April–June	All persons 16–59/64 % unemployed	All persons 16–59/64 Total number unemployed (000s)
1992	9.8	2812
1993	10.4	2928
1994	9.7	2625
1995	8.8	2435
1996	8.4	2296
1997	7.3	1988
1998	6.4	1789
1999	6.1	1728
2000	5.6	1588
2001	5.1	1440
2002	5.3	1529
2003	5.1	1489
2004	4.8	1424
2005	4.8	1465
2006	5.2	1699
2007	5.5	1653
2008	5.7	1776
2009	6.5	2029

Source: Office for National Statistics

which an unemployment rate (the primary figure here) is calculated, and the total number unemployed is then estimated from the (estimated) total size of the workforce. The Labour Force Survey, since 1997 the UK government's preferred way of assessing the true level of unemployment, consistently gives higher numbers unemployed and a higher unemployment rate than the claimant count, though the trends over time that are indicated are the same. Since 1992 the estimated total unemployed in the Labour Force Survey has never been beneath 1.4 million. This survey counts people as unemployed if they have not worked during the previous week, but only if they have actively searched for work, and if they are prepared to start more or less immediately if offered a suitable job. It captures groups who are unemployed but who are ineligible for benefit. These include young people who are not entitled to the Job Seekers Allowance, women returners who are normally unable to claim

Table 3.3 Proportions of working age households where no-one was in employment

Year	Percentage
1984	16.2
1985	17.0
1986	17.3
1987	17.5
1988	16.3
1989	14.9
1990	14.8
1991	15.9
1992	17.3
1993	18.4
1994	18.7
1995	18.7
1996	18.9
1997	17.9
1998	17.5
1999	17.0
2000	16.4
2001	16.7
2002	16.6
2003	16.1
2004	16.1
2005	16.3
2006	15.7
2007	16.1

Source: Office for National Statistics

benefit if partnered by an employed male, anyone who has exhausted automatic entitlement to the Job Seekers Allowance (just six months) and has assets (maybe from a redundancy payment) that exclude them from means-tested benefits, and persons deemed to have retired because they have pensions but who are seeking to supplement their incomes by continuing to work. There are some individuals who feature in the claimant count who are not counted as unemployed in the Labour Force Survey, often because they are not actively seeking work (which they may regard as pointless).

A third way of assessing the level of joblessness is the proportion of households which contain adults of working age where no-one is in employment. This gives the highest estimate – roughly one household in every six. This figure includes groups who do not feature in the claimant count, or in the unemployed as measured in the Labour Force Survey. Households that are dependent on incapacity benefit, lone non-working parents, and people who have retired on pensions before reaching the normal state retirement age are included here. These households contain over four million adults and one-in-six of Britain's children.

For most people unemployment is a temporary experience, and one which they detest. Unemployment is bad for people's physical and mental health, family relationships, standards of living and virtually everything else that they value. And the damage that unemployment inflicts seeps into sections of the workforce who realize that their own jobs are insecure. They know that they cannot rely on finding further jobs of equivalent status immediately. People often manage to escape from unemployment only having lowered their sights and accepted demotion to inferior jobs to those that they formerly occupied. Getting back into work has become tougher since the full employment levels of the 1950s and 60s became distant history.

The official European Union view, and the UK government's, is that the answer to unemployment is faster economic growth which is expected to create more jobs, coupled with better education and training for young people, and for the adult unemployed, so that they will be equipped for the jobs that come on stream. The European Commission claims that new technology has created far more jobs in Europe than it has destroyed, and that the total number in employment in the twenty-first century is higher than ever before (European Commission, various dates). But one important, often overlooked, fact of this matter is that the growth of part-time employment accounts for more than all the additional EU employment over and above the level of the 1970s. There are fewer full-time jobs in the European Union today than there were in the 1970s. It is doubtful whether there really is more paid work around. Unemployment can be concealed by people taking early retirement, young people prolonging their education, and in the 1990s there was an amazing rise in the UK (given the general improvement in health) in the numbers who were recorded as unable to work due to incapacity.

When comparing recent unemployment levels with those experienced before the 1990s, it is important to compare like with like, which means comparing claimant count with claimant count. So in 2009 unemployment was at roughly the same level as in 1980/81 (1.3 million rising towards two million), not the 3.1 million claimants of 1986. A Labour Force Survey in 1986 would almost certainly have estimated unemployment at over four million.

Doing more

These are truly amazing times. Compared with the 1960s, the UK now has more unemployed adults, more who are in and out of jobs, and more who are working part-time. Meanwhile, full-time employees are working longer and harder than ever. The lengthening of working time has been most pronounced in the management and professional grades. This is one way in which some sections of the workforce are now doing more. It is partly a consequence of all the delayering and cutting back core payrolls to the lowest possible levels. Businesses have become reluctant to carry any slack which, in many cases, has meant retained staff carrying heavier workloads. Recessions raise fears of redundancy, which can lead to outbreaks of 'presenteeism'. The present-day worker is often a tired worker. Salaried staff are often expected to take any excess work home and complete it in the evening or at weekend. Warhurst and Thompson (1998) claim that work intensification is in fact the main recent change in people's experience of work.

There are additional senses in which people in jobs are doing more. While seeking numerical flexibility in some grades (generally the lower-skilled grades for which suitable staff can be easily found and replaced), firms have been demanding functional flexibility from their permanent core staff. In some cases this has meant the multi-skilled worker replacing older, specialized trades. Sometimes functional flexibility has been achieved through 'teamwork' which requires all members to be able to cover for each other's absences, and usually requires the team itself rather than managers or supervisors to accept responsibility for the quality and quantity of their work. Multi-skilling often means recurrent training and further education simply to keep abreast of changing technologies and work requirements.

In the 1970s Harry Braverman (1974) forecast a progressive degradation of work which was to result from an increasingly clear division between conception (the responsibility of management) and execution (the worker's role). Braverman anticipated jobs at all levels becoming less skilled and more routine. In practice, the trend has been in exactly the opposite direction. Most employees in all grades report that their jobs have become more demanding, and that doing the jobs requires more skills, training and qualifications than in the past. In this sense there has been a general process of job enrichment. Simultaneously, employees report that they have less task discretion and are supervised more closely. In this sense, Braverman's forecast proves correct. Responsibility is shifted downwards while control moves upwards. Stress levels rise while job satisfaction declines. Meanwhile, 'work commitment' (the importance that employees attach to having a job) remains high. New technology (computers) has been the typical catalyst behind all these trends (see Ashton et al, 2000; Beynon et al, 2002; Gallie et al, 1998; Gallie et al, 2004; Gallie and White, 1993; Penn et al, 1993; Webb, 2004).

Even so, many jobs still require little in the way of qualifications and skills. 34 per cent of the respondents in a 1992 survey said that their jobs needed only low qualifications or none at all, and 22 per cent said that it took less than a month to learn to do their jobs well. 42 per cent said that they had received no training whatsoever in their present jobs (Gallie et al, 1998). In 2001 over a half of all workers in the European Union said that they had received no training during the previous five years (Gallie and Paugram, 2003). Far from technological change racing ahead of the workforce's skills and qualifications, the UK workforce has become grotesquely over-qualified relative to the jobs that are available. 'There are approximately 6.4 million people qualified to level 3 but only 4 million jobs that demand these qualifications.... The other side of the coin can be seen at the bottom of the skills hierarchy. There are 6.5 million jobs for which no qualifications at all would be required to be recruited to them. Yet there are only 2.9 million economically active people who actually possess no qualifications' (Felstead et al, 2002, p 31).

Income inequalities

Another well-documented trend in recent times has been a widening of income inequalities. Since the 1970s the highest earners have been receiving the largest pay increases in both absolute and percentage terms, and this trend is continuing. Company directors and City of London investment bankers have fared best of all, followed by managers and professionals, followed by skilled and office workers, with the least skilled lagging behind everyone else. And behind all of these, the groups dependent on state benefits have seen their incomes falling further and further behind the earnings of those in employment.

The most popular explanation for all this is market forces. At any rate, this is the explanation favoured by politicians and newspaper editors, and probably by those who are doing best and who like to believe that they are gaining only the proper rewards for their hard work and scarce skills. Income inequalities are said to have widened because skill requirements have been rising, and workers with the necessary skills (presumably like the City of London financial professionals who earn six figure salaries plus six figure bonuses) have been able to benefit.

The problem with this explanation is simply that the facts don't fit. This has been known since the 1960s (see Routh, 1965), but the mass of contrary evidence does not seem to prevent the explanation being repeated time and again. The explanation fits classical economic theory which is often confused with how real economies work. All the evidence shows that pay relativities fluctuate only marginally in response to labour shortages and surpluses. In any case, over the last 30 years the workforce's qualifications have improved more rapidly than skill requirements have risen. The number of university graduates has risen steeply, from less than 15 per cent at the beginning of the 1980s to well over 30 per cent of all young people today. If the market forces explanation was correct, this increase in supply should have depressed graduates' earnings. In practice the earnings differential between graduates and other employees has widened. How can this be explained? We shall see that sociological class theory proves far more helpful than classical economics in resolving the paradox. Company directors and senior managers are able to fix their own remuneration. Other grades have to negotiate, individually or collectively, or are simply told how much they will receive. The incomes of state-dependents are determined by politicians whose positions depend on the votes of the population in general.

The changing shape of the occupational structure

The preceding section has identified changes that have swept through the UK economy affecting all sections of the workforce, albeit, as we shall see in later chapters, to different extents and in rather different ways. Here we identify how, amid these tidal waves, the workforce has shifted between different types of jobs. There have been two main shifts: sector shifts – from manufacturing into service sectors, and occupation shifts – from manual into non-manual jobs.

Sector shifts

It is misleading to speak of a collapse of British manufacturing since output is as high as ever. Even so, over the last generation the decline of employment in manufacturing (and extractive) industries has been steep. Well over half of the manufacturing jobs that existed in the 1970s have gone. In some industries the workforces really have collapsed. Huge steel plants have closed. Coal-mining used to employ three-quarters of a million. In 1981 the National Coal Board still had 211 collieries and employed 218,000 miners. By 1994 British Coal had just 17 mines and 8,500 miners (Fieldhouse and Hollywood, 1999). In the early-1980s few people believed that, before the end of the century, Britain's coal mining industry would be all but closed down. Arthur Scargill (the leader of the coal miners union) was accused of scare tactics when he led the 1984–85 coal miners strike against an alleged programme of pit closures. The scale and speed of pit closures following the strike actually exceeded Scargill's forecasts.

The downward trend in manufacturing employment is sometimes described as a second industrial revolution. In the first industrial revolution labour moved from the countryside to towns, and from agriculture into the mines and factories that were then opening. At the beginning of the nineteenth century agriculture was far and away the country's main employer. Today less than two percent of the workforce is in agriculture, but output from the land is greater than in the nineteenth century. Much the same has now been happening to manufacturing for several decades. Output is being maintained – increasing slightly in the long-term – but with far fewer workers. The explanations are the same as applied in agriculture over a century ago – more efficient working practices (enforced in recent times by international competition) and technology boosting the productivity of each worker.

Employment in manufacturing grew during the nineteenth century, and continued to grow until the inter-war years. At that time around a half of all jobs were in manufacturing and mining. Subsequently there was a slow decline, then a steep decline from the 1970s onwards: the effects of new technology and globalization. By 2009 81 per cent of all jobs in Britain were in services.

The steep dip in manufacturing employment since the 1970s is sometimes described as de-industrialization (see Box 3.4). Some old 'rust bucket' and 'smoke stack' industries have been all but wiped out. In addition to coal mining, these include ship-building and steel production. The impact has varied from region to region. Regions that were heavily dependent on older manufacturing and extractive industries (the midlands, the north of England, and Scotland) saw their levels of unemployment rocketing upwards in the 1970s and 80s. South-east England, in contrast, experienced the greatest benefits from the job creation that occurred. Some workers in declining regions stayed put. Family commitments, the social and economic costs of relocation, and fears of being unable to afford housing in the south-east, tied them down. But many moved. So by the end of the twentieth century in the UK, regional disparities in unemployment rates were narrower than at any time since the First World War. The recession that began in 2008 was different from earlier downturns. It began in financial services (banking) where initial job losses were heaviest, then spread fairly evenly throughout the private sector economy, and throughout all regions. Nowadays there are growth spots, and unemployment blackspots, within all regions, though there are still more of the former and fewer of the latter in the south-east than anywhere else. Needless to say, regional imbalances, and population movements, are anything but novel. During the industrial revolution the north and the midlands attracted new labour to the mines and factories that were then opening. In the nineteenth century the countryside was largely depopulated, and levels of unemployment rose in many rural areas. Rural unemployment is still an apparently intractable problem in many parts of the UK, though in the late-twentieth century some out-of-city areas began to experience sustained economic booms as businesses moved onto greenfield sites (see below).

Box 3.4   De-industrialization

This can be a misleading phrase. It is true that manufacturing employment has declined steeply, but this does not apply to output. Some industries have all but disappeared from the economic landscape, but Britain is doing OK in many manufacturing sectors, and excellently in some. Food processing and chemicals are OK. So is motor manufacturing thanks to all the foreign-based (but really trans-national) firms that assemble in Britain, which is far and away the world's number one in producing Formula One. The UK is world class in other high-tech areas – weaponry, aircraft, and pharmaceuticals are just three examples.

The expansion of employment in services (anything that you cannot drop on your foot) has more than compensated for the loss of manufacturing jobs, but we may now be on the verge of a third industrial revolution. From the 1940s up until the 1970s employment in public services expanded. There were more jobs in central and local government, teaching and health services. Subsequently this all-round public sector growth ground to a halt. Financial and other business services were a major source of new jobs from the 1960s up to and through the 1980s, but this trend is now being reversed. Financial services, like agriculture and manufacturing previously, have been introducing labour-saving technology and downsizing in terms of staff. In recent years the main source of employment growth has been consumer services – retailing, hotels and catering, and other leisure industries.

Manufacturing jobs have been lost because Britain, along with other advanced industrial countries, has been unable to increase sales and output sufficiently to maintain the earlier armies of workers. Part of the explanation is the switch of production to less developed, lower-cost countries in the Far East, Latin America and Eastern Europe (an aspect of globalization). New labour-saving technology is another part of the story. Another reason is that in countries like Britain demand for goods is growing more slowly than spending power. People still have a huge appetite for manufactured goods – cars, televisions, videos, computers, mobile telephones, gardening equipment and so on. But as standards of living rise, we all tend to spend higher proportions of our incomes on 'being served' – with holidays and meals out, for instance.

What are the class implications of this? These are explored fully in later chapters, but two implications can be noted immediately. First, there are fewer manual jobs because in some (but not all) service sectors white-collar employees are larger proportions of the total labour forces than in manufacturing. Local government, the civil service, banks, hospitals and universities have top-heavy occupational profiles. However, it is important to bear in mind that not all service sector jobs are white-collar. Hospitals employ porters as well as doctors. The service sector includes cleaning and security businesses, restaurants and supermarkets, as well as banks and solicitors. Indeed, the consumer services in which employment growth is now concentrated have bottom-heavy occupational profiles.

A second class effect of the shift to services is to change the character of the manual jobs that remain. The old working class was employed in coal mines, shipyards, steel plants and engineering workshops. The new working class is employed in supermarkets, security firms, contract cleaners, fast food and other catering establishments, and suchlike. The full implications of this are discussed in chapter 4.

Occupation shifts

There have been simultaneous changes in the distribution of employment between the various grades within some business sectors, and especially within manufacturing. The main shift has been upwards. Manual employment has sometimes been decimated and sometimes trimmed, while white-collar employment has held steady or increased. Production workers have been replaced by technology. Meanwhile, new higher-level occupations have been created connected with the design and management of the new technical systems.

Occupation shifts have combined with sector shifts to reduce the number of manual workers. The working class is no longer the mass of the people as it was at the beginning of the twentieth century. Tables 3.4 and 3.5 (see pages 67–68) present evidence from British Election Studies conducted during every general election from 1964 to 1997. The tables are based on information supplied only by respondents aged 35 and over – those considered to have reached occupational maturity, their ultimate destinations. The pooled samples are divided into birth cohorts, and the left hand column in Table 3.4 adds the class distributions of the fathers of respondents who were born between 1900 and 1909. The tables show how the class distribution of the British workforce changed during the twentieth century. In the nineteenth century 68 per cent of males' jobs were working class. This figure declined gradually to 38 per cent among those born in the 1950s. Among women there was a similar decline from 52 per cent to 23 per cent. Self-employment dipped among cohorts whose working lives spanned the decades of the mid-twentieth century, then rose again. Among men the main growth throughout the twentieth century was in middle class employment – up from 11 per cent to 42 per cent of all jobs. Women's employment also shifted into middle class occupations – from 13 per cent to 36 per cent – but also into lower non-manual jobs – 24 per cent among those born before 1900 to between 35 per cent and 37 per cent for those born between 1920 and 1959. The extent to which, and the speed with which, the working class has declined numerically should not be exaggerated. It still comprised around two-fifths of the male working population among those born in the 1950s, whose working lives continued into the twenty-first century. If we discount the intermediate classes, we are still some distance from having a middle class majority. We are certainly not on the verge of an age when we will all be stockbrokers, accountants, brain surgeons and suchlike. There is still plenty of 'donkey work'. As we have seen, there are still plenty of jobs that require no formal qualifications and very little training.

It is often assumed that the trends described above are still in process and will continue into the future. However, the trends may have stalled in the late-twentieth century. Tables 3.6 and 3.7 (see page 69) bring the time series up to date, as best we can. The class distributions of males and females who were born in the 1950s are repeated in the left-hand columns of Tables 3.6 and 3.7. The centre columns give the class distributions in 1991 of a nationally representative sample of persons born in 1958 (so they were age 33 in 1991). The right-hand column gives the class breakdown for the entire UK workforce in 2004/05. There is no evidence of any change among males. Among women the main trend is out of intermediate (lower non-manual) occupations and into working class jobs.

Table 3.4 Class profiles of males by birth cohort (in percentages)

Class	Fathers of respondents born 1900–09	Pre–1900	1900–09	1910–19	1920–29	1930–39	1940–49	1950–59
Higher middle class	4	7	10	12	16	17	22	23
Lower middle class	7	11	9	11	13	15	16	19
Lower non-manual	4	8	8	9	7	6	4	5
Self-employed	16	12	10	9	9	13	15	15
Skilled working class	36	32	30	31	32	26	23	22
Non-skilled working class	32	30	32	29	23	23	20	16
N (of cases) =	1357	417	941	1393	1840	1617	1095	565

Based on data from Heath and Payne, 1999

Table 3.5 Class profiles of females by birth cohort (in percentages)

Class	Pre–1900	1900–09	1910–19	1920–29	1930–39	1940–49	1950–59
Higher middle class	2	3	2	4	4	7	9
Lower middle class	11	14	14	12	16	19	27
Lower non-manual	24	28	31	35	37	36	35
Self-employed	11	5	5	3	5	7	6
Skilled working class	15	10	11	9	7	6	4
Non-skilled working class	37	40	37	37	31	25	19
N (of cases)=	184	513	868	1311	1121	911	428

Based on data from Heath and Payne, 1999

Table 3.6 Male class distributions (in percentages)

Class	Born 1950–59, positions 1964–97	Born 1958, positions age 33 in 1991	All ages 2004/05
Middle class	42	36	40
Intermediate	20	21	19
Working class	38	43	41

Based on data from Heath and Payne, 1999; Li et al, 2008; Savage and Egerton, 1997

Table 3.7 Female class distributions (in percentages)

Class	Born 1950–59, positions 1964–97	Born 1958, positions age 33 in 1991	All ages 2004/05
Middle class	36	30	37
Intermediate	41	40	25
Working class	23	29	38

Based on data from Heath and Payne, 1999; Li et al, 2008; Savage and Egerton, 1997

During the early and mid-twentieth century, there was strong growth in routine office jobs which were filled mainly by women – typists, secretaries and other clerical employees. However, since the 1970s this trend has been reversed. Technology has taken over in the office. Managers and professional staff are now expected to do their own correspondence (usually by email) and to maintain their own computer-based records. Once upon a time 'office work' was the most common type of female employment, but no longer. Just a fifth of women employees are now in such jobs: twice as many are in working class jobs on the one side, and management and professional jobs on the other. Lower-level office work is still mainly women's work: just six per cent of male workers hold such jobs. Men are more likely to be self-employed (13 per cent compared with five per cent of women). However, there is little difference today in the chances of male and female employees holding management and professional posts. These grades of employment expanded continuously throughout the twentieth century. The proportion of employees in middle class (professional and management) occupations doubled then doubled again. This growth rate could not continue. Indeed, it is likely that the growth has now ended entirely.

Class demographics

The numerical decline of the working class and the expansion of the middle class are not new trends. As explained above, they are very long-term trends

that began before the First World War, and there have been profound implications not just for the size, but also for the character of all the main classes.
A large class (like the working class once was) that is in long-term decline tends
to be overwhelmingly self-recruiting. Most adults in the class today, and yester-
day, were born into it. So for a long time Britain's working class has been composed mainly of lifelong members. In this sense the working class is a mature
demographic entity and will remain so well into the twenty-first century.

In contrast, the growth of the middle class has required many of these positions to be filled from beneath. There was no way in which the new positions
could be filled by the children of middle class parents – there were simply not
enough of them. So, unlike the working class, the middle class has been, and
still is, composed of people with diverse origins. High proportions have been
upwardly mobile (drawn from the working and intermediate classes), as we
shall see in chapter 8. The middle class will stabilize demographically only as
and when its growth rate slows, as it must, and indeed already has, because
no group can double in size again-and-again-and-again because at some stage
it would comprise over half the population and its growth rate would simply
have to slacken. As the middle class grows ever larger, and as the rate of growth
slows, it is becoming increasingly self-recruiting (see Noble, 2000). Well into
the twenty-first century, the middle class is likely to become as well formed
demographically as the working class was in the twentieth century.

An effect of middle class growth has been to create more opportunities for
working class children to experience upward mobility. Again, we shall see in
chapter 8 that throughout the twentieth century the chances were growing
of children who started in the working class moving into the middle class.
More and more working class parents, themselves usually lifelong members
of this class, have seen their own and their neighbours' children ascend. These
changing class experiences become important when we consider the types of
consciousness and political action that have characterized different classes, and
how these have changed over time.

Workforce dispersal

This has been the result of several separate trends, the combined effect of which
has been to break up large, communal concentrations of workers.

Downsizing

Large firms have downsized (another new term), often dramatically, simply
because they have had the greatest scope to save labour by introducing new
technology and new working practices. Just like the decline in manufacturing
employment, large firms have not necessarily declined in terms of turnover and
profits – just in terms of the numbers on the payrolls.

Downsizing has also been due to the spread of sub-contracting (or outsourcing as it is called in North America). Businesses have been stripping-down to their core functions (enabling managements to concentrate on what they do best) and sub-contracting their cleaning, catering and so forth. Oil refineries have become less likely to employ their own staff to repair buildings and transport their output. This development has occurred at all occupational levels. More work is now passed out to various types of consultants – engineers, solicitors, recruitment specialists and so on. This is another way in which enterprises have been making themselves flexible. Specialists are hired only as and when needed. Also, the hirer is able to go to whoever has the most expertise or the lowest price. Sub-contractors often pay their own staff less than the union-negotiated rates in large companies. And the firm which sub-contracts ceases to be hampered by what may be the limited and out-of-date experience and expertise of its own staff. Private and public sector organizations have been equally keen to strip down to essentials.

Self-employment

Meanwhile, small businesses have been growing in number. The number of self-employed persons (with or without employees) has more than doubled from around 1.5 million in the 1970s to 3.8 million in 2009, around 13 per cent of the workforce. Far from disappearing as Marx predicted, the petit bourgeoisie is flourishing. This is another side of the coin of sub-contracting by large organizations – there are more opportunities for small businesses. So staff at all levels – with professional, office and craft skills – have often found that they can earn more, and enhance their career prospects, by moving out of employment and into self-employment.

There are other developments, apart from sub-contracting, that have contributed to the growth of self-employment. In the 1980s there was much talk about the spread of an enterprise culture. It was a myth. There was no sea-change in attitudes. The population did not become more entrepreneurial than formerly, though it is true that, ideologically at any rate, the government at that time was sympathetic and supportive towards small businesses.

Unemployment-push was and remains one of the forces behind the growth of self-employment. There has been a great deal of survival self-employment – people setting-up on their own accounts due to their inability to obtain proper, secure and decently paid jobs.

However, new technology has also played a part in the growth of small businesses. Small is not necessarily beautiful, but it can be, especially in the age of micro-computing. Small businesses can now afford, and are able to use, state-of-the-art technology. So small independent companies are able to produce recorded music of much the same quality (technical as well as artistic) as the giants of the industry. Small radio stations can be commercially viable, as can desk-top publishing.

The shrunken state

Another dispersal has been from jobs with the biggest of all employers – government. There has been no decline in the proportion of the national income that the government spends, but more of its spending is channelled through quasi-autonomous agencies – hospital trusts and suchlike – and via private firms like the train operating companies. They spend public money, but the employees are not public servants. However, the major cut-back in public sector employment accompanied the privatization of a series of nationalized industries in the 1980s and 1990s – steel, British Airways, oil, gas, electricity, coal, water, telecommunications and subsequently the railways. In all these industries there is no longer one large monopoly operator. Competition has been introduced. There are now scores of telecommunications businesses. In 1980 the public sector accounted for 30 per cent of all jobs. By 1990 this was down to 22 per cent and in 2009 it was 20 per cent. The drop in the 1980s represented over two million workers being transferred to the payrolls of smaller (though usually still quite large) private businesses.

What are the implications of this dispersal? The detailed implications for social consciousness and political action are explored in later chapters but here we should note that government employment has always been more secure than jobs in the private sector, and that jobs in large private companies are more secure than those in small businesses. Scattering the workforce out of large organizations has helped to make employment more precarious. It is only large firms that can offer structured career opportunities. And on average very small firms pay less than large companies. There is another, related, difference: large firms' workforces are more likely to be in trade unions and to have collectively negotiated terms and conditions. Public sector employees are the most densely unionized of all.

Collective bargaining

The proportion of workers who are members of trade unions, and whose terms and conditions of employment are subject to collective bargaining, are much lower today than in the 1970s (see Table 3.8). This is another sense in which workers have been dispersed: more confront owners and managements 'on their own'.

Trade unions have lost almost a half of their one-time membership. This has been due wholly to economic restructuring rather than individuals quitting trade unions. There have been steep declines in employment in one-time densely unionized industries such as coal and steel production. The effect has been not only to decimate the size of the trade union movement but also to change its profile. Trade union members today tend to be employed in the public sector rather than by private sector businesses. Government, rather than a capitalist employer, is most likely to sit opposite at the bargaining table. Some of the most densely unionized parts of the public sector have top-heavy occupational

Table 3.8 Trade unions

Year	No. of members	Percentages of workforce
1948	9,363,000	45
1965	10,325,000	44
1979	13,447,000	55
1984	11,086,000	46
1989	8,963,000	39
1992	7,999,000	36
1997	7,117,000	30
2001	7,600,000	29
2006	7,205,000	28

Table 3.9 Trade union membership by occupational groups, 2006 (in percentages)

Occupational Group	Percentage
Managers and senior offices	17.0
Professions	47.2
Associate professional and technical	43.0
Administrative and secretarial	23.7
Skilled trades	24.0
Personal service occupations	12.7
Process, plant and machine operatives	33.4
Elementary occupations	20.5

Source: Grainger and Crowther, 2007

profiles (education, and central and local government administration, for example), and a result is that management and professional grade staff are now more likely than manual employees to belong to trade unions (see Table 3.9). Some of the largest trade unions, with the strongest public profiles, now represent mainly non-manual employees. Trade unionism was originally, but it has now ceased to be, basically a working class movement.

Places of work and residence

Another dimension of the dispersal of the workforce has followed the spread of car ownership. This has reduced, if not eliminated, the advantages of businesses locating close to the hubs of public transport networks, usually in city centres. Sites on city outskirts, or in small towns, or on completely green fields, are often more accessible for car-borne workforces as well as for customers, suppliers and a business's own transport. All of Britain's major cities have lost jobs since the 1970s (Turok and Edge, 1999). The consequences have been disastrous for inner-city residents without their own motor transport. Car ownership has become essential to gain access to the full labour market, or, at any rate, to give oneself the same scope for choice as today's normal, motorized employee. In 1951 only 14 per cent of UK households had a motor car. By 2000 there were at least two cars in 28 per cent of households, and one car in another 45 per cent (Lindsay, 2003). Once people have acquired cars, these enable them to live farther from their workplaces than formerly. At the end of each working day, in most workplaces nowadays, the staff disperse in numerous directions. Correspondingly, most neighbourhoods' residents disperse to a variety of workplaces at the beginning of each working day. An effect is that fewer people have the daily experience of travelling to work and being at work alongside large armies of others all doing similar jobs. Fewer people work and live among the same colleagues. This type of communality has evaporated. All classes have been affected, but the working class most of all, because, in the past (see chapter 4), its ways of working and living were the most likely to be communal.

A further aspect of dispersal has been more people working at or from home. The number of 100 per cent home-based workers is still quite small despite the possibilities opened by information technology. However, by the early-2000s 13 per cent of the UK workforce was operating from a home-base, or working at home, on at least one day per week (Felstead et al, 2005b). People who are totally home-based seem to miss the sociability of a regular workplace. Also, face-to-face interaction appears essential to allow people (suppliers and customers, colleagues, supervised and supervisors) to establish trust relationships with one another.

A possibly more interesting development is towards people (mainly managers and professionals) taking work home, and being able to work at home during evenings and weekends. This has been made possible by information technology, and what becomes possible easily becomes expected of staff. Also, more people are working 'on the move'; in trains, on planes, in airport lounges, motorway cafes, even car parks. 'The emerging new landscape of employment is one in which spaces and times of work and non-work are not clearly separated, work-time is spent in a variety of locations, many of which are not set aside specifically for job-related tasks, workers are required to construct their own sequences and sites of activities, and personal space in the labour process is absent, problematic or contested. We no longer go to the office but, instead, the office comes with us, every where and every when' (Felstead et al, 2005a, p 2). These changes require new types of management control, based on output rather than processes, and sometimes through cultural processes whereby the employer captures the worker's subjectivity. Employees need to cope with new kinds of unpredictability and uncertainty, and may develop new forms of 'resistance', very likely to include open expressions of emotional detachment and disrespect (when far from the employer's gaze).

Workforce composition

Jobs have changed, and so has the workforce. Its demography is different from the workforce of the mid-twentieth century. Age, gender and ethnic divisions need to be examined together because how an age group has fared amid the changes in the labour market has often varied by gender and ethnicity.

Buchholz and her colleagues (2009) have gathered data from 17 OECD countries to try to separate winners from losers during recent economic changes (which have been similar in all the countries). They conclude that everywhere the main winners have been mid-career men, but only if they have been well-qualified, skilled, experienced and established in employment. Mid-career women have fared less well. On returning to employment following periods devoted to family care, they have often found themselves marginalized and downgraded, especially if seeking just part-time hours (see also chapter 4, pp 95–97).

Britain has been different from some other countries in that experienced male manual workers have often found themselves cast out of what they hoped would be career-long employment in manufacturing and extractive industries. The manual workforce in Britain today has an entirely different profile than in the 1970s. It used to be mainly male, employed in manufacturing, and its senior employees were older skilled workers, some of whom had moved into supervisory positions. Today's working class is based mainly in service sectors where the jobs (as in retailing and other consumer services) have traditionally been considered more suitable for women than for men. Nearly a half of all manual employees are now female, and the males are mostly young men (see Egerton and Savage, 2000; Savage, 2000). Ethnic minorities also are higher proportions of manual employees than in the past.

Buchholz and her colleagues note that in all countries late-career employees have been losers. Britain is no exception here. Employers have tended to regard them as inadequately qualified, too inflexible and too costly. The recessions of the 1980s and early-1990s in Britain pushed many older employees into pre-mature retirement. In 1979 two-thirds of 60–64 year old men were in employment whereas by 1999 two-thirds were not in work (Campbell, 1999). In 1901 nearly 40 per cent of men aged 75 and over were still working whereas by 2000 less than 10 per cent above age 65 were in employment (Lindsay, 2003). The recession of 2008–09 will have had similar consequences. Anyone aged over 45 may be regarded as too old to be taken-on (see Riach and Loretto, 2009). The employment prospects of the 65-plus age group became dire in 2008–09 when there was intense competition for any available job (Dispatches, 2009). Gender differences in employment rates have narrowed as labour force participation

Table 3.10 Employment rates by age (in percentages), 2009

Gender	16–17	18–24	25–34	35–49	50–59/64	60/65+
Males	30	65	87	88	73	11
Females	33	61	73	77	71	13

Source: Office for National Statistics

by women has risen (see Table 3.10). Today the main differences are by age. Employment rates for both sexes peak among 25–49 year olds, the years that have long been regarded as prime working life. After age 50, employment rates begin to decline, and dive steeply after the ages when retirement pensions normally become available.

Prior to the recession that began in 2008, employment rates among older workers had been edging upwards. The policies of European governments were encouraging people to work longer into later life, partly because it was feared that their growing economies would lead to labour shortages, but mainly because, with more people surviving into their 80s and 90s, governments knew that unless employees worked longer it would be impossible for them to retire on adequate pensions. The recession then rolled back these intentions.

Buchholz and her colleagues identify young people, especially the less-qualified, as another group of losers. Their employment, when obtained, is typically precarious nowadays, and there are plenty of examples of this in Britain, especially in high unemployment areas where working class youth in the labour market have been marginalized and have often struggled to retain any connection with the employed workforce (see MacDonald and Marsh, 2005).

However, among young people in Britain there has been a group of clear winners, namely well-qualified young women who have moved into professional employment either directly from higher education where females are now the majority of students and graduates, or from intermediate non-manual occupations (see Egerton and Savage, 2000, Savage, 2000). Currently in Britain young women have better jobs overall than older women (the reverse applies among males). Among women this situation will probably be temporary because the young women with professional jobs are now taking maternity leave rather than extended career breaks, and are returning to full-time employment and continuing to progress in their careers.

Another age-specific feature of youth in the labour market is that they appear to adjust to precarious work more readily than older age groups. One response to job shortages has been to stay longer in education. A response to the shortage of secure, stable, career jobs has been to postpone marriage and parenthood. Young people, even the well-educated, appear at ease with career-less working lives. They are able to construct coherent life stories out of successions of jobs that appear to be heading nowhere in particular, and are optimistic as regards their futures. Bradley and Devadason describe them as an 'adaptable generation' that has 'internalized flexibility' (Bradley and Devadason, 2008; Devadason, 2007). Whether this is an age-specific response to current labour market conditions or a sign of generational change by cohorts who have never known or expected anything different, and who experience present labour market conditions as simply normal, will become evident only in future decades.

There are class implications in the new positions of young people in the labour market. To begin with, they are spending smaller proportions of youth and young adulthood exposed directly to workplace relationships and cultures. Perhaps even more significant for the working class, Britain has lost one of the two former routes into adult political careers. One route, now the only significant route, is via student politics during an extended academic education. The other route, which now scarcely exists, was via employment-based trade union and related political activity, all accomplished prior to marriage, child-rearing, and the time squeeze that these life stage transitions enforce. It is also the case that manual workers' trade unions have lost the now early-retired over-50s who once lent immense experience and provided leadership for younger members.

Box 3.5 Labour market segmentation

The key observation here is that labour markets are divided into interrelated but non-competing (in the short-term at any rate) sub-markets or segments. This segmentation arises when workers become trained, skilled and experienced in specific industries and occupations. They are sometimes able to progress upwards through internal (to an occupation, industry or firm) labour markets, gaining benefits that are lost if they move outside. Conversely, outsiders can only enter at the bottom, which will usually involve sacrificing any progress that they have made in their existing or former labour market segments.

Which segments individuals enter depends on their places of residence and qualifications, and gender and ethnicity are often influential as well.

Some analysts (dual labour market theorists) claim that a major division cutting right across the entire workforce is between primary and secondary labour market segments, and that labour market segmentation has disadvantaged particular groups (women, ethnic minorities and the poorly qualified) because they have been likely to become trapped in secondary segments. Today, however, this labour market segmentation cuts through both genders, and creates divisions within all the longer-settled ethnic minorities. Age and qualifications are now the main predictors of the advantaged and disadvantaged labour market segments where individuals will be situated.

The segments themselves are as widely apart as ever. Some Marxists have regarded labour market segmentation as an employer strategy to undermine workforce solidarity. But trade unions and professional associations are often deeply implicated in maintaining segmentation thereby protecting their members' jobs and career prospects from outside competition.

Like women, ethnic minorities have an increased presence in the UK's labour markets. This is a consequence of the immigration into Britain from the new Commonwealth that peaked in the 1950s and 60s. The subsequent growth of these minority populations has been due mainly to natural increase, but since 2004 there has been a new inflow, mainly 'pendulum migrants' from the new European Union member countries (see Box 3.6). Roughly eight per cent of all employees are now from an ethnic minority. The proportion varies from place to place and from occupation to occupation, but there is certain to be a further all-round increase over the next generation.

Britain has numerous ethnic minority groups, each with its own ethnic characteristics. Over time, as they have lost the common status of recent immigrants, their experiences in Britain have become more diverse – in terms of housing, educational attainments, and the kinds of jobs that they obtain – but they continue to share one important characteristic in common, namely, an ethnic handicap in the labour market (see Box 3.6).

Beck and Beck-Gernsheim (2009) argue that we miss the main long-term significance of present-day migration, especially by young people, when we simply compare their achievements in the labour market (and in other spheres) with those of the local populations. They argue that among young people outside the relatively rich western world, there is a new expectation of global equality, that the young people want western standards of living, and if these are not available at home, then they move to where they can be found. Beck and Beck-Gernsheim argue that these migrants are genuine cosmopolitans, with trans-national

---

Box 3.6 The ethnic penalty

All Britain's ethnic minorities have one thing in common – an ethnic penalty in the labour market (see Heath and McMahon, 1997). This is evident in two ways. Compared with British whites with equal qualifications, all the ethnic minorities have:

■ Inferior career achievements.
■ Higher unemployment (except Indians and Chinese).

It is difficult to think of any possible explanation for this other than discrimination, which may not be racial discrimination. There are around two million citizens from other European Union countries in the UK at any time. Around a half of these are from the new (post-2004) member states. They come to Britain (and other West European countries) for the higher earnings than are available at home. In Britain they are under-employed relative to their qualifications and skills. They work longer hours, for lower wages, than comparable British workers. Up to now most have arrived in Britain intending to be temporary, pendulum migrants, and have been willing to trade occupational downgrading for the higher earnings than they could expect at home. They are satisfied if they can return home with some capital saved, which may be used towards a house or flat, or to start a business (see Anderson et al, 2006).

homelands. They may achieve a share of the west's wealth, but in doing so they spread precariousness into western labour markets. These authors claim that a new trans-national global generation is being created, and that its members target any protests not at national authorities so much as representatives of the international order of inequality.

Summary

In this chapter we have seen how globalization and new technologies have ushered in new, post-Fordist economic times, characterized by: greater flexibility (of labour markets, jobs and workers); more precarious, non-standard employment (temporary, part-time and self-employment); higher unemployment; pressure on those in jobs to do more; and wider income inequalities.

Amid these linked waves of change there have been major shifts of employment: from manufacturing into services, and from manual into non-manual grades. Simultaneously, the workforce has been scattered spatially: out of the public sector, large private enterprises, and city centres into self-employment, small firms and greenfield sites. Meanwhile, car ownership has facilitated the separation of places of work and residence. There have been parallel changes in the composition of the workforce: there are more women and ethnic minorities, and fewer under-25 and over-60 year old workers.

Two class effects deserve underlining. First, the numerical decline of the manual working class and the expansion of the white-collar grades, with powerful implications for the demography of all classes. Second, a whole raft of trends in the economy, labour markets and in the composition of the workforce has tended to undermine older employment-based cultures and the associated solidarities, and has made it difficult for new solidarities to develop. These trends are:

- Greater flexibility and mobility (due to car ownership and international migration) in the labour market.
- People spending more time (as a proportion of their lifetimes) outside the workforce: in education when young, during spells of unemployment, and on account of earlier retirement (for men).
- Its rate of expansion means that a high proportion of the present-day middle class is first generation.
- The spatial scattering of labour from local concentrations in particular firms, industries and occupations.
- Less uniformity within all occupational grades in terms of gender and ethnicity.

The Working Class

4

Introduction

Previous chapters have defined class, explained its continuing importance, adopted a class scheme as a guide, and examined the economic and occupational trends which have reshaped Britain's class structure in recent years. In this and the next three chapters we look in detail at each of the main classes, beginning with the working class. This chapter:

- Describes the original working class that was created in Britain following the industrial revolution.
- Reviews the debates of the 1950s and 60s about embourgeoisement and the creation of a new working class.
- Analyses how the working class has fared in post-industrial times.
- Considers whether an underclass or excluded groups have been detached from the working class proper.

The original working class

Roots

Britain's original working class was created in the nineteenth century. It was the world's first industrial working class: Britain was the first industrial nation. At the beginning of the nineteenth century four-fifths of Britain's population lived in rural areas. By the end four-fifths lived in towns and cities. The countryside was depopulated. Towns and cities expanded and kept growing together with their mines, docks and factories. These new industries attracted workers escaping from rural poverty, in search of better living standards and more regular work. The countryside-to-town movement of people was augmented by migration, mainly from Ireland, but also from the continent when Central and East Europe's Jews fled from pogroms (organized persecutions and massacres, at least tacitly condoned by the authorities). The expanding ports, textile, mining and engineering towns were unruly places at first, Britain's version of the Wild West. Employers found it difficult to induce 'green' labour to accept industrial discipline – regular and long hours of work, six days a week when required. This was the background to the nineteenth century campaigns against drink and blood sports, and in favour of 'rational recreation' – playing modern sports, using libraries, visiting museums, and engaging in other so-called wholesome, edifying activities. A motive behind the drive for universal elementary schooling was to accustom children to industrial work routines.

In time, of course, the new workforces did settle, and industrial, urban cultures developed throughout the land. The major enterprises employed scores, often hundreds of workers. Except in textiles, the workforces were mostly male. The work was usually arduous; power-driven equipment was introduced slowly. The work was often dangerous – in steel works, engineering workshops, on the docks which handled imports and exports, in railway construction, and especially in the mines. Workers needed to co-operate in order to do their jobs. They were often dependent on each other for their physical safety. These are the origins of working class comradeship, and the us-them frame of mind. 'They' were the people who imposed on 'us' what they would not have considered tolerable for themselves or their families.

Interdependence in the workplace spilled into out-of-work life. Before the age of mechanical transport, it was necessary for workers to live close to where they were employed. This continued to make sense even when bus, tram and suburban railway services were introduced. Working men's clubs, pubs, beer, football, chapel, brass bands, pigeons – the mixture varied from place to place – became the foundations of working men's leisure. People who worked together also played together. When pits and factories closed for annual weeks, each town would empty and the inhabitants would travel together, and stay in adjacent streets and boarding houses in nearby coastal resorts.

Workplace and neighbourhood relations were mutually reinforcing, but homes and neighbourhoods were primarily the women's domains. It was mostly women who were at home throughout each day throughout each week. Sons often followed fathers into the same pits and factories, and usually continued to live locally. Daughters did likewise. Parents would assist their grown-up children to obtain accommodation of their own by speaking to the rent man. Prior to World War Two, most working class families lived in privately rented dwellings. In the days when families with six and more surviving children were common, neighbourhoods became knit by numerous interlocking kin relationships. Relatives and neighbours would help each other in times of adversity and need.

Needless to say, this communality was stronger in some places, and in some sections of the working class, than in others. Everywhere there was a distinction between the respectable and the rough. Respectable working class families adopted some bourgeois habits, or, at any rate, habits that were being urged upon workers by some sections of the middle class – sobriety, saving, holidays, Sunday schools and, above all, regular work. Skilled workers had the most regular work, and the highest earnings, and were the most likely to be able to lead respectable lifestyles. Early sociological surveys of working class districts distinguished strata of loafers and criminals. All the industrial cities had rough areas, usually where the most recent migrants settled, which were renowned for the residents' irregular work habits, their criminality, the gangs, and the street fights after closing time at weekends.

Mateyness at work and communality in neighbourhoods were hallmarks of respectability, and acted as the soil from which working class organizations grew. For as long as there have been factories, workers have seen advantages in 'combination' – to protect each other from arbitrary dismissal, pay cuts, and to express demands (for more pay, for example) with which entire workforces have agreed. Workers have always appreciated the need to avoid competing against one another, and against workers doing similar jobs in other factories. They have wanted to prevent employers hiring the cheapest and sacking anyone with the temerity to ask for more. In the eighteenth and early nineteenth centuries, combinations of employees were usually unlawful and employers did whatever possible to smash them. Then, in the 1850s, skilled workers began to develop effective combinations, which is how they came to be called 'trade' unions. Employers began to recognize and negotiate with these unions instead of trying to suppress them. The workers who were combining were recognized as respectable and responsible. Subsequently, from the 1880s onwards, trade unionism spread among semi-skilled and unskilled workers, and by the First World War all the main industries and manual occupations had trade unions. At that time the working class amounted to over two-thirds of the population. They had learnt that their strength lay in numbers; that 'the union makes us strong'. Activists have always understood the need for solidarity, and how elusive it can be. Hence the stigma, within the organized labour movement, attached to free-riders, and to scabs or blacklegs.

The co-operative movement was another product of the capacity for effective organization that the working class developed during the nineteenth century. The type of co-operative that turned out to be most successful was the consumers' co-operative: stores owned by the shoppers, and therefore able to pass on any profits (the dividend) to their ordinary members.

The Labour Party, of course, was the other great product of the working class's ability to self-organize. It was established in 1900, principally by the trade unions which had already learnt the limitations of industrial action. They needed political representation to gain legal protection for themselves, and to pursue benefits that could never be won through negotiation with employers. Throughout the twentieth century the trade unions were to remain the Labour Party's main source of financial support. The rise of the Labour Party was aided by the two world wars, and catastrophic splits in the Liberal Party after the First World War. From the 1920s onwards, Labour was the party that attracted most support from the working class, and the main alternative to the Conservatives, but it was not until 1945 that the UK had its first majority Labour government.

Nostalgia

Sociologists started to describe and analyse working class ways of life only when Britain's original working class was already in decline. Until the Second

World War, poverty was the big issue. Material conditions rather than culture and values pre-occupied researchers. For a time, in the 1950s, it was believed that poverty had been abolished and consigned to history. The working class was enjoying a type of prosperity that had been almost beyond the imaginations of pre-war generations, and sociologists set about examining these changes.

Dennis, Henriques and Slaughter (1956) were able to study a Yorkshire coal-mining community (Featherstone) where workforce solidarity was as strong, and community life was as vibrant, as ever. But when Michael Young and Peter Willmott began their widely acclaimed research in Bethnal Green in the 1950s, this was to record a way of life that was then under threat. *Family and Kinship in East London* was first published in 1957, and ever since then sociologists have relied heavily upon it (either at first, second or third hand) for their knowledge about traditional working class communities. This portrait of London's East End surprised much of middle class England in the 1950s. It had been supposed that people disliked living in slum areas. Conditions were supposed to be repugnant. Young and Willmott described an East End to which the residents were strongly attached, a way of life that was warm, and a community whose members were so supportive towards each other that the rest of the country was envious. The story-line in the book was about how Eastenders were being resettled to London's outskirts, on council estates with better dwellings, more spacious neighbourhoods and cleaner air, yet regretted deeply that they had been uprooted, isolated from kin and lifelong friends.

Richard Hoggart's *The Uses of Literacy* was also first published in 1957. This book was based on Hoggart's knowledge of life in Hunslet (now a part of Leeds), where he had been brought-up. His portrait of traditional working class life was basically as in Young and Willmott's account, and came with the same message; that something of real value was being lost. In Hoggart's account, the main threat was not from bulldozers and urban redevelopment so much as the mass media – the press, radio, the cinema, and especially television, but most of all from the imported American culture which was seen as obliterating older sensitivities and forms of sociability, and replacing them with something more shallow and less authentic.

David Lockwood was able to draw on these accounts in his landmark 1966 article, 'Sources of variation in working class images of society'. In this article Lockwood identified two traditional working classes. One was a deferential working class, which was said to have developed in agricultural communities and in small businesses where workers were bound into relationships of dependence on (personally known) employers. Lockwood argued that such contexts bred deferential attitudes, which were liable to spread into politics where the workers were quite likely to vote for the party led by their 'betters'. Lockwood's second and larger traditional working class was proletarian, and subscribed to a power-model, us-them view of society. It was the original working class described above. Lockwood's purpose in constructing these traditional types was to lay-down benchmarks against which to describe a new working class that was coming into existence (as he and others suspected).

The new working class of the 1960s

The embourgeoisement thesis

Sociology began to study the working class thoroughly only when it was believed (correctly as it has turned out) to be changing in fundamental ways, and the change alleged by most commentators in the 1950s and 60s was embourgeoisement (the economic, social, cultural and political assimilation of manual workers into the middle class). This was in the context of the full employment, steady economic growth and regular pay rises that had been maintained since the Second World War. Manual earnings were rising year-on-year, and the earnings gap with white-collar salaries was closing. Goods and services formerly associated with the middle classes – soft home furnishings, television sets, washing machines, motor cars and holidays abroad – were being enjoyed by more and more working class families. The claim was that as manual workers' incomes rose into the middle class bracket, their ways of life, identities and politics would change accordingly. These claims looked plausible in the 1950s when the Labour Party was losing three successive general elections. It was claimed that as fewer and fewer manual workers lived like, and identified with, the traditional working class, then fewer and fewer would support a political party with a working class image. Hence the argument that the Labour Party was in danger of becoming a permanent opposition unless it overhauled its constitution, policies and image, and broadened its appeal (Abrams et al, 1960). This triggered a debate within the Labour Party that was not won decisively by the 'modernizers' until the 1990s.

The embourgeoisement thesis never received much support from sociology. Its main exponents were political scientists and journalists (for example, Turner, 1963). The argument always sounded too simplistic for sociologists to be convinced. Ferdinand Zweig (1961) was probably as near a supporter as sociology produced. He interviewed 600 manual workers from five modern factories and concluded that the new working class, content with the system in which it lived and worked, was more concerned to boost its earnings within, than to question let alone challenge, the prevailing economic and social order. Zweig also drew attention to how affluence made nuclear families less dependent on kin and neighbours, thus weakening one of the roots of traditional working class culture.

The research which interrogated the embourgeoisement thesis most thoroughly was a study conducted in Luton in the mid-1960s by John Goldthorpe, David Lockwood, Frank Bechoffer and Jennifer Platt. Their main book from this project (Goldthorpe et al, 1969), is one of the best-known works in the history of British sociology. It was based on interviews with just 229 (male) manual workers at three establishments in Luton (a car manufacturer, an engineering company and a chemical plant). Fifty-four white-collar employees were also interviewed as a comparison group. It is remarkable that the findings from this small-scale study, or rather the interpretations that the researchers placed upon their findings, were to define British sociology's view of the 'new' working class for the next quarter century. One of the reasons for the study's impact was the choice of location. Luton was selected partly because it was not too far from Cambridge where the researchers were based, but mainly for its 'prototypicality'. Luton was not a traditional industrial town with a history of working class organization and an associated traditional working class culture. It was an expanding town, and in the 1960s many of its employees had migrated from other places. Earnings in the town were well-above the national average. The authors could claim, with justification, that if embourgeoisement was happening anywhere, it should have been evident in Luton.

On the basis of their findings the Luton investigators rejected the embourgeoisement thesis, and as far as sociology was concerned the thesis lay dead and buried. With the exception of Peter Saunders (1978, 1981, 1990, see below), hardly anyone of note in British sociology has felt it necessary to take the embourgeoisement thesis seriously for over 40 years. The Luton investigators had excellent grounds for rejecting the thesis. First, the vast majority of their respondents identified with the working class. Second, they were nearly all not only trade union members but regarded trade union representation as indispensable. Third, 71 per cent had voted Labour in the most recent general election (a higher figure than for the working class nationally). Fourth, the manual workers had few if any white-collar friends. They were not rubbing shoulders with factory managers in local pubs or visiting each other at home. Kin and neighbours were the manual workers' main associates outside their workplaces. Unlike the white-collar respondents, they were not joining formal leisure-time associations, or developing wide networks of friends.

The Luton investigators had good grounds for asserting that the acquisition of a middle class income did not lead automatically to social integration into the middle class, or the adoption of a middle class identity, values and political preferences. In terms of their work and market situations, the Luton sample remained emphatically working class. They were on the receiving end of authority at work. They were paid per hour and according to how much they produced. They did not identify with their jobs or employers in the ways considered characteristic of the middle class. The Luton workers had no long career ladders to ascend. Their prospects of betterment depended, as ever, on making collective gains, alongside colleagues. There were no signs of the traditional class divide at work even fraying let alone collapsing.

A concurrent study of compositors endorsed this conclusion (Cannon, 1967). Print workers, although highly paid, homeowners, and so on, retained proletarian identities and loyalties due to the strength of their craft-based working lives and trade unions.

Privatized and instrumental

The Luton investigators rejected the embourgeoisement thesis but they were still impressed by contrasts between the evidence from their sample and the ideal

caricature
*

types of traditional working classes that David Lockwood had constructed. Two keywords signal these contrasts.

First, privatism: in Luton there were no deferential relationships of dependence on superiors, but neither was there much of the workplace mateyness associated with the proletarian working class. In their factories, employees were positioned at individual work stations, as along car assembly lines, separated from each other by noise and machinery. The work process did not require them to collaborate. In this sense their lives at work were privatized. Few members of the Luton sample had plenty of kin living locally. Their houses did not open directly onto streets or common 'backs' but were separated by gardens. Kin and neighbours were the workers' main social contacts, but their lives outside work were basically home-centred. The affluent workers had been buying soft home furnishings, carpeting and, most crucially, televisions. At the end of a working day they did not hang around with mates. Nor did they go out to pubs to spend time with their mates during the evenings. If they did go out occasionally this would be as a couple or family group. The sample's life projects were nuclear family-centred.

In the Luton investigators' account, this lifestyle was spreading by choice. There was little of the sense of loss reported in the Bethnal Green study, or in Jeremy Seabrook's (1971) concurrent account of working class life in northern cities. Maybe the difference was that so many of the Luton sample had chosen to leave their home areas of their own accord. However, neighbourhood life was collapsing throughout the length and breadth of the country at that time. More married women were taking paid jobs. They were no longer around all day to knit neighbourhoods together. More working class children were getting on and leaving their home districts (see chapter 8). Families were smaller so, in any case, there was less chance of a child remaining local. Above all, television was keeping people 'in', while the motor car was enabling them to go out in private, and was turning streets into thoroughfares rather than places for children's play and other forms of community life. Also, although this attracted little comment in The Affluent Worker study, Luton in the 1960s was becoming a multi-racial town, and many old working class areas throughout the land were likewise being transformed into multi-ethnic inner-city districts.

The second keyword in the typification of the new working class in the Luton study was instrumentality. The workers' lives were home and family-centred, and all their engagements with the outside world tended to be instrumental, means to ends, rather than ends or values in themselves. This certainly applied to their orientations towards work. These were pecuniary. The workers were not worried if their jobs were not intrinsically satisfying, or if they were not bound into fraternal work groups. None of this was either sought or expected. Many of the sample had been attracted to Luton by the well-paid jobs, and if the pay was right the workers were satisfied. The Luton investigators queried whether their respondents could be regarded as alienated at work if their jobs were offering what they wanted. They worked in order to earn the wages to support home-centred lifestyles. Homes and families were the places where the workers had emotional investments.

There appeared to be a similar instrumentality in the workers' attachments to trade unions and the Labour Party. They supported trade unions because this was the best way of obtaining and protecting even fuller pay packets. In a similar manner, their support for the Labour Party seemed to have a calculative base. They judged Labour to be more likely than any of the alternatives to implement policies that served their private interests. Their support was pragmatic, and, by implication, fickle, rather than solidaristic.

False diagnosis?

The new working class thesis did not win instant acceptance in British sociology. At the time of the book's publication, the near-revolutionary (on the continent) events of 1968 were still fresh in mind, and the spirit was still in the air. Wildcat strikes and cost-push inflation were the big issues in Britain's industrial relations. Governments were trying, unsuccessfully, to curb shop-floor power. Trade union activists appeared to be more militant than the national leaders. It was not wholly implausible to imagine capitalism being toppled if only the working class received radical leadership. One point made against the new working class diagnosis was that the cash nexus was likely to prove more brittle than the analysis suggested. It was argued that workplace and local community loyalties may have inhibited the spread of class-wide solidarity and political action in the past (Westergaard and Resler, 1975). Throughout the 1970s many sociologists continued to believe that the working class was but a short-step from becoming a truly revolutionary force. Whether workers really were satisfied with assembly line jobs, provided they were well-paid, was queried. It was argued that the Goldthorpe team had underestimated the resentment, anger, and the dehumanizing character of the work, testified by the cheers that would ring through car plants whenever a line broke down, and the sabotage that ensured that break-downs occurred reasonably frequently (Beynon, 1973).

Some critiques of The Affluent Worker study queried whether a 'new' working class had been discovered. It was argued that instrumental, pecuniary orientations towards work were in fact long-standing. Workers had always been concerned about their earnings. Many had always been most concerned about 'number one', and sometimes their immediate families. The tidyness with which the Luton researchers had distinguished deferential, proletarian and new working classes was queried. It was shown that agricultural workers were not consistently deferential (Newby, 1977), and that shipbuilding workers were not as consistently proletarian in outlook as the typology suggested that they should be (Brown and Brannen, 1970). It was counter-argued that, in practice, all sections of the working class were more likely to hold muddled mixtures of radical and conservative, rather than coherent views about their own circumstances and the wider society (Abercrombie and Turner, 1978; Mann, 1970, 1973; Nichols and Armstrong, 1976).

Recently Mike Savage (2005) has re-examined the original fieldnotes from the Affluent Worker study, and has concluded that the interpretations offered by the original investigators were very much influenced by their own theories. Savage found plenty of evidence of contradictory attitudes and a general hesitancy when discussing class. On Savage's reading of the fieldnotes, most of the Luton respondents had not made any clear distinctions between white- and blue-collar, middle class and working class. Rather they had stressed how they were just 'ordinary', not 'stuck up', definitely not upper class (a class that was mentioned by nearly everyone), and with no such pretensions.

A further criticism was that there had always been Lutons – expanding towns attracting migrant labour, when, at the stage of the cycle in question, there was no tradition of local community life or workplace organization. Given time, it was argued, Luton would change. Luton has indeed changed, and its affluent workers were re-studied in the 1980s (Devine, 1992). By then many had kin who had joined them in the town, or family ties had developed locally with the growth of a second generation. Extreme privatism in the 1980s, when it occurred, was due to constraint rather than choice – long and unsocial hours of work, or financial constraints which prevented people from socializing in the local pubs and clubs.

The working class in post-industrial times

It is only at this point that we encounter the economic trends reviewed in the last chapter – globalization, new technology, labour market flexibility, more non-standard employment, spatial scattering, job insecurity and unemployment. The digression into history has been necessary, first, because, albeit in a partial way, the history is part of the memory of the present-day working class, a template for experiencing and evaluating current conditions, and second, because the post-1970s economic trends have not created a totally new working class but have reshaped what already existed.

Myths and real trends

We need to be clear about exactly what has happened to Britain's working class since the 1970s. First, there has not been a steep decline in the number of manual jobs. Rather, a long-term slow decline has continued and may now have bottomed. We saw in chapter 3 that around 40 per cent of both male and female employees are currently in working class jobs. The proportion of female employees in intermediate (office) occupations has fallen. Women have either moved up into the professional or management grades, or down into the working class. Second, unskilled jobs have not been especially vulnerable. In fact the steepest decline has been in the skilled manual jobs in manufacturing and extractive industries which used to be filled by men. The idea that jobs which require no formal educational qualifications or extended training are disappearing is plain bunk (see Box 4.1).

Box 4.1   Lousy jobs and lovely jobs

'There has been a growth in lousy jobs (mainly in low paying service occupations) together with a (much larger) growth in lovely jobs (mainly in professional and managerial occupations in finance and business services) and a decline in the number of middling jobs (mainly clerical jobs and skilled jobs in manufacturing)' (Goos and Manning, 2003).

Top 10 occupations by job growth, 1979–1999 (in rank order):

- Care assistants and attendants
- Software engineers
- Management consultants and business analysts
- Computer analysts and programmers
- Educational assistants
- Hospital ward assistants
- Actors, entertainers, stage managers and producers
- Treasurers and company financial managers.

Other low paying jobs where employment has increased include:

- Bar staff
- Shelf fillers
- Sales assistants
- Retail cash desk and check-out operators
- Waiters and waitresses
- Beauticians.

Non-routine jobs which are complementary to (rather than replaceable by) technology include skilled professional and managerial jobs but also many unskilled jobs like cleaning that rely on hand-eye coordination that virtually all human beings find easy but machines find enormously difficult. So labour has declined mainly in middling jobs that have required routine manual and cognitive skills.

The main trends have actually been a shift of manual employment from extractive and manufacturing industries to services, from large to small establishments, from city-centre locations and older industrial estates to out-of-town greenfield sites, and increases in the proportions of women and ethnic minorities in the manual (as in the non-manual) workforce. Overall there has been a decline in the quality (in terms of pay and skill levels) of working class jobs. The service sector contains a lot of low-level, part-time and casual jobs (see Walsh, 1990). The new working class is employed in shops, or more typically supermarkets and hypermarkets, in restaurants and hotels (the hospitality industries), and other businesses connected with leisure, sport and tourism. There is more work in call-centres, in security firms, and with contract cleaners. Many of the new jobs require an emotional input. The work is often demanding, though not skilled in the traditional sense. Employees are required to market themselves and to supply 'aesthetic labour'. Their appearances and demeanour in shops and restaurants are part of the service that the businesses offer. This also applies in air travel (see Tyler and Abbott, 1998). This work can be stressful, and demeaning. It requires tacit skills rather than formal qualifications and training. There is still plenty of straight 'donkey work' but many of the new working class jobs require the occupants to appear human, interested, and committed to the customers' satisfaction. Many of the new working class jobs have continued to be regarded as more suitable for women than for men – a main source of an alleged crisis in working class masculinity.

However, a section of the working class is still employed in what are now regarded as traditional, quality jobs, done mainly by men. Yaojun Li and his colleagues (2002) report from survey evidence that around a third of objectively working class adults claim to be experiencing careers and are engaging in forward planning. There are still plenty of traditional working class jobs in construction. Darren Thiel (2007) studied a group of such men in London (participant observation plus 32 interviews). He reports that being working class was not an explicit part of the men's identities, but even so, their identities were rooted firmly in aspects of traditional masculine working class culture. They were men who did physical work, dirty work, real masculine jobs, and enjoyed considerable autonomy on the job.

Nevertheless, even for those manual employees who have hung on to decently paid jobs, life at work has become tougher. In the larger firms which still offer quality jobs, managements have been asserting their right to manage. Even if the workforces are unionized, the trade unions are not necessarily consulted. Personnel management has been replaced by so-called human resource management. Businesses have made themselves lean and mean. No slack is carried. 'Featherbedding' and heavily ratcheted overtime rates have been eliminated on the docks, in coal and in print. None of these are 'the greatest game' any longer; not for the employees at any rate (see Prowse and Turner, 1996; Turnbull and Hass, 1994). Managements have asserted themselves not out of malice, but because they have been exposed to stronger competitive processes (a result of globalization), and the availability of new technology has magnified the potential rewards for re-vamping the entire labour process. The Fleet Street bosses never wanted to carry excess staff in their print works. Computer technology made it possible to off-load the lot. Firms have embraced total quality management. This means expecting top standards from everyone, all the time. Customers are prioritized. Costs are reduced wherever possible. Workers have little choice but to acquiesce. They know that their own jobs could go in the next round of downsizing, delayering or outsourcing. Labour market conditions have meant that a typical route into such 'quality' jobs has been to succeed against hordes of fellow applicants, often for positions that are initially temporary or part-time, then hope to be made full-time and permanent.

For other members of the working class, their real occupational identities are rooted in the past, but are kept alive, and thereby remain part of the present. Robert Mackenzie and colleagues (2006) report findings from 125 interviews with redundant steelworkers in Wales (93 per cent were men). Most were currently unemployed or were doing lower-skilled and lower-paid jobs than those that they had held in the steel industry. Although this was gone, the men's former jobs, and their former occupational communities, remained an important part of their current identities. They would often meet with ex-workmates with whom they would re-affirm their real status, and they still talked the language of the working class. They spoke of 'them and us' in accounting for their treatment in their former industry, and their subsequent experiences.

Richard Sennett (1999) has written about a 'corrosion of character'. We saw in chapter 3 that there has been no decline in the average time spent in a job, but employees at all levels now feel less secure. They know that their employers have no long-term commitment to them, and that at any time all their experience and skills could be declared dispensable. Sennett argues that this makes it difficult for employees to maintain self-respect. They lack stable anchorage points for their lives outside work. At home they are unable to act as role models that they wish their children to emulate.

Labour market flexibility

Britain's labour markets are among the most flexible in Europe. Labour market flexibility is supposed to be beneficial since it allows firms to adapt rapidly to changes in technology, and to conditions in global market places. The flexibility in Britain is due to relatively weak regulation through 'corporatist' agreements between government, employers and organized labour. Britain was the first industrial nation. Countries that developed later were faster to regulate. In recent times, the cross-national trend has been deregulation, and here Britain has been at the forefront (Lash and Urry, 1987). This is despite the minimum wage and the ceiling on compulsory working time that were introduced, somewhat reluctantly and half-heartedly, in Britain in 1999. The minimum pay was then extremely low, and the ceiling on working time is still easily breached. The other indicators of Britain's unregulated state are the relatively low rate of trade union membership, and the low proportion of the workforce covered by collective agreements, especially national agreements (see below), few restrictions on employers' ability to hire, fire and to declare redundancies without consultation or negotiation, and the similar prerogative claimed by employers to run their businesses as they see fit, legally subject only to their shareholders. Since the 1970s British governments have stood at arm's length from economic life. 'Lame ducks' have been allowed to sink. Owners and managers have been told to do their best or face the consequences.

Deregulation and its associated labour market flexibility in Britain became possible largely as a result of radical reforms to trade unions and industrial relations that were implemented in the 1980s and early-1990s. These required trade union officials to be elected periodically, banned the closed shop, required ballots prior to industrial action, banned most forms of secondary (sympathetic) industrial action, made the unions responsible for the actions of all their officials, including shop stewards, imposed heavy restrictions on picketing, and placed the unions' funds at risk in the event of any breaches. These reforms made it easier for employers to opt out of national bargaining, and to limit workplace negotiations to matters of their own choosing like basic rates of pay and hours of work, but not working practices or incentive systems let alone investment decisions. Trade union membership has declined across Western Europe, but more steeply in Britain than in most other countries. In Britain at the end of the 1970s over a half of all workers were in trade unions; it is now less than 30 per cent. The proportion of the UK workforce covered by collective agreements has also declined steeply to well beneath the European norm (see Ebbinghaus and Visser, 1999; Traxler, 1996).

The European Union has classified European industrial relations regimes using the typology in Table 4.1. The UK is part of a 'liberal' group; the only other European countries in this group are Cyprus, Malta and Ireland. The USA would be in the same group but the typology lists only EU countries. The proportions of the labour forces that are in trade unions are substantially higher only in the Nordic, organized corporatism group. However, the liberal group differs from all the others except the post-communist 'transition' states in the extremely low proportion of workers and jobs that are covered by collective agreements. The UK is the only large 'old' EU member state where so few employees have the protection of collectively agreed terms and conditions.

The decline in trade union membership, and in the collective regulation of working life, have occurred mainly in the private sector, and manual workers

Table 4.1 Typology of European industrial relations regimes

Regime	Countries	Mean union density (%)	Mean bargaining coverage (%)
Nordic, organized corporatism	Denmark, Finland, Sweden	74.7	86.8
Central social partnership	Belgium, Germany, Luxembourg, Netherlands, Austria, Slovenia	35.4	82.8
South, state centred	Greece, Spain, France, Italy, Portugal	20.2	75.4
West, liberal	Ireland, Cyprus, Malta, UK	33.9	35.3
Transition countries		22.8	34.5

Source: European Commission, 2009

have been the most affected. They have been the most affected by the transfer of jobs from the public to the private sector, the public sector being the most highly regulated of all sectors of the economy, and by far the most strongly unionized. This transfer of jobs and labour has been largely due to the series of privatizations in the 1980s and 1990s – steel, oil, British Airways, gas, electricity, water, telecommunications, the railways, coal and others. A subsidiary source of the shift has been the outsourcing of non-core functions from public services – catering, cooking and laundering from schools and hospitals, for example. Also, instead of performing direct works, local authorities are now more likely to contract-out. This has happened to refuse collection and the management of some local authorities' leisure services. An outcome is far fewer blue-collar public sector jobs. Managers and professional staff are still employed directly by schools, hospitals, universities and so on, which is the main reason why, across the country, these grades are now the most likely to be unionized. Roughly two million jobs have been shifted from the public to the private sector since the 1970s. The employees have found themselves in smaller, often non-unionized firms, in more competitive environments. Some sections of the privatized workforces have done rather well. Train drivers, for example, are now among the country's best paid manual workers. Elsewhere, pay and other conditions of work have been degraded. Privatized jobs are invariably less secure (see Davidson, 1990; Nichols and Davidson, 1993). Until the 1970s public sector employment was expanding, and, in some ways, in times of full employment, set the standards that private businesses had to match. Nowadays the public sector is more likely to be 'market tested' against private sector efficiency and practices.

Disempowerment and devaluation

The working class has lost the trade unions in the sense that most manual workers are no longer members, and they are no longer the section of the workforce that is most likely to be unionized. This is due entirely to sectoral shifts in the workforce rather than manual employees deserting the trade unions and the middle classes joining these organizations. There have been massive job losses in what were once densely unionized manufacturing and extractive industries (mines, steel, textiles, and also dockwork where technology has now replaced most humans). The public sector has long been more densely unionized overall than private sector businesses. Large establishments have always been more densely unionized than small firms, and the state is by far the largest employer of all. Lower grade staff in central and local government, and in hospitals, are still densely unionized, but overall the public sector has a top-heavy workforce. Teachers, doctors and lawyers have always been well-organized, and in the public sector overall there are more staff in these grades than in working class occupations. The trade unions have always claimed to speak for all employees. This has not changed. However, the public voice of the unions is no longer an identifiably and distinctive working class voice.

In the 1990s the working class also lost the Labour Party: the leadership made it clear that it did not wish to be associated with any particular class, and that it valued its links with employers as much as its relationship with organized labour. The Labour Party's parliamentary leadership saw this 'modernizing' move as essential if the party was to regain power since the working class no longer comprised the majority of voters.

The Co-op has become just another retailer. Working men's clubs and other community, free-time organizations have been largely replaced by television and commercial leisure. Consumer culture, promoted through marketing, is now primarily a middle class consumer culture. Individual middle class house-holds always had more money to spend than individual working class house-holds, but the much greater numbers in the working class once gave that class the greater aggregate spending power. This has ceased to be the case. The days when stores such as Woolworth's commanded the mass market have gone. In eating-out, holidays, clothing and virtually everything else, there is now more money to be made by courting middle class spenders.

The value of a working class identity may currently be in a period of historical transition. Forty-three in-depth interviews with residents in Cheadle (a suburb of Manchester) which outside observers, including sociologists, would prob-ably have regarded as lower middle class, found that this was not how most residents described themselves. Most had backgrounds in manual work and the district was mixed in terms of current occupations. Among those who iden-tified with any class (42 per cent declined to identify with any) twice as many described themselves as working class as middle class. What did they mean by working class? The working class identifiers, and also those who refused any class label, saw themselves as part of a social mainstream, a respectable main-stream, as a result of how they worked and earned their livings (hard graft), plus their respectable family and consumption practices (Savage et al, 2004).

In contrast, among the subjects in Beverley Skeggs' (1997) ethnographic study, conducted over 12 years among a group of 83 young women from working class backgrounds who were taking care courses at a further educa-tion college in an industrial town in north-west England, working classness was treated as a stigma. The young women's abiding concern was to become respectable, not common. This was expressed in their concern about dress, accent, and the places where they preferred to be seen. The girls in this study did not mention the word class. Skeggs considers that they were avoiding the term at all costs. The word was never mentioned. Skeggs takes 'respectable' and 'common' to be codes for middle and working class, but we need to bear in mind that there has been a long-standing distinction between the 'rough' and the 'respectable' within the working class.

Skeggs (2004) has subsequently examined recent media and political dis-courses, and has noted how frequently the working class is denigrated for its lack of relevant skills, poor work habits, its need for social housing, its children's misbehaviour, and unhealthy lifestyles. Stephanie Lawler (2005), using exam-ples mainly from journalism and other popular writing, argues that disgust is the most common response to working class lives by present-day middle class commentators. Diane Reay's (2004) focus groups with 454 10–11 year olds in London schools have revealed how, within this age group, particular schools and groups of pupils are demonized in everyday discourse. However, Reay emphasizes that 'respectable' working class families as well as the middle class were avoiding these schools and their pupils.

One sentiment expressed in many working class neighbourhoods is regret that the old communities have gone. The workplace and neighbourhood communities from which the original working class acquired solidarity have vanished. The reasons include economic change, television and the motor car, and also the fact that many of these neighbourhoods have become multi-ethnic. It is not necessarily that the white households are racist, but they can still feel that their own culture is under assault, that their quality of life has suffered, and that they need to rely on themselves because no-one else now speaks for them (see Evans, 2006).

Not only in Britain

The recent trends in Britain's economy, and the experiences of its working class, are anything but unique. All the older industrial countries, now the world's richest countries, have experienced the de-industrialization of their labour markets. They have all experienced the latest ICT revolution, post-Fordist practices, and they are all exposed to global markets.

All the world's richer societies are now net immigration countries. This applies to all the countries that were part of the pre-2004 European Union. There are always local specificities in immigrant-host relations depending on the origins and cultures of the migrants, and the receiving contexts. That said, everywhere immigrants have tended to settle in districts where working class residents have been experiencing the consequences of a decline in the quantity and/or quality of working class jobs, and immigrants have often been blamed for all the ills. This is the background to the pan-European emergence of populist political parties that seek to restrict immigration (and maybe resettle existing immigrants), while defending and privileging the natives and their cultures. Talja Blokland (2004) has illustrated some of these processes in Hillesluis, an inner-city district in Rotterdam (Netherlands), where immigrants (the largest group were from Morocco) were blamed for the loss of a largely imagined past working class community.

Ulrich Beck and Elisabeth Beck-Gernsheim (2009) argue that the formation of factions among upcoming generations is now being driven by global forces, and that in sociology methodological nationalism is no longer adequate. They argue that young people all over the world have a new expectation of global equality, which they are likely to seek through migration to richer countries where their presence spreads economic, social and cultural insecurity.

In some ways Britain's working class has been exceptionally exposed to the costs of change by the country's relatively unregulated labour markets.

However, the findings from the GLOBALIFE project, reported by Sandra Buchholz and a team of German colleagues (2009) are highly instructive (see Box 4.2). There have been similar winners and losers from globalization in all countries, but in the least regulated economies and labour markets flexibility and insecurity have been spread around most widely and thinly. In the more strongly regulated systems, either a division between insiders and outsiders has been strengthened or, in the case of 100 per cent official regulation, jobs have gone elsewhere. Fabrizio Bernadi and Luis Garrido (2008) offer the case of Spain. Between 1994 and 2005 employment grew in total from 12.3 to 19.3 million and the number of immigrants estimated to be working in Spain rose from 0.5 to 4.0 million. During this same period Spain experienced a major expansion in low-skilled, low paid service sector employment, including jobs as domestic cleaners, gardeners, nannies etc. These jobs have been filled mainly by immigrants and Spanish women who tend to remain indefinitely in this kind of work. Spain has a strongly regulated primary labour market where employees have permanent jobs from which dismissal is difficult. Spain also has a very weakly regulated labour market sector where most low-skilled employment in services is based. Young people are unlikely to obtain permanent career jobs until they are age 30. Until then they 'mark time' in the secondary sector and

---

Box 4.2   Globalization: winners and losers

The GLOBALIFE project (see Buchholz et al, 2009) gathered data from 17 countries in an attempt to identify winners and losers from globalization.

- In all countries men in mid-career tend to have been the main winners, provided they have been qualified, experienced, and already established in stable types of employment.
- In contrast, women have been at risk of marginalization in flexible forms of employment.
- Young people have been losers. They have faced increased uncertainties, precarious and atypical forms of employment.
- Late-career employees have also been losers. Companies see them as inadequately qualified, inflexible and too costly.

However, there have been some differences between countries. These include:

- In liberal, flexible market regimes (as in the UK and USA) flexibility has been spread around widely and thinly.
- In countries with low degrees of labour market flexibility (Central and Southern Europe) there has been a strengthening of the division between insiders and outsiders.

remain living with their families. Thus employers can treat them as second-ary earners who do not need full adult salaries, and in turn the young people are obliged to remain in their parents' homes. Other service sector employees never move out and up. Hence Bernadi and Garrido's hypothesis that Spain is currently developing a separate service-sector based proletariat.

The underclass and social exclusion

The underclass debate begins in Britain

British sociology began to debate the possible formation of an underclass at the end of the 1960s. Initially this was in response to the post-war growth in non-white immigration, and to earlier claims that assimilation and integration difficulties were just normal and temporary immigrant-host rather than race relations issues (Patterson, 1965). In their 1960s study in Birmingham, Rex and Moore (1967) noted how new Commonwealth immigrants were excluded from owner-occupation by their lack of capital, and from council housing by their lack of 'points' accumulated by length of residence. As a result they were being concentrated in privately-rented accommodation, typically in multiply-occupied dwellings, in inner-city districts that were being deserted by whites. During the 1970s it became evident that, for some immigrant groups, similar processes were operating in the labour market. The immigrants were entering and then remaining stuck at the bottom (see Rex and Tomlinson, 1979). By then, as unemployment had risen, there was discussion about the likelihood of long-term unemployed whites who were displaced by economic restructuring then failed to regain work, and school-leavers who were unable to establish themselves in stable employment, becoming an underclass (Giddens, 1973). Since the 1980s the existence of an underclass has been at least tacitly accepted in much of British sociology. The list of classes proposed by Gary Runciman in 1990 included an underclass. The versions of John Goldthorpe's class scheme adopted as the official classification in the UK, then in the European Union, list an underclass (though not under that title). By the 1990s the earlier practice of classifying everyone (including all the retired and those currently out-of-work) by their normal occupations had been abandoned.

During the 1980s, Britain's debate about the formation of an underclass spread beyond sociology into politics and the mass media, where the issue became 'hot' rather than purely intellectual. By the end of the 1980s John Westergaard (1992) was able to distinguish 'left' and 'right' versions of the underclass thesis. Both camps agreed that an underclass was being formed, but disagreed on the reasons. The left blamed high unemployment which was depriving many of the chance to earn their livelihoods, and the manner in which government policies had allowed state benefits to fall further and further behind typical earnings (Field, 1989). The right had a different diagnosis: the underclass was said to comprise 'workshy scroungers' who refused to 'get on their bikes' to search for work in favour of living on state hand-outs. Young single mothers who allegedly became pregnant in order to qualify for council housing and a life on benefits, and the feckless fathers, were major folk devils.

The underclass in the USA

By the 1970s the USA had its own underclass debate. This had arisen in a specifically American context. During the Great Depression in the 1930s, completing high school at age 18 or 19 had become normal in all social classes. Then, after the Second World War, college enrolments rose steadily and included a half of all young Americans by the end of the 1960s (it is now around two-thirds). However, not all young Americans were extending their education. Around 15 per cent were failing to complete high school and they became known as drop-outs. They were not drawn equally from all sections of American society. Rather, they were concentrated in inner-city districts populated mainly by black Americans. In many such districts dropping-out rather than completing high school remained the norm. The drop-outs had spectacular rates of unemployment, high rates of criminal convictions, and were mainly from female-headed single-parent households. The main objective of the civil rights movement that formed during the 1950s was an end to blatant race discrimination like the colour bar that remained in force in much of the old South, but a parallel set of demands was for genuine equal opportunities, to be delivered by affirmative action where necessary, to compensate for the historical discrimination that all black Americans had suffered.

By the end of the 1970s there was agreement across the USA that affirmative action programmes, which included positive discrimination in college admissions, were creating an enlarged black American middle class. This has become strikingly evident in American government where Colin Powell and Condoleezza Rice were successive Secretaries of State during George Bush junior's presidency (2000–2008), followed by the election of President Barak Obama in 2008. However, by the 1980s it was equally clear that not all black Americans were benefitting from the post-1960s reforms. Some were being left behind in the inner-cities where unemployment and crime rates, and rates of single-parenthood, remained as high if not higher than ever.

There was agreement among American commentators on the existence of a mainly black underclass in the inner-cities, but disagreement on why these Americans were being left behind. The main academic protagonists were the sociologist, William Julius Wilson, and the political scientist/policy analyst, Charles Murray. Wilson (1987) argued that the more able, ambitious and better-qualified young people had exited the inner-cities, but that jobs had exited even more rapidly. Hence the higher rates of unemployment and the acute shortage of potential male 'breadwinning' fathers and husbands. The solution, in Wilson's view, had to be somehow joining together inner-city residents and jobs. Murray's diagnosis was different (Murray, 1984). He claimed that the root cause of underclass formation was over-generous welfare which offered the alternative of living without official work. Mothers were able to support themselves and their children on welfare, freeing males to work in America's unofficial, largely criminal economy.

In American politics (though not in sociology) Charles Murray won this argument. All presidential administrations since the 1980s (those of Ronald Reagan, George Bush senior, Bill Clinton, George W Bush junior and now Barak Obama) have practised 'tough love'. Welfare is now limited to a maximum of five years in a normal working lifetime. Mothers with infant children who claim welfare are required to be available for work for up to 40 hours per week. No-one is any longer offered 'something for nothing'. Welfare claimants are required to enrol in education or training, or to accept 'workfare' – working for the community in exchange for their benefits. As far as most Americans are concerned , 'tough love' has worked. Welfare rolls have fallen. Communitarians believe that rolling-back big government creates scope for local communities to address local problems. In Europe similar ideas are advocated by the Social Capital Foundation.

Charles Murray in Britain

At the end of the 1980s and in the early-1990s Charles Murray made two short visits to Britain, on each occasion jointly hosted by the Sunday Times (a Thatcherite newspaper at that time) and the Institute of Economic Affairs (then and still a right-wing think-tank and publisher). Murray was invited to consider whether the kind of underclass that he had identified in the USA also existed in Britain. He made brief excursions to some of Britain's unemployment blackspots. On his first visit Murray concluded that an underclass was 'emerging' (Murray, 1990). On his second visit, four years later, he concluded that 'the crisis' was deepening (Murray, 1994). The clinching evidence, according to Murray, was the sheer number of unemployed, able-bodied young males, the spread of single parenthood among young women in high unemployment districts, and rising crime rates in these same areas. Murray's proposed solution for Britain, as for America, was less generous welfare.

Murray's style of writing has consistently engaged and enraged both academic and wider audiences. Such was the attention that Murray attracted in Britain that the term 'underclass' and Murray's name and views became conjoined. In sociology, anyone using the term underclass became a suspected Murray sympathizer. Thus the term was dropped from sociological discourse. The term also slipped out of mainstream UK politics and the media. During the 1990s the right in Britain (the Conservative Party then led by John Major) was seeking to cultivate a softer, post-Thatcher image.

Social exclusion

While the UK and the USA were arguing furiously about the processes that were creating underclasses, continental Europe, orchestrated by the European

Community (soon to become known as the European Union) was engaged in calmer consideration of the possibility that member countries could acquire socially excluded groups. The context on the continent was basically the same as in Britain. All the West European states had become net immigration countries. They were all undergoing similar economic restructuring to Britain: de-industrialization accompanied by rising levels of unemployment. Immigrants were known to have exceptionally high rates of unemployment. Hence the possibility that some unemployed groups (especially unemployed immigrants) might be physically within, yet remain economically, socially, culturally and politically outside the mainstream continental societies.

By the mid-1990s British commentators had adopted European terminology. Excluded groups, plural, seemed far more appropriate than underclass for designating impoverished pensioners, long-term unemployed adults, repeat young offenders, single parents, and so on. While in opposition prior to 1997, *New* Labour (as it had titled itself) was developing policies to improve the prospects and lives of these disadvantaged groups. Its flagship policies, implemented after 1997, were first, the series of New Deals, initially for the young unemployed (18–25 year olds), then lone parents, the disabled, high unemployment communities, and then others; second, tax credits to supplement the earnings of low paid working adults, especially those with children; and third and fourth, a minimum wage for the employed and a minimum income guarantee for the retired.

While in opposition prior to 1997 New Labour stressed the need to address poverty and unemployment rather than social exclusion. However, immediately following its 1997 election victory, a Social Inclusion Unit was created within the Cabinet Office, which was to coordinate the work of new Policy Action Teams (PATs) that were formed in all government departments with domestic responsibilities. Simultaneously a series of research projects was funded to discover how best to include the socially excluded.

Ruth Levitas (1998, 2004) has distinguished three New Labour social exclusion discourses, and has traced changes in emphasis over time.

- First there was a RED (re-distribution) discourse. This was strongest when New Labour was seeking office, then immediately following its success in 1997. The emphasis was on spreading the benefits of economic growth (income and jobs) to all sections of the population.
- A SID discourse (social integration through employment) became ascendant as successive New Deals were launched. New *Labour* was living up to its name: its preferred route to inclusion was always via employment.
- MUD (moral underclass discourse) became pronounced when many of the intended beneficiaries proved (or appeared) reluctant to grasp the new deals that were on offer. Many of the excluded were believed to be held back by a lack of motivation and poverty of aspiration. There was particular emphasis on preventing social exclusion being transmitted across the generations. The NEETs (young people not in employment, education

or training) became a prime target for state interventions. In 2001 Connexions replaced the Careers Service and was given the priority aim of reducing the size of the NEET group. Sure Start initially aimed to improve parenting skills (and if not to compensate for poor parenting) among at risk children. In 2008 New Labour announced that the 'participation age' (in some form of learning) would rise to 18 from 2015. Also in 2008 the UK began to introduce its own version of American workfare. There was to be a presumption that anyone claiming the Job Seekers Allowance would participate in some form of pre-employment education or training, or work experience, until they were able to progress into mainstream employment.

By the time that New Labour exited government in 2010, Charles Murray's analysis of the underclass was long discredited, but all its principal claims had resurfaced in a social exclusion rhetoric.

Do the concepts fit the evidence?

Many sociologists have never been convinced that either an underclass or socially excluded groups really exist. These could be examples of reification: inventing a word, then using it so frequently that the users imagine that their term corresponds to something 'out there'. This matter remains unresolved. Whether investigators have declared 'for' or 'against' has depended on how low or high they have set the evidence test bar (see Boxes 4.3 and 4.4).

Box 4.3   Underclass and social exclusion: evidence for

The clearest affirmative evidence has been from investigators who have felt it sufficient simply to demonstrate that Britain has plenty of long-term, chronically unemployed. Alan Buckingham (1999) analysed data from the nationally representative sample of individuals who were born in 1958 (known as the National Child Development Study, NCDS). By age 33 Buckingham decided that 5.4% could be described as part of an underclass.

■ They had spent at least 15% of their labour market careers not in employment (on average they had been unemployed for 40% of this time).
■ They had all experienced at least one period of welfare dependence.
■ They were not home owners.

At age 33 the men were typically unmarried and the women were typically single-parents. Buckingham's underclass had low ability (according to childhood test scores), had left school with poor (if any) qualifications, and had little or no post-school education or training.

Full Employment UK (1990) had previously identified a chronically unemployed underclass who had effectively detached themselves from the labour market.

- They were hostile to the idea of low-paid unskilled work.
- They did not expect to be offered worthwhile jobs.
- Fiddling benefit was the norm.
- They were contemptuous of government training schemes, Jobclubs, Restart interviews, and all official offers of help.

Selected groups of young people, especially male early leavers from education, living in high unemployment districts, who in official discourse would be described as NEET, appear to match what is commonly understood by 'underclass' and 'social exclusion'. Ian Taylor and colleagues (1994) reported a discussion group with young men in Sheffield, all serving probation sentences. This experience '...confirmed the existence in that city of a significant number of young men for whom the idea of employment in the legitimate labour market was understood to be unrealistic and who spent the bulk of their day on the look out for opportunities to steal or to be otherwise employed in the local hidden economy of crime' p283.

There is a wealth of additional case study evidence from particular districts revealing the development of distinctive social practices and knowledge among some chronically unemployed groups of young people (and adults as well in some cases): detailed knowledge of the benefit system which enables individuals to ensure that they claim all their entitlements, sometimes coupled with a reluctance to 'sign-off' for fear of being unable to qualify again (Jordan and Redley, 1994); treating fiddly (unofficial) jobs as a normal way of topping-up benefit (MacDonald, 1994); and, in some cases, developing criminal skills and knowledge, and relying on these for a livelihood (Craine and Coles, 1995).

Box 4.4   Underclass and social exclusion: evidence against

Tania Burchardt (2000) set her evidence test bar at a much higher level. She used data from the first five annual sweeps of the British Household Panel Study (BHPS), a large scale survey with a nationally representative sample that commenced in 1991, and found that hardly anyone could be described as comprehensively excluded. Four measurements of social exclusion were used:

- Income less than 50% of the average, standardizing for household composition.
- Unemployed.
- Political: not voted and not a member of any political organization.
- Lacking emotional support.

The findings included:

- The proportions excluded at Wave 1 ranged from 10% (unemployment) to 18% (income).

■ In all sweeps at least 38% of the sample qualified as excluded on at least one of the criteria.

■ No more than 11% (politics) were continuously excluded in all five sweeps on any single criterion.

■ Only 0.3% were excluded on all four criteria at any one time.

Burchardt concluded that the numbers who could be described as comprehensively excluded were negligible.

The fairest tests of an underclass/social exclusion hypothesis are exactly the same as for any other alleged class. First, there must be a distinctive economic position, and in this instance the distinctive position is not having paid employment and, as a result, a relatively low income. As in other classes, people will have to occupy these positions for extended periods of time, then a core of generational continuity will clinch the case for recognition of an economically and demographically formed class. There is in fact a wealth of evidence that unemployment tends to run in families (Payne, 1987, 1989). Second, such a class might then acquire distinctive social, cultural and political characteristics. An underclass or excluded group might be distinctive in lacking socio-emotional support (one of Burchardt's criteria) (see Box 4.4), but alternatively members of the class or group could lend strong support to one another. A well-formed underclass or excluded group might have a distinctive relationship to the political system. This might be total disengagement (another of Burchardt's tests) but it might also be support for a particular kind of politics – revolutionary, nationalist or whatever.

Up to now sociologists have been most successful in demonstrating that, as yet, Britain does not have specified kinds of underclasses or excluded groups. For example, in 1994 Duncan Gallie showed that the long-term unemployed were no lower in work commitment (the desire to have a paid job) than people in employment, and that their politics were typically those of normal members of the working class – support for collectivism and for the Labour Party. In other words, the notions that the long-term unemployed were workshy, and somehow different in their political proclivities than the employed working class, were pure bunk. There is plenty of additional, corroborating evidence that most of the long-term unemployed are ready and willing to seize any opportunity to work regularly, and that if given the chance they have little difficulty in adjusting to work routines (Marsden, 1982). These studies have stressed how unemployed adults typically struggle to maintain 'respectable' lifestyles, and to ensure that a work ethic is inculcated into their children (Allatt and Yeandle, 1991; Coffield et al, 1986; Wright, 1994). Studies of young blacks have recorded some spectacularly high unemployment rates in inner-city districts, but have consistently found that their work aspirations and political views are thoroughly conventional (Connolly et al, 1992).

Robert MacDonald and Jane Marsh (2005) have reported their findings from a series of studies of 18–25 year olds, all from some of the most deprived neighbourhoods in Britain, and all on Teesside. They prefer to describe their respondents as 'disconnected' rather than either an underclass or socially excluded.

■ All the young people had experience of paid jobs, albeit unstable and insecure jobs. Some jobs were official, others were unofficial fiddly jobs. They were not completely detached from the labour market or employment. They were simply marginal members of Britain's workforce.

■ Theirs had been a normal working class experience of the labour market in their neighbourhoods, for adults as well as young people.

■ They saw their own lives as normal rather than different.

■ They were making real choices when seeking work, as in the rest of their lives, but always within tight constraints.

Actually there is evidence that the experiences of adults in deprived neighbourhoods are somewhat more varied than MacDonald and Marsh suggest. Lydia Morris (Morris, 1992; Morris and Irwin, 1992) studied and compared three groups of adult males in Hartlepool (like Teesside, also in North-East England, and another prime example of de-industrialization). One group of Morris's respondents had been continuously employed throughout the previous 12 months, a second group had been continuously unemployed, while the third group had been unemployed to begin with but had restarted work at some point during the year. In some senses, the continuously unemployed were different – in their labour market careers, of course, but also in tending to have friends and kin who were also unemployed. However, all three groups lived in the same neighbourhoods, and in their everyday lives there were no clear boundaries between them. The middling group who had been in and out of work linked the continuously employed on the one side and the continuously unemployed on the other (see also Byrne, 1995).

The historical context

History always matters. The present always contains legacies from the past. Memories of the past, real or imagined, shape how we view the present. As regards the underclass and social exclusion, it can be useful to identify what is historically novel, and what, if anything, is different today apart from the terminology.

Prior to the 1980s researchers and policy-makers recognized a condition called 'multiple disadvantage'. Various kinds of disadvantage – poverty, unemployment, poor housing, ill health and so on – were each known to be liable to trigger or aggravate each other. It was known that disadvantages tended to cluster in particular families and neighbourhoods. There was particular interest in an alleged 'cycle of disadvantage', meaning the inter-generational transmission of multiple disadvantages. Rutter and Madge's (1976) research was conducted in the context of this 'cycle of disadvantage' debate. Their study found that only approximately a half of all children who were reared in extremely deprived circumstances became similarly deprived adults. The authors used this evidence to argue that a deprived background did not need to be a lifetime handicap, and that whether individuals escaped depended on the job opportunities that were available to them, and the assistance that they received. However, if just a fifth of children were being reared in heavily disadvantaged circumstances (and the real figure was well-beneath this in the 1970s), a 50 per cent rate of inter-generational continuity represented heavily (and unfavourably) skewed life-chances.

One of the explanations offered for this cycle of disadvantage was a 'culture of poverty', a phenomenon originally identified by Oscar Lewis (1959) in Mexico, but which appeared to have relevance all over the world. Lewis illustrated how people who lived in desperately deprived circumstances tended to become resigned, apathetic and fatalistic, and abandoned all efforts to improve their conditions. Debates about whether this culture was cause or consequence of the perpetuation of poverty in particular families and communities mirror the dispute between 'left' and 'right' versions of the underclass in the 1980s. The fact is that structure and agency are always implicated in each other and that each can help to sustain the other.

Before World War II researchers usually identified a stratum beneath the employed working class; people who were variously described as loafers, roughs and criminals. Karl Marx wrote about a lumpenproletariat, and had an extremely low estimation of their likely contributions to the revolution that he hoped to foment (see Box 4.5). In 'respectable' society fear of the mob has a long history, as does a tendency of the privileged to blame the victims for their poverty, or at least to try to distinguish between the deserving and the undeserving poor (see Bagguley and Mann, 1992; Mann, 1991).

Marx's lumpenproletariat, loafers and suchlike largely disappeared from Britain (and the rest of Europe) after the Second World War. These groups were drawn into the employed, more respectable sections of the working class by full employment and the development of strong welfare states, not least the replacement of slums by council housing. These conditions were not products of economic growth alone. They were achieved during the era of strong labour

---

Box 4.5   Karl Marx on the lumpenproletariat

'...thieves and criminals of all kinds, living on the crumbs of society, people without a definite trade, vagabonds, gens sans feu et sans aveu...discharged soldiers, discharged jailbirds, escaped galley slaves, swindlers, mountebanks, lazzaroni, pickpockets, tricksters, gamblers, maquereaus, brothel keepers, porters, literati, organ-grinders, ragpickers, knife grinders, tinkers, beggars...this scum, offal, refuse of all classes' Marx (1962).

movements (trade unions and the political parties that they supported), which made full employment and the elimination of poverty priorities in economic policy.

In the 1950s and 60s it was realistic for probation and rehabilitation officers to aim to establish their clients in employment as a first step towards their full social integration. This first step was generally regarded as absolutely essential. Subsequently, in tougher labour market conditions, the job prospects of the groups in question have become bleak. Employers have become less willing, because they have less need, to take a chance and to carry 'passengers'. This applies even with employers who, in research interviews, express support for the principle of assisting marginalized groups to obtain employment (see Roberts et al, 1997).

Exactly what has changed since the 1970s, and what have been the catalysts? It is implausible that those concerned somehow self-transformed into an underclass or excluded groups. The catalysts have been de-industrialization (of employment) and the advent of a new era of post-Fordism and globalization. Government economic priorities have changed towards attracting and retaining investment. Regions that were once well-stocked with 'traditional' industrial jobs have experienced heavy job losses, steep rises in levels of unemployment, and an overall deterioration in the quality of the working class jobs that remain. Since the 1960s there has been a big increase in the volume of low paid employment in Britain, and a decline in the relative earnings (compared with the average) of low paid employees. Work today is less likely to protect a household from poverty than in the 1960s (see Hills et al, 2002). The best of the 'new deals' that New Labour appeared able to offer in the 1990s and 2000s were a minimum wage and tax credits that enabled the unemployed to join the working poor, just slightly better-off than the non-working poor.

It is still far too early to eject the concepts of underclass and exclusion from sociology's vocabulary, though the earlier concept of multiple disadvantage retains much value. Disadvantages can occur in many different combinations, thereby creating more than one disadvantaged group. That said, we can note that all the groups shade into and are not really outside or separate from the employed working class. This applies to adults displaced from their former occupations, retired persons who are dependent entirely on state benefits, and the young unemployed, some of whose problems are aggravated by drug or alcohol (ab)use or criminal records.

All these groups are unlikely ever to coalesce into a single solidaristic class. Nevertheless, some of the groups already exist as demographic and economic entities, specifically those continuously unemployed or threatened by unemployment, and whose only alternative is low paid, insecure jobs. Full class formation – the acquisition of social, cultural and political characteristics – always takes generations. These characteristics, if they are formed among some of the disadvantaged groups, cannot be predicted solely from the material circumstances of the disadvantaged groups themselves. Much always depends on the political and ideological contexts. At present, full class formation looks unlikely, first, because the disadvantaged, the underclass or the excluded have no label, no name, with which all members are likely to identify, and there is no mainstream political party, and no mainstream ideology, that takes their side. Maybe a blunt truth is that these groups are superfluous to economic requirements in what is still, possibly more so than ever before, a work-centred society. Thus the disadvantaged are most likely to remain fragmented, marginal, semi-connected, and another blunt truth is that they are all products of our society, not under or outside, or aliens from elsewhere.

Summary

This chapter has described how Britain's original working class, then comprising the working masses, the bulk of the workforce, was created following the industrial revolution. Its culture arose from people's first-hand experiences of interdependence at work and in their neighbourhoods. Working class culture became the 'soil' in which working class organizations developed – brass bands, the Co-op, trade unions and the Labour Party.

We then discussed the debates (within and beyond sociology) of the 1950s and 60s about the effects of the spread of affluence and other post-war changes on the working class. The embourgeoisement thesis was rejected by most sociologists. Rather, it was argued that a non-traditional, privatized and instrumentally oriented working class was being created.

The impact of the post-1970s economic changes, examined in detail in chapter 3, on the working class, was then examined. The changes have been bad news for Britain's working class. It has shrunk in size and it has been disorganized by the spread of unemployment and job insecurity, the loss of (mainly males') jobs in extractive and manufacturing industries, the loss of members and erosion of trade unions' rights which were both cause and effect of the industrial relations legislation of the 1980s and early-1990s, ethnic diversity, and the crisis of working class masculinity. The good jobs that remain have become less secure and the workers in these jobs are now under greater pressure in the workplace. Meanwhile, sections of the working class have been impoverished. They are concentrated in the inner-cities and on 'sink' council estates which have spectacularly high levels of unemployment, single parenthood and crime rates, and low educational standards.

Has a separate underclass been created? Not yet, but disadvantaged groups have been separated from the more or less continuously employed working class. It is unlikely that that these groups will congeal into a single underclass, but some of the groups could become more and more distinct, socially and culturally, especially if recent levels of unemployment, and the gap between state benefit levels and average earnings, are allowed to persist.

Intermediate Classes

5

Introduction

All other things being equal, one would expect class formation to be weak in the intermediate classes. This is partly because they are intermediate; neither at nor very close to the top with clear advantages to defend (like the middle class), and not at the bottom (like the working class) with everything to gain, so it might appear, from radical change. If classes are small, this will also work against their demographic integrity. One would expect high absolute rates of both inward and outward inter-generational mobility. In other words, the core memberships with inter-generational continuity should be quite small. Moreover, both the inflows and outflows from intermediate classes are most likely to be both upwards and downwards. It is different in the working class where, if we discount the alleged underclass, the only way to move is up. Conversely, in the middle class the characteristic concern is to avoid descent. Such tidiness is less likely in classes which are literally in the middle. All told, therefore, we should not expect to discover well-defined lifestyles, forms of consciousness and political orientations. But all this assumes that all other things are equal, and in the real world this never applies.

Two intermediate classes are examined in this chapter – lower non-manuals and the petit bourgeoisie (the self-employed and owners of small businesses). These classes are very different from each other. They have little in common except that both are intermediate – neither working class nor middle class.

The lower non-manuals used to be a fairly large, mainly female occupational group (35 per cent of females against just five per cent of males born between 1950 and 1959 were in this type of employment). The class is still mainly female, but now accounts for just 20 per cent of female employees. As we shall see, the lower non-manuals are demographically unstable inter-generationally, and socially amorphous with no distinctive lifestyle or political proclivities. This was the case in the past, remains so, and is most likely to be so in the future. The lower non-manuals' most significant class characteristic is arguably that they have not been absorbed into either the working class or the middle class.

The petit bourgeoisie is small, recently growing but currently stable, and mainly male (15 per cent of males and six per cent of females born between

1950 and 1959), and has impressive inter-generational continuity. We shall see that its members have not just a very distinctive work situation (working for themselves) but also a distinctive work-centred lifestyle and political enthusiasms, and they have played important ideological and organizational roles in Britain's (and in other countries') politics.

It is possible to argue that additional intermediate classes could be identified and examined. The two main candidates are, first, foremen, chargehands and other supervisors of manual employees, and second, technicians and technologists. Present-day conventional sociological practice does not treat either of these groups as separate intermediate classes. Supervisors of manual workers are subsumed within the working class – part of the old and present-day aristocracy of labour. There are strong arguments for this placement. The role of supervisor is rarely a career-long status. Supervisors of manual workers are usually ex-workers. It is most likely that those concerned will regard themselves as having risen within, rather than out of, the working class when their working lives remain shop floor-based.

Technicians and technologists are treated differently in the new official classification). Some, like laboratory workers, are grouped with the lower nonmanuals. Others are treated as part of the working class – another section of the aristocracy of labour – with better-paid jobs, which usually require vocational qualifications, and where there is no grime. Computer technicians, and personnel who control production processes from computer consoles, and who maintain such technical systems, are treated in this way. Other technical grades are merged into the middle class. These include research and development, and other occupations into which university graduates may be recruited prior to gaining full professional status or rising to management positions. The limited evidence that is available justifies this treatment. Marks and Baldry (2009) interviewed 76 software engineers in five software businesses in Scotland. They all regarded software engineers, with whom they felt a collective identity, as middle class, maybe professional, on the basis of their education, incomes and lifestyles. Most identified themselves as middle class or its equivalent: 31 per cent said just middle class, eight per cent said upper middle and 28 per cent said professional. However, 38 per cent described themselves as working class: they were invariably using their family backgrounds as the key marker.

Lower non-manuals, and laboratory staff, are different, in that all the evidence suggests that they are best treated as genuinely intermediate, different from both the working class and the middle class proper.

Lower non-manuals

This intermediate class now accounts for approximately 20 per cent of women employees (if they are classed by their own occupations) and six per cent of men. It is not a tiny class, but it would be very small if women were not placed by their own occupations. Until the 1980s there were more women in these jobs than in any other class of work. Today, as has long been and still is the case among men, there are more women in both the middle class and the working class.

The earlier size of the lower non-manual class (it once accounted for around 40 per cent of all female workers) was the result of the growth of this type of employment which began before the end of the nineteenth century, then accelerated throughout the first technological revolution in the modern office when typewriters, various types of calculating machines, duplicators and other mechanical aids were introduced. This wave of new technology did not reduce office employment. The effect was the exact opposite. The technology enabled offices to provide enhanced services for managers and customers. The mechanized office facilitated the growth of large corporations. The offices co-ordinated everything, or enabled managers to do so. This was the era when big firms grew bigger, when central and local government were increasing their functions, and the size of their bureaucracies. The result was armies of office workers who flocked into city centres every weekday morning and departed in the late-afternoons. Large organizations appeared to have insatiable appetites for qualified (mainly female) school-leavers who could fill these positions, and following the 1944 Education Act an expanded secondary school system delivered the labour supply that was needed.

We are now well into the second technological revolution in the modern office. Ours is the age of electronic information technology – the computer, word processor, fax, email and photocopier. Many of the old office jobs have been lost. Some new non-manual office occupations have been created, but fewer in number than the jobs that have gone. The overall effect has been to reduce employment while, in some organizations, intensifying administration and enhancing the service. It is now possible to despatch thousands of standard but personalized letters during a few minutes at a keyboard. Airlines can now profile individual passengers' travel routines and send out offers accordingly. Prior to the technology being introduced, these operations would not have been mounted. Meanwhile, some types of work have been withdrawn from offices. I am personally keying in this text. It was different before we all had PCs. Manuscripts used to be written by hand then typed up by secretaries. Making alterations was labour intensive. Nowadays we generate more output but have fewer secretaries in the department office. Elsewhere, as in universities, managers and professional-grade staff can often do it themselves just as conveniently as through an office. It is as easy to check one's own email as to ask someone else for a print-out. Some organizations have found that customers can be enabled, and may actually prefer, to serve themselves, ordering online and using automated cash machines rather than dealing with human bank staff, for example. So many organizations, including the major banks, have been reducing employment in their office grades. The recent expansion has been higher up, in management and professional positions.

It has never been easy to specify exactly what all lower non-manuals have in common. They have never all worked in offices. This is just convenient shorthand though the office has been, and is still the class's most common workplace. The lower non-manuals include laboratory staff, customs officers, nursing and teaching assistants. Some non-office occupations were demoted (in class schemes) into the working class during the twentieth century. This happened to gardeners, domestic cleaners, ancillaries in hospitals and other care establishments, and most shop and supermarket staff. The character of the jobs (their work and market situations) changed, and hence how the jobs were regarded in society-at-large and in sociology. It is a long time since anyone in sociology treated the non-manual label literally. All jobs involve some physical activity. Measuring the extent to which jobs are manual and non-manual is not part of the process of placing them in any of the current class schemes. This makes it quite remarkable that the terms manual and non-manual remain part of everyday discourse. People seem to know intuitively which group most occupations fall into. Sociologists can argue that lay people are responding to differences in occupations' work and market situations that they experience without knowing exactly what it is that makes the difference. That said, the lower non-manuals are a class that is defined by what it is not, rather than by what it actually is. The occupations have some middle class features, like hierarchical relationships at work so that most staff are senior to someone else, and have at least modest career ladders to ascend. These features separate the occupations from the working class, but the occupations are clearly not management or professional.

Actually it was only been during the last half of the twentieth century that we were able to say 'clearly' not management or professional. At the beginning of the twentieth century most future managers and professionals started in the office, usually at age 16, then worked up. At that time clerks were definitely part of this milieu – perhaps lower middle class, but definitely middle class. At that time, attempts to define the middle class usually settled upon style of life, attitudes and culture. Non-manual jobs were too heterogeneous to supply definitive characteristics. This was at the time when most jobs were manual. The working class was by far the largest class, and, in a sense, the most important feature that other occupations had in common was that they were not working class. By the 1940s and 50s the middle class was generally perceived as threatened: by higher taxation and the material advances that were being achieved by the working class which were seen as undermining the middle class's way of life and status, and also by the expansion of the white-collar grades which was creating diversity and specialization (Lewis and Maude, 1949). Many commentators at that time deplored the threat to the English middle class, just as, later on, the passing of the original working class was regretted (by some). It was at this time that a clearer division was opening between the new middle class proper of managers and professionals on the one hand, and other non-manual grades – those that subsequently became clearly intermediate.

Office work is very different today than it was 100 years ago, but we need to digress into history in order to understand the current class locations of office staff. The grades were initially placed in modern organizational hierarchies at the same time when the original working class was being formed, and the grades have tended to remain where they were initially placed. There is a parallel in the working class: the original working class culture has weakened but it is still not extinct.

The blackcoated worker

No-one talks about blackcoated workers any longer, except possibly in sociology. The term has lived on in sociology because it was the title of a book by David Lockwood, first published in 1958, but still a standard reference. Even in 1958 the blackcoated worker was almost extinct. The phrase refers to the standard working attire of male middle class employees in the nineteenth and early twentieth centuries. They wore black jackets and striped trousers – a modified version of the morning suit (still often worn at weddings). By the 1950s the attire was worn for work only by a few bank staff in London and by some city solicitors and barristers. Other men were wearing the dark 'lounge suit' which remained normal male office attire until 'dressing down' began to spread in the 1990s. By the 1950s it had become more common to describe the relevant staff as 'white-collar' rather than blackcoated. 'White-collar' was appropriate at that time because the men all wore white shirts and ties. The white shirts usually had detachable starched collars which would be changed every day while the shirt might be worn all week. People had less extensive wardrobes than nowadays, and before the days of automatic washing machines clothes were not usually washed after being worn just once. Office dress codes are somewhat different today; even when men are still expected to wear suits, their shirts can be coloured, so white-collar has become another dated term. Do we need a replacement? Probably: dress remains a way in which people signal their class positions.

It has puzzled some, and annoyed others, that office workers have always tended to locate themselves above the working class (though nowadays they are just as likely to describe themselves as working class as middle class). Things have changed in this respect, but it still holds that despite their employee status, and, in many cases, lower than average manual earnings, many still regard trade unions as not for them and fail to support the working class's normal political choice, the Labour Party. Marxists used to dub these people as falsely conscious.

This was the context in which David Lockwood (1958) conducted his historical study of modern office work and workers. His book, now regarded as a sociological classic, charted developments from the nineteenth century up to the time of writing in the 1950s. The book's argument was that office workers who regarded themselves as middle class were not falsely conscious, but were responding to objective features of their market, status and work situations. Until the 1950s, few (non-Marxists) doubted that office workers were part of a single, if not solidaristic and completely homogeneous, middle class. They were described by others, and mostly described themselves, as lower middle class, definitely not working class (Crossick, 1977; Lewis and Maude, 1949; Wright-Mills, 1956). In a sense, Lockwood provided a sociological justification/explanation for this.

It had always been the case that, just like manual employees, office staff sold their labour power, but Lockwood pointed out that in the early part of the twentieth century recruits into offices had required additional, scarce skills; namely, the standards of literacy and numeracy needed to handle correspondence and to keep ledgers by hand. Their rewards for these skills were not necessarily higher pay, but greater security and fringe benefits, such as sickness pay, holiday leave, and sometimes pensions, that were not offered to manual workers. In other words, office staff had distinctly superior market situations.

Lockwood argued that the status situation of the blackcoated worker was also rather different to the manual employee's. Future office workers were likely to be educated separately, in secondary schools. Normal street attire (like black coats) could be worn when going to and from work, and while at work. Hours of work were shorter in the office which was usually physically separate from 'the works'. With their superior rewards, office workers were able to live in better, respectable districts, and do respectable things like spend annual holidays away from home. Lockwood argued that office staff had not been deluding themselves if they believed that their status was superior.

The typical work situations of office staff were also different. Most worked in small offices or counting houses in the businesses that handled cash. Even in large organizations, the white-collar employees would be scattered across numerous small offices, all performing specialist functions. There would be cost clerks, sales clerks, wages clerks, and so on. In these office environments, workers would experience personal relationships with superiors, and sometimes, in the smaller businesses, with their employers. Office staff were invariably graded. There was always a hierarchy. So newcomers could anticipate promotion, which was more or less certain to come their way in time. Their dream was that eventually they might become so experienced and knowledgeable about their bosses' affairs as to be considered indispensable, and offered partnerships. This rarely happened, but office staff did rise progressively in seniority. Usually everyone in an office would have a different rank, signalled by job title, amount of working space, and maybe physical proximity to the employer. Promotion was a normal expectation, and a normal part of the office worker's experience, unlike in the works where it was exceptional.

Lockwood noted that during the twentieth century superior clerical occupations had been created in some large businesses such as banks and insurance companies, and in central and local government. These positions offered higher pay, but there was no possibility of partnership, the dream of office staff in smaller enterprises.

Of course, all this was most typical in the early part of the period about which Lockwood wrote, before the Second World War and earlier in the twentieth century. *The Blackcoated Worker* told the story of how, over time, the market, status and work advantages of office staff had been gradually eroded. The work situation in offices was changing. Open-plan designs had become increasingly common from the inter-war years onwards, creating situations similar to factories where large numbers of employees, all on the same grade, did very similar jobs. Also, machinery had entered the office – the first technological revolution was well-underway by the 1950s. As a result, many office staff were being treated in much the same way as manual employees; as appendages to machines. The mechanized office bore a resemblance to the factory production line. Over time, the status advantages of office staff had also been eroded. After 1944 everyone attended a secondary school. Manual workers were being rehoused to suburban council estates, and they were receiving better treatment at work. They were being provided with washrooms and industrial clothing at the workplace which enabled them to journey to and from work in normal street clothes, if they wished. The office worker's market advantages had been eroded also. The standards of literacy and numeracy that mechanized office jobs required had become near universal. The welfare state had made pensions, sick pay and holidays into universal entitlements. Finally, office staff were encountering the kind of promotion blockage than had always existed above the working class. Large organizations had begun recruiting higher education graduates directly into their management grades and as professional trainees. So lower-level office staff were facing earlier or tighter career ceilings. In other words, their prospects were deteriorating.

Even so, Lockwood was at pains to stress that these changes were not from one extreme to another. There had always been office recruits who had been fast-tracked up the hierarchies. In the past these individuals had sometimes been exceptionally qualified, but they were more likely to have been relatives, or sons of friends, of the owners. Non-privileged staff might have felt resentment, but there was no resistance. They continued to emulate rather than display antagonism to those ahead of themselves, and there seemed to be no reason why increased graduate recruitment should change this.

Nevertheless, as the above changes had occurred, office staff had become more likely to join trade unions. By the 1950s there were already high levels of unionization among central and local government staff, in some other public services, and in banking and insurance. It was possible to envisage the entire office grades coming to regard their jobs as basically working class, and themselves as part of the labour movement, available for mobilization by the Labour Party. So even if manual workers became a minority of the workforce, as was imminent in the 1950s, there would still be a working class majority. However, Lockwood pointed out that trade unions had become common among office staff only in some business sectors, reflecting, in his view, that although many office staff had lost some of their former advantages, the occupation was far from fully proletarianized.

Lockwood also noted (he could not have failed to notice) that as the relative position of office staff had deteriorated, the occupations had been progressively feminized. At the beginning of the twentieth century, the typical office worker had been a male clerk – the blackcoated worker. At that time women were permitted only limited inroads. Very early on the job of typist was deemed suitable for women, but by the 1950s very little was still deemed unsuitable and there was a clear female majority. Office work had been largely feminized. What difference, if any, was this making to the class location of the employment?

White-collar proletariat

Between 1979 and 1981 Rosemary Crompton and Gareth Jones (1984) conducted another major sociological study of office staff. This was not a historical investigation. It was a 'What's happening now?' type of enquiry. It was a study of office jobs and staff in a bank, an insurance company, and a local authority in a city in south-east England. The business sectors were chosen because they had been responsible for much of the expansion of office work over the previous 20 years.

Crompton and Jones' verdict was that, by the 1980s, in the organizations that they examined (and by implication in many others also), in a strictly technical sense clerical work had been thoroughly proletarianized. Most recruits were early (16 year old) school-leavers. Neither exceptional ability nor qualifications were really necessary. The jobs were at best semi-skilled. Recruits were expected to acquire the necessary skills on a learn-as-you-go basis. There was nothing akin to apprenticeship or professional training. Newcomers were expected to be learning on-the-job and earning their salaries virtually from the start. Promotion prospects were limited. Individuals had realistic chances of progressing into more skilled and senior clerical jobs, and possibly into supervisory posts in the offices, but not into management. Earnings in the office grades were usually inferior to those of skilled (mostly male) manual workers. Even so, Crompton and Jones did not accept that clerical employees were clearly separate from what Goldthorpe had described as the service class (the middle class in this book). Clerks were, after all, still in offices, not the works.

Needless to say, by the time of the Crompton and Jones enquiry, the feminization of office work was even more advanced than in the 1950s. The vast majority of the employees who were studied were women, and Crompton and Jones realized that the sex of the staff was making a difference. It has often been said, in respect of women's work, that men would not stand for it. Crompton and Jones were certain that the employers would have been unable to fill their office vacancies with equally qualified males. They were able to seek, and obtain, 16–18 year old females with good qualifications (for their age). As we shall see in chapter 8, women with most levels of qualifications have tended to obtain inferior labour market returns to equally-qualified men. Young men with the qualifications preferred of office staff by banks, insurance companies and local authorities might nowadays seek apprenticeships, possibly in jobs in which they will be trained-up to professional status, and at the time of the Crompton and Jones study they were more likely than young women to remain in full-time education taking three or more A-levels, then seek places in higher education.

Notwithstanding all this, Crompton and Jones did not attach undue significance to the gender balance and divisions within the offices that they studied. They noted that males and females tended to perform rather different tasks, and that the males were the more likely to study for further qualifications, and to receive promotions, but only to the higher rungs of the clerical grades. For both sexes, there was a technical base for the development of proletarian attitudes, but also good reasons why this was unlikely to happen, in the short-term at any rate.

In their book Crompton and Jones speculated as to why the employers wanted well-qualified recruits in their offices. The jobs did not appear to require this, at least in a technical sense. Crompton and Jones noted that qualifications were a way of sifting out the less reliable, less compliant (the well-qualified would have been 'good pupils' at school), and others who might be unacceptable in office environments. They also noted that the qualifications that were demanded defined the jobs as superior to others that 16 year old school-leavers might seek.

Female recruits into such jobs in the early-1980s, and today also, are likely to be only too willing to believe that they themselves, and the jobs that they are entering, are a cut-above. The main alternatives for 16–18 year old females are still in factories, shops, cafes etc. Starting higher up (as a professional or management trainee) requires higher education. Office jobs are still superior in all respects to the alternatives for 16–18 year old female school and college leavers – the pay, security, prospects, being able to dress-up for work and having a clean environment to work in. Office staff have mostly performed better at school than female contemporaries who take jobs in factories and shops. In this sense, for young women at any rate, given the gender segmentation that persists in the workforce, it remains as true today as in the period covered by David Lockwood's study, that there are objective grounds for office staff continuing to regard themselves and their jobs as rather better. One difference is that there are now fewer office jobs. Many have fallen victim to the second technological revolution in the modern office. So girls now need to aim higher and progress through higher education, otherwise they are more likely than in the past to find that their futures are in a shop or factory rather than in an office.

Trade unions

Since the 1970s the significance of trade unionism in debates about office (and other) workers' class locations has been re-assessed. Previously, ever since white-collar trade unions had been studied, from the 1930s onwards in practice, the prevalence (density) of white-collar trade union membership had been taken to indicate the extent to which an occupation had been proletarianized, and the extent to which the workers identified themselves as working class and with a broader labour movement. So David Lockwood noted the growth of white-collar trade unionism as evidence of a trend, but stressed the trade unions' limited inroads as a sign that office work was still well-short of full proletarianization. By the time of Crompton and Jones' study, the levels of trade union membership in banks, insurance companies and local authorities (high in all three) were regarded as only marginally relevant to the workers' class locations and identities.

During the intervening years the meaning attached to trade union membership in the wider society had changed. In the 1960s Kenneth Prandy (1965) had contrasted two types of occupational associations – professional bodies and trade unions – that recruited professional-grade employees. He argued that professional bodies were basically status organizations – they tried to advance their members' interests by raising their status in the eyes of employers and the public-at-large. Trade unions, he argued, were class organizations which operated through bargaining strength. Prandy argued that professional organizations could possess some class features, and that white-collar unions could possess some status characteristics. This line of thought was developed by Robert Blackburn (1967) in a concurrent study of bank clerks where he argued that a high level of trade union membership had been achieved only by a loss of unionateness, meaning characteristics hitherto associated with blue-collar unions such as willingness to strike and engage in other forms of collective action.

It is now clear with hindsight that things were changing. Just as it only takes enough manual workers to purchase washing machines and foreign holidays for these to cease to be middle class status symbols, so, in a similar way, it is necessary only for enough non-manual employees who regard themselves, and are regarded by others, as middle class, to join trade unions for the behaviour to lose its working class connotations. By the 1970s researchers were noting that white-collar trade union membership levels were responsive to much the same circumstances as blue-collar membership. White-collar employees were most likely to be unionized when they were employed in large concentrations, and when in both objective and subjective senses they were separated from management. It was also noted that white-collar trade union membership rose when unions were recognized by employers, and when the political climate was favourable, meaning when collective bargaining was being encouraged rather than discouraged by the government of the day (Bain, 1970). By the 1970s trade unionism had come to be, and was recognized as, something that could be linked to various types of consciousness and used for a variety of class and other social objectives. It could indicate proletarian circumstances and outlooks. Alternatively, trade union organization and militant action could be used by white-collar workers to prevent their proletarianization, or in attempts to improve their standing vis-a-vis other non-manual groups (Roberts et al, 1972; Roberts et al, 1977).

Already in the 1970s there appeared to be a convergence in the significance of trade unionism within working class and non-manual occupational groups.

Manual workers' attachments to their unions had often become instrumental rather than solidaristic (see chapter 4), motivated by a desire for personal or sectional rather than class-wide benefits. White-collar trade unionists usually have exactly the same motives.

Demographics

Most office jobs have been and still are filled by men and women from working class backgrounds (Goldthorpe, 1980; Marshall et al, 1988). They greatly out-number the inter-generationally static and those downwardly mobile from the middle class. This is a product of the changing shape of the class structure. The working class was by far the largest class up to the Second World War. Subsequently there was a sustained expansion of office jobs, and it was structurally inevitable that most of these positions would be filled from outside, in practice from beneath since the working class was the largest, and a contracting, class. Throughout the twentieth century, obtaining an office job was the main way in which girls, and rather fewer boys, from working class homes were able to 'get on'. In the latter decades of the century, office work became a step upwards for girls from ethnic minority backgrounds.

The outflow picture has been a little more complicated. Here there has been a clear difference between the life-chances of boys and girls whose fathers occupied lower-level white-collar positions. Very few such boys (only just over 10 per cent) have entered the same type of employment. They have either moved up into the middle class or down into the working class. Ever since the Second World War it appears that routine non-manual fathers have considered their type of employment unsuitable for their sons. Dale's (1962) study of clerks in industry found that only seven out of the 208 who were interviewed wanted their sons to become clerks. The occupation was perceived, accurately from all the evidence that we have, to be declining in attractiveness. Fathers who were spending their own careers in the office grades appeared to feel that their sons would be better advised to train for skilled manual work if they were unable (as the fathers would usually have preferred) to qualify for management or professional careers.

The situation with girls has been rather different. Around 40 per cent of the daughters of lower-level white-collar fathers have entered office jobs them-selves, whereas only around 30 per cent have risen into the middle class proper, and approximately 20 per cent have entered working class jobs. Far fewer daughters than sons have descended into the working class. There has been much more inter-generational continuity between lower-level white-collar fathers (and presumably mothers also) and their daughters, than between the parents and sons. The inter-generational step upwards from the working class into the lower non-manual grades appears to have been more secure for females than for males. In the next generation the males have been the more likely to step backwards, though neither the fathers nor the sons have neces-sarily have seen it this way. The explanation will be partly that there have been far more women's than men's jobs in the office grades, partly that there has been an outlet into apprenticeships in skilled manual trades for males, and partly because parents, teachers and others may well have taken the view that a job in an office is fine for a reasonably qualified girl, but less so for an equally qualified boy.

Times are changing. Girls with good academic qualifications are now more likely to go to university than to leave education at age 16 or 18 and take a job in an office. The girls no doubt hope that higher education will lead to professional or management positions, but in practice many still find that their initial jobs are in the intermediate grades. Some work in call centres. The graduate secretary has become more common – a status symbol for senior managers. And what about the three-fifths of all girls who still do not enter higher education? After age 16 they are less likely than boys to study technical subjects. In the sixth forms they tend to read arts or social sciences. On vocational courses they are most likely to study 'care' or business/commercial options. There are still plenty of young women competing for, but fewer than in the past are actually entering, office jobs. The contraction of employment in these grades has created a huge surplus of adult females with relevant experience, and young women (those not entering higher education) who are keen to obtain office jobs. This is why it is possible for firms to employ large numbers of office 'temps'. The office is the place where temporary employment has become most widespread. This applies in the public sector as well as in private businesses. Indeed, the proportion of staff who are officially temporary is now highest in the public sector (see Conley, 2002). Office work is no longer more secure than working class occupations. This is one of its one-time advantages that has been lost.

Class and gender in the office

When office work became thoroughly feminized, the interest of class researchers waned. This was at the time when most sociologists believed that only male occupations mattered as far as class was concerned. There have been plenty of studies of women and employment over the last 20 years, but these have paid much more attention to how their situations are gendered than to their class positions. Beverley Skeggs' (1997) study of young women in north-west England, and Valerie Walkerdine and colleagues' (2000) study of girls growing up in London, are rare exceptions. In studies of women at work, there have been occasional pieces on office staff (see, for example, Truss, 1993), but far more on the smaller numbers of women who enter management, engineering and other professions. We have learnt about how these women have been obtaining post-entry qualifications and opting for nearly-unbroken full-time careers yet still encounter disadvantages, but are nevertheless breaking through former glass ceilings and pressuring males' promotion prospects (see, for example, Crompton and Sanderson, 1986). Males with intermediate, ambiguous class locations have received more attention than secretaries.

In addition to the self-employed, technicians and technologists have been the subjects of some enquiries into whether they are a genuinely intermediate group, or best regarded as a new aristocracy of labour, or part of an enlarged middle class (see Bain, 1972; Carter, 1985; Smith, 1987).

Maybe all that needs to be said about female office workers has already been said. Office jobs were initially designed for men, and, by agreement among all commentators and the men themselves, the jobs were then on the fringe, but definitely part of the middle class. Those were the days when office workers gained an intimate knowledge of their employers' business. They needed to be trustworthy and rewarded sufficiently to secure their loyalty. Then came office mechanization, a vast expansion of office employment, and an influx of women. A gendered division of labour was established very quickly. Men managed and supervised while women operated the machinery, and took on other feminine tasks, including customer-care in recent years (see Halford and Savage, 1995). The gendering has been strongest in the manager-secretary relationship. The latest generation of new technology has been absorbed into relationships that were already gendered. At first computers were considered masculine, but very quickly this was restricted to systems analysis and programming, and women were left with operating computers.

In their study, Crompton and Jones (1984) chose to stress how all clerks, males and females, had limited promotion prospects. These prospects were being squeezed by the growth in the number of clerks, and the simultaneous growth in overhead recruitment into management and professional careers. Crompton and Jones proceeded to discuss the possibilities, and the impediments to, the development of a proletarian consciousness throughout the clerical grades. Yet it was already known that men and women in lower-level white-collar jobs were usually performing rather different tasks, and were in somewhat different career situations. The males were, and still are, administering, and were, and still are, by far the more likely to be promoted, because women in the grades who become mothers (the majority) rarely pursue full-time continuous careers. This is why, in respect of the males, the Cambridge class researchers (see chapter 2) have argued that it is possible for lower-level non-manual occupations to be proletarianized, but not the incumbents (Stewart et al, 1980). It can be argued that, rather than occupying distinctly intermediate locations, males in lower-level non-manual occupations are better conceptualized as located on the lower fringe of the middle class proper, as in the days of the blackcoated worker. It has been different for women. This could change as more females with higher education enter the non-manual grades. These lower-non-manuals might re-connect the office with the middle class proper. Up to now, however, female office staff have been more likely to occupy intermediate positions for life, or to experience demotion into working class jobs following career breaks. This could change as career breaks shorten, if more of the women return to work on a full-time basis, and claim their equal opportunities to be trained for career progression. But is this really likely? Young males and females with all levels of educational attainment, and who enter all types of occupations, may be equally career-minded (Bynner et al, 1997; Roberts and Chadwick, 1991). But the current and likely future career rewards of those in ordinary office (and manual) jobs, and the relative (to earnings) costs of child care, are very different from those of women and their partners in the core middle class occupations. Lower down the class structure, the male breadwinner model has been, and remains, a more rational family strategy (Creighton, 1996).

Some of the continuities since David Lockwood wrote *The Blackcoated Worker* are startling. There are still superior office jobs in banks and insurance companies. The difference is that the old prospects of partnership in other firms, and of promotion to management from the basic entry grades for non-graduates in the superior office jobs, have all but disappeared completely. And the other change, of course, is that by the 1960s most of the employees were, and the majority still are women. There is no reason to expect anything to change while 16–18 year old female school-leavers still face the same basic choice – if not higher education, then shop, factory, office or, nowadays, a 'care' or some other service sector occupation. As in the past, office work will be considered attractive by those with the necessary qualifications, from working class homes. Valerie Walkerdine and colleagues (2001) and Beverley Skeggs (1997) have both emphasized how keen these young women are to leave the working class. The office occupations that they enter are intermediate par excellence. There is no distinctive consciousness, lifestyle or politics. Ethnic diversity has simply added to the variety rather than broken up a distinctive culture linked to lifestyle and politics. The class identities that women office workers adopt continue to depend heavily on their fathers' or husbands' occupations, types of housing and so on. They are never likely to align overwhelmingly and unambiguously with either the working class or the middle class, or to develop a characteristic consciousness and politics of their own.

The petit bourgeoisie

Growth

Until the 1970s the petit bourgeoisie was in long-term decline. As Marx had predicted, small enterprises (pre-capitalist relics) were being squeezed out of the market or absorbed by larger companies. This process was most evident in retailing, the business sector with by far the largest number of small enterprises. By the 1970s the march of the supermarkets was already well-advanced. In retailing the decline in self-employment has in fact continued. National chains selling clothing, toys, computers, carpets and so on have filled the new city-centre shopping precincts and out-of-town retail parks. Their advertising shapes consumer demand. Sometimes their bulk purchasing power enables them to pass on lower prices to customers. Smaller, independent shops have been unable to compete. We all deplore the demise of the small retailer. We would love the convenience of being able to pop out to the corner shop. But we still do our main food shopping by car, at more distant supermarkets, and head for the major stores at other times. Shop-keepers are still the largest, albeit contracting, single occupational group among the self-employed, but in other business sectors there has been a turnaround. The number of small enterprises doubled during the 1980s, the number of self-employed persons rose to 13 per cent of the UK workforce, and it is exactly the same percentage today, equivalent to just under four million people. There has been a similar recent upward trend in all the advanced industrial countries, and Britain still has a lower rate of self-employment than most European Union states. This is due mainly, though not entirely, to there being fewer small farms in Britain. The prospects for further growth in the number of small enterprises in Britain are rather good. Most of the factors which have led to the recent growth are still operating.

One reason for the growth of self-employment has been unemployment-push (see Bogenhold and Stabler, 1991). People who have been made redundant have sometimes used their lump sums (redundancy pay-offs) to establish their own companies. Many individuals who have been unable to find jobs have taken the initiative in creating their own. There has been a great deal of survival self-employment. It has not always been the entrepreneurs' first choice. In the 1980s and early-1990s a government-operated Enterprise Allowance Scheme provided modest financial assistance for the unemployed who qualified and who wished to start their own businesses. Many of these businesses struggled. Robert MacDonald (1996) found that only 14 out of 86 young entrepreneurs who had been first-studied when they were setting-up in the late-1980s were still in business in 1995. The young unemployed who try to create their own businesses have an extremely high failure rate (Kellard and Middleton, 1998), and well under 10 per cent of all the unemployed exit for self-employment (Metcalf, 1998). This does not mean that it is always inadvisable for the unemployed, even for the young unemployed, to try self-employment. Britain has probably the world leader among organizations that aim to assist disadvantaged young people to become self-employed. This organization is The Prince's Youth Business Trust (see BMRB International, 1997). The secrets of its success are being highly selective over who to assist, and providing continuing support throughout and following the start-ups.

Government policies have assisted new businesses, not just with the Enterprise Allowance that was available to the unemployed at one time, but also with the various support services – advice centres and suchlike – that have been created. In the 1980s the government claimed to be fostering an enterprise culture and cited the growth in the number of small businesses as evidence. In practice there was no evidence of cultural change. Self-employment is a very old dream, especially within the working class. Nevertheless, the government in the 1980s did create a favourable ideological climate for, and offered modest forms of material assistance to, business starters. Enterprise was taught in schools and on Youth Training schemes. Taxes on incomes and wealth were reduced. A climate was created in which there was no shame, but pride, in being able to flaunt success and money. All governments have continued to be supportive towards small enterprises for one very good reason – they have realized that such businesses have been responsible for most of the new job creation and net employment growth in recent years.

Unemployment-push has certainly not been the only factor in the growth of small enterprises (see Meager, 1992). New technology has been another, and it is an underlying and continuing factor in this growth. The latest generation of new technology has two important relevant features – it is small and cheap. This means that it is no longer necessary to be a giant company to do things the cheapest way and to obtain top quality results. Quality publishing is now possible in any office, even from home. Small independent companies can produce recorded music of the same quality as the multi-nationals. New technology has applications in most industries and occupations, so the effects are pervasive. Typists, design engineers and even radio broadcasters can do it from home.

Outsourcing (see chapter 3) by large companies has been another engine behind the growth of small enterprises. This has been a way in which big businesses have made themselves flexible, and it has created new business opportunities, sometimes for staff displaced from the larger enterprises. People with office, craft and professional skills have often discovered that they can earn more in total, and provide themselves with greater security, by going self-employed and obtaining contracts from a number of businesses rather than by working full-time for any one of them.

Demographics

Small businesses and their proprietors are clearly a very mixed group. There are many types of businesses. Even when the various kinds of professional consultants are excluded and placed in the middle class, we still have a motley collection of cleaning and security firms, shop-keepers, garages, builders, other service businesses, and so on. Should they all be grouped together? An alternative, in class analysis, is to return all concerned to the classes in which employed members of their occupations are located. The case for grouping them together is that they have such a distinctive, and common, work situation; namely, working for themselves, being the boss.

The businesses vary in size, turnover, profits and solidity. There are much higher annual birth and death rates among small businesses than among large companies. Some new businesses never grow beyond the micro-fragile stage. Others are quite substantial concerns with employees and turnovers in millions of pounds. Some are long-standing 'family businesses'.

The amazing thing is that the proprietors, if not the businesses, do in fact share a great deal in common. First, they are mostly men. Over four-fifths of the people who are self-employed as a main occupation are male (Taylor, 1994). This is one of the two classes (the active section of the upper class is the other) which are most dominated by one sex (men in both cases). There are niches in business for women – in hairdressing, typing and fashion, for instance – but generally the business culture is masculine. As we shall see, the self-employed pride themselves on masculine values such as competitiveness, independence and individualism. And their work schedules are usually too long, and the hours are too varied, to be compatible with major domestic responsibilities.

Second, young people are under-represented. Self-employment is usually not career-long. Most people who start businesses, especially those who then stay in business, do so having gained some experience in someone else's. The main exceptions are when children join family businesses, but even in these cases they are most likely to start off as employees rather than bosses.

In terms of ethnic mix, the self-employed are less dominated by whites than any other class. The Chinese, Pakistanis and Bangladeshis are very much over-represented (see Table 5.1). This applies among both males and females. Black Africans are the only under-represented male group, and Black Africans and Black Caribbeans among females. Britain's ethnic minorities have transformed the restaurant trade, and have also made a major impact in retailing. Business is one of the ways in which members of the over-represented ethnic groups are achieving individual and collective upward mobility in Britain.

What about mobility flows? Roughly two-fifths of self-employed men have fathers who were also self-employed. This is a very respectable rate of inter-generational continuity; approximately three times the level that would occur in an equal life-chances society. It is likely that the motivation, and some of the skills, that are needed to run a small business successfully are passed down the generations in business families. Of those who are recruited inter-generationally from outside, there are roughly three times as many from the working class as from the middle class. There are slightly more self-employed males with working class (around 45 per cent) backgrounds than with business

Table 5.1 Percentages of all workers who were self-employed by ethnic group, 2004/05

Ethnic Group	Males	Females
White	13	5
Black Caribbean	12	2
Black African	6	2
Indian	13	5
Pakistani/Bangladeshi	22	7
Chinese	20	11
Other	12	4

Based on data from Li et al, 2008

(self-employed) family backgrounds (around 40 pcr cent), and relatively few whose fathers were managers or professionals (around 13 per cent).

The outflow picture is rather different. There are similar numbers of sons of business fathers who themselves run businesses (29 per cent) and who enter the middle class (28 per cent), and rather more who enter the working class (37 per cent). Inter-generationally, setting-up in business is more likely to be a step upwards, or at least an attempted step upwards, from the working class than a step down from the middle class, no doubt due partly to the fact that the middle class has been expanding and the working class contracting over recent generations, and this trend is continuing. However, in the subsequent generation, the sons of business fathers are more likely to fall back into the working class than to continue their families' inter-generational ascent. We have seen that this applies also to males in the other intermediate, lower non-manual, class. All the evidence shows that intermediate positions are less secure than positions in the middle class proper. This is one justification (there are several others) for separating a middle class of managers and professionals in sociological class schemes, rather than lumping all non-manuals plus the self-employed into a single middle class.

With women as with men, there is a high rate of inter-generational continuity in business (fathers to daughters). Approximately 30 per cent of self-employed females have self-employed fathers. However, they are outnumbered by the 45 per cent from working class family backgrounds. Just 20 per cent are from middle class families and the remaining six per cent are from the lower non-manual class. Daughters are less likely than the sons of self-employed fathers to continue in business (10 per cent against 29 per cent). Thirty-five per cent of the girls enter intermediate non-manual occupations, another 35 per cent enter working class employment, and just over 20 per cent rise into the middle class. As for men, so among women, self-employment is typically a step up from the working class in one generation, often leading to a step back in the next.

Consciousness and politics

It is all the more surprising given their diverse occupational make-up, the variations in the size, stability and longevity of the businesses, and the mixed origins of the self-employed in terms of social class and ethnicity, that they tend to share a very distinctive consciousness and political proclivities. With the exception of the ethnic minorities (see chapter 9), the petit bourgeoisie is the most Conservative of all the social classes except possibly the upper class (Marshall et al, 1988). Conservative here has a capital. The self-employed are not conservative in the sense of being content with the status quo. They tend to be angry, sometimes radical, Conservatives. But Conservatives they nearly all are. They have been the Conservative Party's infantrymen, providing cash and organizational inputs at local levels, just as big business has at the national level.

The self-employed have a distinctive set of values (see Bechoffer and Elliott, 1981; Blanchflower et al, 1987; Nugent and King, 1979). They are individualistic, and proud of it. They believe that people should stand squarely on their own feet. They believe in independence. They also believe in hard work and discipline. They are low on gambling spirit. Success is believed to follow hard work and enterprise, not pure luck. These values are likely to have driven the self-employed into, and are probably sharpened by their experience in, business.

The petit bourgeoisie have little time for government or most politicians. They discriminate among politicians in their own preferred party. In the 1980s Margaret Thatcher was their hero. The self-employed were among the staunchest Thatcherites in the country (Edgell and Duke, 1991). Thatcher appealed not just because she was a grocer's daughter but also for her evident determination to clamp down on state spending and reduce taxes (though she achieved neither), and to disempower the trade unions (where she was more successful). Usually the self-employed do not like government. They object to the number and levels of the taxes that they have to pay. They also object to the torrents of paperwork that the government requires – for income tax, national insurance, VAT and so on. They resent all the health and safety, equal opportunities and other regulations that are liable to trip them up.

The self-employed do not like big companies. They are scathing about salaried managers and professionals (and civil servants, of course) with their inflated salaries, cushy jobs, security and pensions to follow. Many depend on trade that is put their way by large firms, but they dislike the way in which these customers will pay no more than rock-bottom prices, then pass on fantastic mark-ups. Then there is the speed, the leisurely speed, with which big firms tend to pay their bills. What is just normal bureaucratic delay in big companies means heavier interest charges on small businesses' bank overdrafts.

Needless to say, the self-employed have no time for trade unions. Their own workforces are rarely unionized. Many of these employers are adamant that they would not let trade unions through the door. Their view is that everyone should be independent and prove their own worth. Collective representation (for others) is anathema.

Nevertheless, the self-employed are not adverse to having their own interests collectively represented by trade associations, chambers of commerce, and the Institute of Directors, for example. All these organizations confirm that the self-employed are difficult to organize. The business community does not like to be regimented. However, it sees clear advantages in having its voice heard in local councils and at national government level.

Intolerance of others is a personality trait associated with self-employment (Blanchflower et al, 1987). Of course, bosses can afford to be intolerant, within their own enterprises at any rate. This character trait will be nurtured in business, though it could also be the case that some of the self-employed would never have been comfortable working under someone else.

It must be said that the self-employed have grounds for feeling that they themselves earn everything that they receive. They have a distinctive, work-centred lifestyle. They work long hours. Homes are usually workplaces even if the businesses have bases elsewhere. Every small business has hordes of competitors. Actions by central and local government, and by big companies, over which the self-employed can exert little control, can make a crucial difference. The withdrawal of a large order can be crippling. A new competitor can always open across the street. A new road, or new parking restrictions, can decimate a business's custom. New parking charges, or failing to provide sufficient car parking space in a commercial district, can blight all the local businesses. Hence the small business community's perpetual vulnerability. They know it, and they feel it.

The significance of the contemporary petit bourgeoisie

The self-employed are not a historical relic, and they play an important role in the contemporary class structure. First 13 per cent is not a negligible proportion of the working population. They are never going to be the main targets for political parties' election campaigns or in consumer advertising. But, to begin with, they employ more people than their own numbers, and the proportion of employees in small businesses has been growing. Over two-fifths of all employees are in establishments with under 50 people on the payrolls. The petit bourgeoisie have not been the prime movers, but they have been deeply implicated in the processes that have weakened the working class. Small might be beautiful for some employers, but this is rarer for the workers (see Rainnie, 1985). Wages are lower than in large companies. The workforces in small enterprises are unlikely to be unionized. The jobs are often chronically insecure. There is no chance of a career. Working conditions are, well, varied. These are the employees who are most likely to have benefitted from the statutory minimum pay, and their employers are quite likely to have been vocal in their opposition to this example of government interference and the burden imposed on small businesses.

Second, the petit bourgeoisie are the people who keep the Conservative Party in being, financially and organizationally, throughout the country. The party would no doubt survive without them, but everyone would notice the difference.

Third, the petit bourgeoisie play an ideological role by their very presence. They are the living proof, or so it can be said, that we live in a society where anyone with talent and enterprise can make it.

Summary

The intermediate groups prevent the class structure becoming polarized. Rather than 'clear sky', the two main classes are separated by 'muddy water'. The character of the intermediate classes also prevents the population coalescing into a middle mass: the classes that are intermediate are distinct from the working class on the one side, and the middle class proper on the other.

Lower non-manuals, mainly women, became a distinctly intermediate class during their expansion and all the technological changes following the nineteenth century. At one time roughly 40 per cent of women's occupations were in this class, but the current proportion is around 20 per cent. The class is demographically unstable, and has never developed a separate and distinctive subjective class identity, lifestyle or politics. Most members of this class are in cross-class households, thus further blurring the class divisions beneath and above their own occupations.

The petit bourgeoisie is currently stable in size rather than expanding or contracting, though new businesses are still being born while others die as rapidly as ever. Most of the self-employed are men, and they have arguably the most distinctive of all work situations – working for themselves. They also lead distinctive work-centred lifestyles, and are the source of a distinctively angry and radical brand of conservatism. Just under a third of the sons of business fathers remain in the petit bourgeoisie – an impressive level of inter-generational continuity for a class that accounts for just 13 per cent of the working population. The petit bourgeoisie has an ambiguous relationship with the working class. On the one hand, they are the suppliers of some of the poorest jobs. On the other hand, these are the employers who are closest to their workers, and not just in terms of working alongside them. Few manual workers can realistically hope to become managers or professionals, whereas self-employment is a realizable dream. It is most likely to involve hard work for modest rewards, maybe failure, but there is the possibility of real success, a high income, wealth accumulation and a status position in the local community.

Both of the intermediate classes, albeit in rather different ways, play highly significant roles in the overall system of class relationships in present-day Britain.

The Middle Class

6

Introduction

Previous chapters have described the economic and occupational changes that have reshaped Britain's class structure in recent years. We have looked in detail at the implications for the working class and the intermediate classes. Here we turn to the middle class.

- First we deal with its recent growth (very rapid) and current social composition (extremely diverse).
- Second, we consider the middle class at work, and its members' typical reasons for both celebration and discontent.
- Third, we examine divisions within the middle class: by levels, between those in the public and those in the private sector, between managers and professionals, and by lifestyle. The key issue here is whether the divisions are sufficiently severe to make it unrealistic to bunch everyone into a single class.
- Fourth, we look at the typical pre-occupations, and the types of consciousness and related political action, that characterize the contemporary middle class.

A cautionary note is necessary. Knowledge of Britain's working class is not necessarily an asset when approaching the middle class if it leads to a search for directly corresponding features. It is not difficult to demonstrate that middle class occupations are distinctive in their work and market situations, or that the incumbents satisfy the demographic criteria to be treated as a class. The difficulties arise when we seek distinctive middle class social, cultural and political characteristics. We find no equivalents to the shared recreation of Britain's original working class, or an equivalent solidaristic sense of 'us'. This may lead to queries as to whether the middle class is really a class. We need to accept that what is common and distinctive in middle class lifestyles and cultures may be entirely different: individualism can be a common, distinctive characteristic.

Another point to bear in mind before proceeding is that, as explained fully below, today's middle class is a different formation than the middle class of the early-twentieth century. The working class has changed: it has shrunk and has become weaker as a socio-cultural and political entity. The middle class has grown, and it has changed fundamentally in character rather than simply strengthening or weakening.

The rise of the new middle class

Growth

The middle class is now roughly the same size as the working class. Each accounts for approximately 40 per cent of the workforce. During the second half of the twentieth century the proportion of the workforce in middle class occupations more than doubled. Some time during the twenty-first century the middle class could become Britain's largest.

The present-day middle class needs to be distinguished from an older middle class whose core members were self-employed professionals and proprietors of businesses. The present-day middle class is newer: in fact it is Britain's newest class, even though its origins can be traced back to the nineteenth century. The Northcote Trevelyan Report (1853), implemented from 1870 onwards, was a landmark. This report recommended that recruitment to government employment should be on the basis of competitive examinations (previously positions had been filled by patronage and the purchase of office). Civil service and army reform acted as a catalyst, but also reflected broader cultural changes. During the same period some older craft guilds and new aspirant professions began to tighten their entry requirements and adopt the examination system. The universities, likewise, introduced matriculation (entrance) examinations which were rationalized after the First World War into a national system of secondary school examinations, from which our present-day GCSEs and A-levels have developed.

The reformed civil service adopted the 'army model' of a separate officer (administrative) class, but this type of career organization was slow to spread. Industry's production managers and engineers continued to be drawn mainly from shop floors. Individuals who progressed gained any further qualifications through part-time study, in technical colleges, on the so-called 'alternative route'. This is how twentieth century Britain came to have (apparently) under-educated leaders of industry compared with competitor countries. Until the Second World War Britain's university system was tiny. There were very few occupations that required a university qualification. This was necessary in order to enter directly into the civil service's administrative grades, to become a medical doctor, or a secondary (but not an elementary) school teacher. University was also a common route into the Anglican ministry. In contrast, all types of engineers, accountants, solicitors, bank clerks, journalists and social workers normally started work on completing secondary school then worked their way up. Anyone with a university degree joined the normal career streams rather than a separate grade. This was the era when clerks (lower non-manuals) were definitely part of the middle class (see chapter 5). Some organizations have retained the single grade entry system to this day: banks and the police service, for instance, though nowadays both allow university graduates to be fast-tracked.

In the first half of the twentieth century the growth of government employment was a main source of growth in the new middle class. The functions of central and local government were extended. So there were more jobs in administration (management) and in public sector professions – education, housing, social work and health care, for example. The economy was becoming dominated by large companies (the number of small businesses was then declining, while large firms were growing forever larger), and these businesses began to seek bright secondary school and (more rarely at that time) university leavers to fast-track into management positions and professional occupations. However, it was not until after the Second World War that the growth of the new middle class really took off. The newly nationalized industries adopted versions of the civil service model (ever since the Northcote Trevelyan reforms, paper qualifications have been more vital in public than in private sector employment). Higher education expanded. It became normal for large and even medium-sized companies to recruit designated management trainees. More and more occupations became closed to non-graduates. Business and management schools were established in universities from the 1960s onwards. Initially their courses were post-graduate, but since the 1980s business/management has become one of the most popular undergraduate subjects.

During these developments the new middle class expanded rapidly. The core members of the old middle class – business proprietors and independent professionals – became peripheral. Genuinely middle class occupations became more distinct from the lower non-manuals. That said, Britain's managers and professionals are still poorly educated compared with their counterparts elsewhere. This is a legacy of history, and also a feature of Britain's relatively unregulated labour markets (see chapter 3). The 'alternative route' is still open. It remains possible for individuals to rise to management without gaining any particular qualifications provided they can demonstrate the necessary ability. People in some 'professional' occupations, in financial services for example, can be completely unqualified.

Social composition

Nowadays men and women are equally likely to be in middle class occupations, but men are still more likely than women to reach the higher levels. Women have tended to stick lower down, and this is still the tendency, even though times are changing in this respect. The professions may have been designed originally by and for men (Witz, 1992). Nevertheless, these are the occupations in which more women are now getting in, gaining post-entry qualifications, and pursuing long-term, scarcely broken, full-time careers. Glass ceilings have

Table 6.1 Percentages of employment in middle class occupations by ethnic group, 2004/05

Ethnic Group	Males	Females
White	40	37
Black Caribbean	28	43
Black African	39	37
Indian	47	42
Pakistani/Bangladeshi	23	23
Chinese	45	41
Other	40	41

Based on data from Li et al, 2008

been cracking in most businesses and professions. The proportions of women in some senior positions are increasing spectacularly in percentage terms, but from very low baselines, like just two per cent of university professors being women in the 1970s. There are now roughly seven times as many – around 14 per cent.

Overall, Britain's ethnic minorities are not under-represented in the middle class. Indian and Chinese males and females, and Black Caribbean females, are slightly over-represented. Male and female Pakistanis and Bangladeshis, and Black Caribbean males, are heavily under-represented (see Table 6.1). The main contrast today is not between whites and all the minorities but among the latter. Within the middle class the minorities are currently more likely to be in professional than in management positions. In the professions the entry criteria are clearer, and paper qualifications rather than less formal judgements of suitability play the major role, during the initial entry stages at any rate, but up to now ethnic minorities have remained much better-represented in the lower grades than in the higher grades. Also, as explained in chapter 3, the minorities are sometimes channelled into specific niches, like work in the 'inner cities'. Equal opportunities policies have been in operation since the 1960s, and the current ethnic composition (like the gender composition) of the middle class is most likely still to be in a fluid, intermediate stage, perhaps en route to full equality. Political initiatives to accelerate this process are somewhat compromised by the minorities' under-representation at higher levels in the government's own departments, and in politics itself.

The expansion of the middle class has been responsible for the gradual rise in the absolute rate of upward social mobility from the working class which occurred throughout the twentieth century and is still ongoing (see chapter 8). A consequence of the rate of middle class growth is that its current members have varied origins. We shall see in chapter 8 that roughly two-thirds of the present-day middle class have been upwardly mobile. Those with middle class parents are quite likely to feel that they themselves needed to earn their positions by obtaining the necessary qualifications. They will know people from similar backgrounds to their own who have experienced social demotion. The composition of the present-day middle class cannot but tell those who are 'in' that entry has been possible whatever an individual's starting point. Unless they have studied sociology, they are unlikely to feel that they are beneficiaries of an unequal opportunity society.

The trend in the twenty-first century will be towards a growing proportion of the middle class being recruited from within. The inter-generationally stable core will grow and, as this happens, a characteristic consciousness and politics may become clearer. At present, the best that we can hope to see are indicators. Simultaneously, in the twenty-first century people who start life in the working and intermediate classes will have improved chances of reaching the middle class. These developments might appear incompatible, but chapter 8 will explain in detail how both are possible. Once people are in the middle class, they personally are unlikely to experience demotion, but there are significant, even though diminishing, chances of their children failing to maintain their positions. Hence the middle class's concern about their children's opportunities and progress in education.

The middle class has always been vocal and politically active, but the class is now more numerous than ever before. We shall see that the middle class has already become culturally and politically dominant. Its concerns already shape and dominate political agendas.

The middle class at work

Can it really be true that two-fifths of the workforce have good jobs as professionals and managers? There have been suspicions of these ranks being artificially inflated by people being given symbolic rewards in the form of job titles when in reality they are just sales, office and laboratory staff. Some call-centre staff are called 'banking consultants'.

As far as we can tell, these incidents have not been happening recently to any greater extent than may always have been the case. We know that around a quarter of the people classed as managers and administrators say that in practice they do not have any management duties, but there are almost as many people in other classes of occupations who say that they do manage (Rose and O'Reilly, 1997). How many people are crystal clear about what management is? Does a manager have direct control over other staff, or a budget? Can a university head-of-department be described as a manager? A fact of this matter is that in large organizations management is a process. Most decisions are governed by rules or taken by committees. It is a function of particular grades of occupations, rather than specific individuals within them.

We know that jobs classed (by the employers) as management and professional have not become less onerous. Reported skill and qualification requirements have risen in recent years at all occupational levels, including management and the professions (Gallie and White, 1993). In most organizations there is a clear division between the offices and laboratories (the intermediate grades) on the one hand, and management-level grades on the other. The jobs differ not just in titles but also in the salary scales, the overall composition of compensation packages, and promotion prospects. All the evidence suggests that the normal rewards of middle class status still accompany the job titles.

To recap, middle class occupations have privileged work and market situations. These employees are not closely supervised at work but are trusted to use initiative and discretion responsibly. The decisions taken by middle class staff, individually or collectively, and even decisions taken by those outside the main lines of command, have implications for the work of others. Middle class employees also have superior compensation packages, especially when account is taken of all the fringe benefits and, in particular, the promotion prospects. The jobs are distinguished by the opportunities for progressive careers. There is considerable distance between the bottom and top rungs in the management and professional grades, not least in terms of salaries. And career ascent is still a normal and realistic expectation. As ever, the opportunities are greatest in expanding firms, professions, business sectors and regions. In recent times, south-east England appears to have acted as an escalator region. People have been able to move in, and possibly out again at a later career stage, having reached a higher level than they would probably have attained had their intervening years been spent outside the south-east (see Savage et al, 1991).

Congestion

However, there is a sense in which a degree of 'proletarianization' has been inevitable. Clearly, when two-fifths of the workforce is in the middle class, it is impossible for them all to enjoy well-above average status and salaries. Things were rather different before World War II when less than 15 per cent of the workforce was in the professions or management. Nowadays it is inevitable that many middle class careers will start off on below-average earnings, and that many will never progress far above the average. The growth of the middle class has not been accompanied by a corresponding expansion in the room at the very top – on boards of directors of large companies, for example. So the growth of the middle class has led inevitably to an increase in career congestion.

There is also increased congestion at the points of entry to middle class careers. Nowadays the normal preparation for such a career is higher education. This is now the most common, but, as already explained, it is not the only route in. There are still plenty of 'non-credentialled' managers and formally unqualified people in 'professional' occupations. It is still possible, though rare, to start in the working class, then to progress through the skilled to technologist and into the professional grades. Likewise, there are still promotions from the office grades into management. In Britain today just over a third of all young people now enter higher education at age 18/19. Given that alternative routes are still open, it is impossible for all these graduates to be recruited straight into the middle class, and for them all to spend their entire working lives in middle class occupations. So there is more competition, more scrambling, for entry positions in the management and professional grades, then, once in, there is equally intense competition to progress up the career ladders.

Discontents

In recent years the mathematically inevitable consequences of the expansion of higher education and middle class employment have interacted with two independent developments. First, the drive to cut costs, boost labour productivity, and reduce staffing levels which began among manuals has spread through offices and has infected the management and professional grades. Here there has been delayering, and pressure on the remaining staff to do more, often reinforced by target-setting and staff appraisals. Second, mergers and takeovers have sometimes led to site closures, rationalizations and redundancies, and sometimes to businesses taking on new functions, or widening their product ranges. For example, most banks and building societies have become multi-purpose financial service providers. An outcome has been the creation of new management and professional specialisms, which has required staff to adapt, and it has created dangers of becoming trapped in contracting niches. A net result of these developments has been that recent studies of the middle class at work have uncovered widespread unhappiness. This is despite the fact that the long-term growth of the middle class has meant more jobs, and, overall, more opportunities to get ahead.

The Institute of Management has found that its members have been making more job changes than in the past, and that more of these changes have been enforced rather than voluntary. 'Enforced' here includes cases where individuals have jumped before being pushed. Also, more of the moves have been sideways or downwards rather than upwards. The 'onward and upward' view of management careers is said to be outdated (Inkson and Coe, 1993).

Building society managers have been griping. Until the 1980s most branch managers were 'expected to stay' until the normal retirement age. By the 1990s the normal expectation was 'hope to remain'. The managers were under new pressures. Their employers were marketing wider ranges of financial products, and the managers were under pressure to sell. They were being set performance targets. They knew that staff of their level and seniority had been offloaded during previous bouts of re-organization, and that they could be next. Delayering had made promotions less frequent. Organizational pyramids had been flattened and this had led to more career congestion in the upper, as well as at lower career levels (see Redman et al, 1997).

Research and development staff in the pharmaceutical industry complain about deprofessionalization. Competitive pressures, rationalization, drives to cut costs and demands for measurable results have created a sense of autonomy being lost and promotions becoming more difficult (see Randle, 1996).

Damien Grimshaw and his colleagues (2002) report research in four service sector organizations where delayering had left large gaps between the rungs on career ladders. Despite the development of certificated training, promotion depended ultimately on appraisal and selection by more senior managers. The outcome was a 'winner takes all' distribution of career opportunities. Some careers whizzed upwards while colleagues were left standing and could not understand why.

Kate Mulholland's (1998) research among managers and professionals in privatized electricity and water companies has portrayed an all-round loss of commitment among staff who would once have been loyal organization men. In these businesses the staff recognized a split between 'survivors' and 'movers and shakers''. The 'survivors' (from the days when the organizations were nationalized utilities) were typically in their 50s. They were fully aware that employees such as themselves had come to be regarded as a cost, and that all costs had to be cut wherever possible. They knew of scores of former colleagues who had either jumped or been pushed. They knew that their own positions were vulnerable. They believed that their experience and technical expertise were still valuable, but felt that this was no longer recognized by their employers. Since privatization they had been joined by new, younger colleagues, the 'movers and shakers'. These were not all accountants by profession, but they were all part of the accountancy-led cost-cutting culture. They knew that they were expected to deliver – to find ways of reducing costs, in which case they could expect to get on. They also knew that failure meant that they would have to move on. So the recent recruits to the businesses were uncertain of their own career prospects. They were all constantly reading job adverts and looking for their next career moves.

Some large organizations appear to have been stripped of commitment. Manual employees feel vulnerable, and it appears that this is equally the case nowadays in many offices and even in the management and professional grades. Investors remain only while they can expect a better return on capital than is available elsewhere (see chapter 7). Organizations recognize no long-term commitment to any grades of staff and the feeling is reciprocated. This is how the large organizations that were reliable fixtures on the Fordist landscape have been 'hollowed out', drained of solidity.

However, morale has not sunk to rock bottom among the managers and professionals in all organizations. Fiona Devine and colleagues (2000) report the results of interviews with 48 managers, senior partners and junior staff in accountancy, actuarial, law and corporate finance businesses in Manchester. The businesses were operating in more competitive markets than in the past. There was a perception of heightened career insecurity, and there was considerable job mobility in the early stages of careers, but no-one who was interviewed had ever been unemployed, and the occupations were really extremely advantaged. Employees were working long hours, but these schedules were not experienced as particularly onerous. Everyone recognized that the salary rewards were extremely good.

New careers?

There has been no decline in middle class career opportunities. The distance between the bottom and top of management and professional hierarchies has widened as a result of the fastest salary growth taking place at the top. Middle class employment is still expanding. The trends in these grades are not basically the same as in the working class. The change in the middle class has been in the social organization of careers. New technology and globalization have played a part, as in the restructuring of manual employment. Organizations and professions themselves have lost much of their former solidity. Careers are not as predictable as formerly. Promotions are no longer regular, like clockwork. But overall there are more opportunities, and the higher-level middle class jobs are better-rewarded, than ever before.

Susan Halford and Mike Savage (1995a) have looked in detail at employment in banks and local government. They confirm that there has been no overall decline in the statistical chances of middle class employees in these fields experiencing career advance. But in both banking and local government some old career paths have closed, and new, often more specialized, career tracks have been created. There are no longer as many distinct layers in the organizational hierarchies, or on career ladders. All employees' performances are now systematically monitored. People have targets, they are appraised regularly, and have to apply for promotions: these are no longer simply delivered. Then there is the new possibility of redundancy. Also, women are now competing for promotion with men. And many jobs have been redefined socially in ways that advantage feminine rather than paternal qualities. Sales has been re-imaged as customer care (Halford and Savage, 1995b). These are some of the reasons for the middle class griping. There are losers, but also winners. Some 'new' managers and professionals have been able to make spectacular progress.

It may be useful to unpack some of the principal changes in middle class careers. In real life situations the changes are always merged and coloured by firm, industry and occupation specifics. However, one general trend has been towards more regular and formal staff appraisals, thus making everyone more 'accountable', and giving rise to feelings of loss of autonomy and control. Second, promotions are now less likely to be automatic: people have to apply and compete with one another. Third, many middle class careers have ceased to be linear and now involve more retraining and repositioning. The rewards available in middle class careers have not shrunk, but the 'rules of the game' have changed.

Studies that have concentrated on the downside have been complemented by those that highlight the upside, and which have identified new types of management and professional careers (see Arthur et al, 1999; Martin, 1998; Watson and Harris, 1999). These studies have portrayed new bricoleur professionals, flexecs, wandering troubadours, who treat jobs as projects in which they can extend their competencies, their portfolios of skills, and add to their CVs. Image and reputation within professional and management networks are now vital career assets. These people are said not only to create their own careers, but to develop every job that they take, and sometimes create new businesses of their own – management consultancies and professional partnerships in leading edge fields such as IT and advertising, for example. The flexecs are not all young. There are examples of 50-somethings who have quit large organizations, jumped prior to being pushed in some cases, then thrived. However, it is important to bear in mind that as many small enterprises flounder as prosper.

Whether the entire middle class can become successful flexecs and bricoleurs is still not clear. All the studies in large organizations (which is where most of the middle class still work) find far more evidence of old careers disintegrating than new careers being created (McGovern et al, 1998). The graduates who initially struggle to get in are less likely than in the past to find secure career plateaux from which they can make regular, if unspectacular, progress. There are no longer any secure positions in many organizations, and any upward movement needs to be won.

Divisions

Recent research on the middle class has sought to identify, first, how their work and market situations are changing, and second, whether they really have a typical class situation from which the social, cultural and political dimensions of class formation could develop. Some analysts have stressed the divisions that exist within the contemporary middle class or classes. Growth is said to have led to greater diversity. Four types of divisions have been highlighted: by occupational level, between those who work in the private and public sectors, between managers and professionals, and by lifestyle. The disorganization of the working class combined with an alleged fragmentation of the middle class may be seen as adding-up to a death of class. However, differences, which there most certainly are, need not amount to divisions, or, at any rate, not as basic as the division between the working class on the one side, then, on the other, the middle class or classes.

Levels

There is obviously a great deal of inequality among managers and professional employees; more so than among manuals. Some junior managers and professionals earn less than the overall average in the present-day UK. Others have telephone number annual salaries. Are they all in the same class? There always were inequalities, but these have widened considerably in recent years. Hence the plausibility of a division of interest being created between upper-level and 'proletarianized' layers of the middle class.

In Goldthorpe's original class scheme, the lower level of the 'service class' was described as a cadet grade through which entrants could rise into the service class proper. So junior hospital doctors eventually become consultants, junior managers become senior managers, and so on. Things are really more complicated than this. Some professions are higher than others. On the one hand, there are well-established professions – law, medicine and accountancy – which have been successful in retaining high proportions of jobs in the upper-ranks, and have avoided the degree of career congestion that is now found in the basic grades in banks, among teachers, social workers, and so on. There are also graduates who are recruited into fast-track trainee management posts with blue-chip multi-nationals and firms of consultants. Access to these positions tends to be restricted to young people who achieve good degrees (firsts or 2.1s) from older universities (preferably Oxford or Cambridge), who performed well in the A-level and GCSE examinations, and who can also survive days of personality and role-play tests to prove that they are the right type of person. These selection processes tend to favour individuals from established middle class families who are privately educated, or who attend other selective schools (see Jackson, 2009). This leaves the lower middle class positions to be filled by the upwardly mobile, from state comprehensives, new universities, and with lower class degrees from older institutions (see Brown and Hesketh, 2004; Brown and Scase, 1994). It has been argued that the professions and man-agement positions into which women and the upwardly mobile are recruited have been seriously degraded, and that men from elite family and educational backgrounds have gone into the financial sectors and high-tech fields where the rewards are considerably greater (Walkerdine et al, 2001).

There are two problems, or at least qualifying points, that have to be entered against this diagnosis. First, it understates the amount of intermingling that occurs in schools and higher education, and in the early career stages, between eventual high-fliers and also-rans. Some graduates from older universities do not become high-fliers. There are wide inequalities within the established pro-fessions. There are small town solicitors who depend on conveyancing and legal aid work as well as big city firms that handle the business of large cor-porations. The same applies among accountants, and in medicine. There are people from modest backgrounds who have made fortunes in the city, and in e-commerce.

Second, there is the matter of gender. As feminist critics note, although times are changing, the high-level middle class positions still tend to be occupied by men, while women are still far less likely to reach these same heights. This is despite the fact that more women in middle class occupations are pursuing full-time, scarcely broken, careers. What must also be said is that most of these women marry middle class men. There is a powerful tendency for like to marry like, so there are now more middle class households than formerly that benefit from two middle class salaries. Neither salary needs to be particu-larly large to provide the base for a standard of living that is entirely different from working class ways of life. The new middle class buys services, including domestic services, from the new working class. The former hires live-in nannies (in some cases), nursery child-care (in rather more instances), gardeners and cleaners (see Gregson and Lowe, 1993). And members of the middle class are able to pay to have their cars repaired and serviced, and their houses decorated and renovated. The new middle class is also able to afford to use out-of-home services in restaurants, hotels and theatres. There are more and less successful and prosperous managers and professionals, but are the differences among them really as basic as between the household cleaner and her employer?

Public and private

The argument here is straight-forward and arises from the prominence of taxation as an issue in British politics ever since the 1980s. Managers and professionals who work in the private sector are said to have vested interests in low levels of taxes on incomes, enabling them to keep more of their earnings in their pockets or bank accounts, and a corresponding willingness and ability to accept the inevitable cutbacks in state services and benefits because they are able to buy alternatives privately. Public sector managers and professionals are said to have entirely different interests: their jobs, salary levels and career prospects are at risk. No surprise, therefore, that the public services' white-collar employees have been at the forefront of campaigns to defend the National Health Service and state education. A new political cleavage can be envisaged between working class users together with public sector managers and professionals on the one side, and the private sector middle class on the other.

There are several problems with what might initially appear a persuasive argument. First, there is nothing new about this division of interest, or between the trade-off between higher top earnings in the private sector, and greater job security in state employment. Nothing has changed here. Second, these differences were sharpest in politics in the 1980s when Margaret Thatcher's governments were emphatically pro-private enterprise, hostile to the public sector, and against high taxes on earned incomes. Even then (see Table 6.2), although controllers (the middle class in this book) who worked in the public sector were more likely than

Table 6.2 Percentages voting against the Conservative Party in 1987

Employee Classes	Percentage
Workers, public sector	57
Workers, private sector	51
Controllers, public sector	42
Controllers, private sector	35

Adapted from Edgell and Duke, 1991

their private sector counterparts to vote anti-Conservative, and the same was true of public compared with private sector workers, both middle class groups were less likely to vote anti-Conservative than both working class groups.

Third, there are just as good reasons as ever why the public-private sector split is unlikely to become as clear as the longer-standing class division. Public sector professionals may have been keen (and largely successful) in protecting the state services in which they are employed (education and health, for example) but they have not saved the nationalized steel, coal, railways, gas, electricity, and other industries which had larger blue-collar workforces. Nor have public sector professionals and managers prevented the contracting-out of the cleaning, laundering and catering from their schools and hospitals. Moreover, the state services that their middle class employees are keenest to protect are used by managers and professionals in public and private sector employment, as well as by the working class. There are more middle class children in state schools than are educated privately. Very few middle class pensioners are able and willing to meet all their health-care costs from private resources. Finally, doctors who work in the National Health Service and senior civil servants are not all adverse to having their children educated privately, or using private medicine. Many are no doubt as keen as anyone to have taxes on their incomes kept as low as possible, and to have government spending held down, provided only that their own jobs are not threatened.

Professionals and managers

These words are nearly always coupled when describing the middle class. They can be treated as different types of occupations which share common middle class characteristics. Alternatively, they can be treated as having distinct work and market situations; maybe sufficiently distinct to create a class division between them, or at least to prevent the middle class developing common and characteristic types of consciousness and politics.

The latter point of view has been developed by Mike Savage who has constructed what he calls an asset-based, realist theory of middle class formation which explains how middle class groups are able to become real entities which can act causally. Such middle class groups, according to Savage, can have bases in three types of assets – in property, bureaucracy or culture (Savage et al, 1992). Various mixtures are possible, but Savage's view is that the main sections of the contemporary middle class are based primarily on either one or another. The propertied middle classes can be set to one side for the time being. They are the petit bourgeoisie (see chapter 5) and the upper class which will be considered in chapter 7. For present purposes the crucial distinction is between bureaucracy and culture, which are said to be the bases of the managerial and professional middle classes respectively.

Now it is very easy to make stark contrasts in terms of ideal-types in which managers are shown to owe everything to their positions in organizations (bureaucracies) and the control that they exercise over organizational assets. Managers are portrayed as acquiring particularistic skills and knowledge (specific to the organizations). Their entire (ideal-typical) careers are said to be spent within the same organizations where they may well become indispensable on account of the detailed knowledge that they acquire about the organizations' working methods, suppliers, customers, various departments, and so on. These are the archetypal organization men (and women nowadays) (see Whyte, 1957) whose working lives, careers and prospects are inextricably bound to the organizations in which they work. They depend on their organizations, and the organizations depend on them. Managers' loyalty is rewarded with security and career progression.

The careers of ideal-typical professionals, and their claims to middle class status and treatment, are based on culture, meaning in practice, skills and knowledge that are certified and validated by professional associations. The core functions of professional associations are to restrict entry to those properly qualified, and to regulate professional conduct. Professions are based on expert knowledge and related practices, which, it is claimed, are so esoteric that the only competent judges of whether work is of a satisfactory standard are other professionals. This creates situations where occupational groups can elevate their status in the eyes of the public, including actual and potential customers, thereby elevating the rewards that they can command, through professional organization. Professional associations distinguish the competent from quacks, and discipline, and may ultimately expel, any members who do match-up to the standards set by the professions. People who embark on professional careers need to invest initially in acquiring the appropriate cultural capital (qualifications). Thereafter their main loyalty is to their professions. Their careers will often involve movement between numerous employers. They always have a wider loyalty, namely, to their professions. They may work in professional organizations which are, in effect, controlled by the professionals (hospitals and universities, for example). They may work in smaller professional practices. The crucial point is that they have options.

Studies which compare managers and professionals invariably find that the latter are the relatively advantaged group, and since the 1970s the advantages of professionals appear to have increased. Hence the claim that the professional-manager divide is deepening. Mike Savage believes that property and culture have always been more secure bases for middle class positions than organization-based assets, and that in post-Fordist times the latter assets have been devalued even further. This is said to have occurred during the waves of mergers and take-overs, rationalizations and delayering, which have rendered many packages of particularistic skills and knowledge completely redundant (Savage et al, 1992). Professionals appear to have been less vulnerable. They have been less likely to experience demotion (Fielding, 1995). Moreover, it appears that cultural capital is more easily passed down the generations. Professionals' children are more successful in education than the children of managers and, therefore, are more likely to avoid socio-economic descent (Egerton, 1997).

The problems with the neat manager-professional division only become apparent, but then become glaringly obvious, when we move from ideal-types into the real world. First, managers' careers have always had a cultural base. Initial positions on management career ladders are typically awarded partly on the basis of qualifications, and, although this may be nit-picking, the particularistic knowledge and skills that make managers valuable to their organizations are 'cultural'. Conversely, professionals often pursue careers in professional organizations in which they climb bureaucratic ladders. Also, non-professional organizations may develop their own professionals who can combine broader-based skills and knowledge with a deep acquaintance with company culture (company lawyers and accountants, and army doctors, for example). Organizations themselves can be places within which expert professional-managers are created. Rionach Casey and Chris Allen (2004) describe how this has happened to housing managers who work in local authority housing departments, and nowadays in housing associations also. The new performance ethos with its target culture has enabled housing managers to claim professional status, and to advance their own careers, on the basis of personal accredited achievements vis-a-vis the targets.

Second, professionals' careers often criss-cross between line management and professional positions. University academics may move into academic management. Some become vice-chancellors (chief executives). Doctors in hospitals do likewise. Accountants, engineers and so on often move into line management posts in their companies (Mills, 1995). Some find that this move is necessary in order to keep their careers advancing. Out in the real world, the distinction between managers and professionals has always been blurred. According to Tom Watson and Pauline Harris (1999), few managers embark on their careers with the set aim of becoming managers. They explain how they simply drifted into management, often from professional backgrounds, and stayed because they found that they could 'swim'.

Third, the respondents who are identified as professionals in surveys are sometimes distinguished from managers basically because the former are the better-qualified rather than on account of their membership of professional bodies. The well-defined lifestyles that can be distinguished, mainly within the professional middle class (see below), probably owe much more to their higher education, higher social origins, and higher incomes than to their membership of professional bodies.

Fourth, it can in fact be argued that, rather than widening, the distinction between managers and professionals is currently weakening, though qualifications (cultural capital) are undoubtedly becoming more important than ever as a base for middle class careers. On the one hand, more careers in management are being launched on the basis of higher education, and there are more management qualifications available. There are MBAs and a variety of qualifications in marketing, personnel and other management fields. Some managers have always been able to benefit by possessing skills and knowledge applicable across entire industries rather than specific to one firm. So there have been oil men, car-makers, and suchlike. Nowadays there seem to be more cases where people can claim generic management skills and move between organizations in entirely different industries, often moving upwards in the process. Some claim that management itself is now a profession, and a high status profession judged by the popularity of higher education courses with management in their titles.

Meanwhile, there are ways in which professionals are becoming more like managers. The traditional high status professions – medicine, law and accountancy – are no longer typical. These occupations developed a public service type of professionalism, not because their members necessarily worked in the public sector, but on account of their strong professional associations which set great store, in theory if not always in practice, on prioritizing the public interest. The present-day professional is more likely to practise a commercial type of professionalism (Hanlon, 1998). The commercial professional is a certified expert who hires out skills to deliver whatever customers want, which is invariably plain expertise rather than moral guardianship. The clients of these professionals are usually organizations rather than individuals, and the customers set the ground rules. Professionals' careers benefit when they are able to deliver. Their strictly professional reputations (in the eyes of peers) are of secondary importance to their reputations in the eyes of customers. Janette Webb (1999) has noted the development of such a division among public sector middle class employees. On the one hand, there are those who have embraced an entrepreneurial ethic. They are intent on making their departments lean and efficient, and on getting-ahead in their own careers. These public sector 'entrepreneurs' tend to be males, in higher-level positions. On the other hand, there are staff, mainly females in lower-level positions, who still subscribe to a traditional, caring, public service ethic. Note that the contrasts found by Webb were within the public sector middle class.

Yaojun Li (2002) argues strongly that today's managers and professionals are part of a single service (or middle) class. The two groups are equally secure in their class positions. There is no difference between their (low) risks of unemployment. Professionally qualified personnel move freely into line management, and managers are increasingly as highly qualified as professionals.

Of course, there is a difference between the better and less-educated sections of the middle class (professionals plus managers), and between those who commit their careers to specific organizations and those who move between employers while remaining in the same occupations. There are differences between those who become high-fliers and those who stick at lower levels, and between those who work in the public and private sectors. In class analysis it is important not to lose sight of the crunch questions. These are, first, how the differences within the middle class compare with the division between the entire middle class and the working class, and second, whether the differences within the middle class are sufficient to prevent the development of characteristic socio-cultural patterns and practices, and political proclivities.

Lifestyles

Researchers are agreed that whether they are managers or professionals, in the public or the private sector, and whether they are on the lower or upper rungs of career ladders, those concerned are so different from the working class (in their work and market situations) that they must be assigned to a different class or classes. The question then arises (as above) as to whether middle class occupations and careers have sufficient in common with each other to be regarded as constituting a single class, or whether we need to recognize two or more middle classes.

Lifestyles are relevant because during class formation social and cultural commonalities may be built upon a common economic position. Here the issues that arise are basically the same as when considering middle class occupational careers. Researchers currently agree that all the middle class groups have lifestyles that distinguish them from the working class. Working class lifestyles are more uniform, and much more TV-dominated (see Ophem and Hoog, 1998). The controversial issue is how to interpret the lifestyle differences – which all researchers acknowledge – that are found within the middle class or classes.

A number of middle class lifestyle groups have been identified: healthy ascetics who play sport and take other forms of exercise and who are careful about diet; those who are interested in art, theatre visits, concerts and wine; a country set or sets; and inner-city gentrifiers. All these lifestyle groups involve mainly persons from the professional 'branch' of the middle class (see Butler, 1995; Cloke et al, 1995; Savage et al, 1991; Wynne, 1998). Alan Warde (1995) has shown that the lifestyles of managers, whether in terms of their choices of foodstuffs, or their leisure spending and activities, tend to be 'undistinguished', meaning that they simply spend more on or do more things that are common within the working class. The problem for class analysts concerns the significance of the intra-middle class differences.

There is an 'omnivore thesis', initially formulated in the USA by Richard Peterson in 1992. The original claim was that the middle class had ceased to be distinguished by its exclusively highbrow tastes (if it was ever distinguished in this way) and that its members had become omnivores who enjoyed both high and popular forms of culture. The working class, in contrast, were univores, consuming popular cultural forms only (see also Peterson and Kern, 1996). These findings have subsequently been replicated in all the western societies where the relevant evidence has been assembled, including Britain. Tak Wing Chan and John Goldthorpe (2007) have shown that the main schism by patterns of cultural consumption in the UK is between those who consume pop only and those who consume both popular and other kinds of culture. Tony Bennett and his co-researchers (2009) have expressed this contrast even more starkly. They claim that the main division in Britain is between omnivores and people whose cultural consumption consists (almost) wholly of TV-viewing. These researchers also found that higher- and lower-level professionals, but only higher-level managers, were typically cultural omnivores. Lower-grade managers' levels and patterns of cultural consumption set them alongside other 'intermediate' classes. Thus these researchers' realist map of the class structure, based on cultural tastes and practices, has a reduced middle class (24 per cent of the population), an enlarged intermediate, business-oriented class (30 per cent), and a disengaged working class (46 per cent) (Roux et al, 2008).

The middle classes are not just cultural omnivores (with wide ranging tastes in music, reading matter and the visual arts), which was the original claim; they are also more general leisure omnivores. Compared with the working class, they eat out more frequently and use a wider variety of restaurants offering different kinds of cuisine (Warde et al, 1999). The same can be said of their participation in sports, holidays and, indeed, across the whole of leisure. Middle class omnivores are also voracious consumers with huge appetites (Sullivan and Katz-Gerro, 2007).

Middle class omnivorousness exists at a collective and at an individual level. It applies to the tastes and activities of the middle class as a whole (whether defined to include all professionals and managers, or excluding lower-level managers), and to particular middle class individuals, couples and households. However, no-one can do absolutely everything. Individuals enjoy playing and watching particular sports, eating out at particular kinds of restaurants, listening to particular kinds of classical and popular music, taking particular kinds of holidays, and so on. Gindo Tampubolon (2010) has identified two kinds of omnivores in the UK. One likes classical music, opera and dance. The other likes jazz, plays, musicals, folk, pop and film. There is little overlap in taste between these two groups. In a sense, each individual, couple or household can have a unique set of tastes and lifestyle. Is this further fragmenting the middle class(es)? Clearly, the present-day middle class is not bound in the same way as the original working class, when workmates would drink together in the same pubs and clubs, take their holidays during the same weeks, and spend these weeks at the same regional holiday resorts.

Bonnie Erikson (1996) originally observed that omnivorousness itself could serve as a mark of distinction, a point subsequently reiterated by Alan Warde and his colleagues (1999), following which voraciousness has been added by Oriel Sullivan and Tally Katz-Gerro (2007). According to this argument, the middle class is united by its members' ability to share and discuss their various tastes with one another, and by having sufficiently broad lifestyle knowledge to sustain this kind of discourse. Those who are unable to do this, the univores, are locked out, excluded from or marginalized in present-day middle class socio-cultural networks.

Consciousness and politics

The traditional and new middle classes

It is still too early, historically, for a precise and confident verdict as to whether the new middle class will develop common and characteristic forms of consciousness and politics and, if so, what their key features will be. We have seen that the middle class grew steadily throughout the twentieth century, but especially from World War Two onwards. It more than doubled in size, and a consequence is that most current members have been recruited from beneath. Collectively they have very mixed origins, but this will not continue indefinitely. The inter-generationally stable core will grow in size, and the rate of middle class expansion will decline even if the trend continues (see chapter 8).

At the beginning of the twenty-first century we are in a similar position vis-a-vis the middle class, in trying to identify its likely political and societal impact, as analysts were vis-a-vis the working class at the time of the First World War. During the nineteenth century the working class had been created as an economic entity, and working class cultures had developed throughout the land at local community and workplace levels. Trade unions and the Labour Party had been created. Even so, it was impossible in the early twentieth century to be certain as to the extent to which working class power would be mobilized, or the uses to which such power would be put. Revolutionary, reformist and conservative (a domesticated, quiescent working class) prognoses were equally plausible.

It is important to recognize that, during its twentieth century growth, the middle class was reconstituted. Today's middle class is not simply a swollen version of the middle class at the beginning of the twentieth century. Up to the Second World War, the core members of the traditional middle class were proprietors of businesses and self-employed professionals. Other white-collar workers identified with this middle class core. Their market, work and status situations may have encouraged this, but the various outer-sections were bound to the traditional middle class basically by the threat of working class power. Middle class fear is not new, but until the 1950s the characteristic fear was quite different from concerns that we hear today. The recurrent and unifying fear earlier on was the advance of the working class. This threatened to erode the middle class's advantages. It threatened to tax their incomes to provide the working class with services that the middle class already enjoyed. So the middle class applauded everything that the working class was believed to be against: individualism, enterprise and independence. The traditional middle class was opposed to trade unions and the so-called 'nanny state'.

The new middle class is different. Its core members are salaried managers and professionals. Many of them work in the public sector. They are simply too numerous for them all to feel privileged, and for the defence of middle class privileges to be an overriding common concern. Moreover, working class power has waned. The middle class has been organizing – joining trade unions as well as professional associations, for example. The working class is now weakened. It is no longer a threat. If the present-day middle class is concerned about what is happening beneath, the worries are less likely to be about militant trade unions and a socialist Labour Party than the effects of unemployment and poverty on crime, the costs of welfare, and the general quality of life in their towns and cities.

Pre-occupations

Up to now we have no national congress of professional associations or white-collar trade unions. There is no political party with policies that make an explicit, and provenly effective, appeal to specifically middle class interests. 'Middle Britain' (which all the main political parties aspire to represent) is not really an equivalent. This middle is too elastic, too big a 'tent', capable of including anyone who is not 'poor' at one end, and people earning four times the average at the other. The Conservative Party had the support of the traditional middle class, and retained this support for as long as Labour was regarded as a working class party, and a threat. We now know that Thatcherism did not solidify new middle class support for the Conservatives. New Labour was successful in the late-1990s in developing policies, or at least an image, that appealed to all classes. Throughout the early years of the twenty-first century the Conservatives have been unsure of how to regain even their traditional, once taken-for-granted, middle class support.

It is impossible to say which policies will appeal, but it is possible to identify three pre-occupations which are specific to, and resonate throughout, the new middle class. As one might expect, these arise from the middle class's typical work and market situations.

First, the middle class expects a 'service' relationship with employers. Managers and professionals expect to be trusted, to be given responsibility, autonomy and discretion. Otherwise they feel mis-employed and under-utilized. They are willing to play their parts in the service relationship. Managers and professionals are willing to 'put in the hours' without overtime payment. They may complain about the stress and strains imposed on family relationships, but they are just as worried if their employers have no need for such commitment. It is not usually fear of the sack that motivates managers and professionals to work 50-plus hours a week at the office, and to carry more work home in their briefcases and on their laptops. They are more likely to be, or want to be seen to be, work enthusiasts, keen to demonstrate their indispensability and promotability. They accept that relocation to another part of the country may be part of the package despite the additional strains on personal relationships, especially between dual career couples. According to Janette Webb (2004), trust is eroded only when seniors devolve responsibility (blame for failure) without conceding discretion and authority. This leaves junior managers and professionals feeling exposed and vulnerable. The service relationship that the middle class seeks is rather different from the more widespread desire for 'interesting work'. The characteristic middle class pre-occupation also goes beyond vocationalism – pride in, and identification with, professional or craft skills. The middle class is willing to give more, and expects to give more, and those concerned are most likely to feel entitled to all the rewards that accrue. They are quite likely to approve of higher taxes on the rich but unlikely to place themselves in this category.

The conservatism of the middle class, in so far as the class is conservative, stems partly from the service relationship sought with employers. While this relationship is maintained, the middle class is unlikely to recognize any basic division of interest vis-a-vis a class above. The middle class depends on employers for its advantaged work and market situations, just as employers depend on salaried managers and professionals to protect and secure returns on their capital. The rewards that successful managers and professionals receive from work in the private sector are, in part, shares in profits rather than straight-forward payments for work done. Middle class salary levels are difficult to explain in terms of contributions (functional importance) to society, or with classical economic theory. They are easier to explain in terms of the value of the work to their employers. The higher echelons of the middle class are effectively integrated into the upper class. Top managers (at director level) are usually rewarded with share options. They may not become major shareholders in the companies, but the managers become wealthy individuals with vested interests in the returns that accrue to their own capital investments. Middle class careers can be a route into the upper class. This is neither a normal career destination nor the most common route in, but it is a possible, and a highly attractive, reward for a successful middle class career. A broader section of the middle class has been able to become personal share-owners as a result of the privatizations and building society conversions of the 1980s and 90s. Approximately a half of all managers and professionals now own shares (Saunders and Harris, 1994). Also, it is the middle class rather than the working class that has been able to take most advantage of the government-provided tax shelters for savings – TESSAs, PEPs and subsequently ISAs. The really wealthy have off-shore tax havens, and the middle class has something similar. Upper and middle class interests are far from identical (see chapter 7), but up to now the two classes have been so interdependent that neither has been likely to confront the other.

'Career' is the second distinctively middle class pre-occupation. The middle class seeks and expects careers. Managers and professionals expect to advance progressively in their organizations or professions. They may achieve this by following structured career routes, or by forging new careers, but they all expect to advance. If necessary, they will switch employers and localities. These are accepted prices that may need to be paid in order to get on. The middle class is willing to undertake additional study and training, and to top-up qualifications, in order to keep its careers moving. Managers and professionals are far more likely than any other occupational group to receive post-entry, often recurrent and ongoing, training, and to engage in qualification accumulation. They are often willing to do whatever is possible and necessary to position themselves directly beneath promotion opportunities. They are equally concerned that their children should do well. Middle class children are taught by their parents that school work is important. These are the parents who shop around, relocate if necessary, and sometimes pay for private education, in order to give their children the best possible starts. For their part, the children become aware of their parents' financial and emotional investments. Failure becomes unthinkable – the ultimate act of family betrayal (see Walkerdine et al, 2001).

A common middle class gripe nowadays is about career blockages. Many present-day managers and professionals are dissatisfied with their career progress and opportunities. This is a reason why more have been joining trade unions (see Redman et al, 1997). The present-day middle class is anxious rather than complacent and comfortable, but this does not necessarily or normally lead to a challenge to class divisions. The normal middle class response is to try even harder, to seek a personal solution: hence the willingness to train, move house, top-up qualifications, and so on. Otherwise the frustrated middle class tends to increase its psychic investments in out-of-work life. Those concerned may become home and family-centred (psychologically at any rate), and adopt instrumental, calculative approaches to their jobs (Scase and Goffee, 1989), just like the 'new working class' of the 1950s and 60s.

The third characteristic middle class pre-occupation is meritocratic, of a specifically middle class type. The middle class believes that positions and rewards should be earned, largely though not entirely on the basis of qualifications. They are opposed to virtually every other form of discrimination – by gender, race, religion, social background, country of origin, nationality. The one type of discrimination that the middle class endorses is according to qualifications. On qualifications they are arch-conservative rather than radical. According to Milner (1999), a qualification meritocracy, which may well be deemed classless, is the dominant ideology of contemporary intellectuals. Members of the middle class expect their own qualifications to be appropriately rewarded and will defer only to those who are even better-qualified.

Middle class pre-occupations and working class interests

These are no longer diametrically opposed, as they were when the middle class had a 'traditional' core. It is realistic nowadays for politicians to seek to appeal simultaneously to both the working class, including the poor, and the middle class (or middle Britain, as they usually prefer to say). However, middle class and working class aspirations are not identical. It is still possible to address one set while ignoring, or at the expense of, the other.

The new middle class is not particularly conservative in either party political or broader social and economic terms. As the shape of the class structure changed during second half of the twentieth century, with the working class diminishing in size, the proportion of the popular vote commanded by the Labour Party gradually declined. At any rate, this was the long-term trend from the 1950s until 1997 (see Table 6.3). It is less often noted, though more remarkable, that over the same period the Conservative Party failed to become more popular as a result of the expansion of the white-collar classes. The proportion of white-collar workers voting against the Conservatives, though not necessarily for Labour, increased gradually, then shot upwards in 1997 (see chapter 9). The Conservative Party has never regained the share of the popular vote that it won in most general elections between 1945 and 1992. Hence, despite the unpopularity of the Labour Party in 2010, the Conservatives were unable to win the share of the vote that would have given them a House of Commons majority.

The socio-occupational profile of the non-Conservative middle class is well-known. They tend to be well-educated (university graduates), usually in arts or

Table 6.3 Percentages of total votes received by Conservatives, Labour and Liberals

Year	Conservatives	Labour	Liberals*
1945	40	48	9
1950	44	46	9
1951	48	49	3
1955	50	46	3
1959	49	44	6
1964	43	44	11
1966	42	48	9
1970	46	43	8
1974	38	37	19
1974	36	39	18
1979	44	37	14
1983	42	28	25
1987	42	31	23
1992	42	34	18
1997	31	43	17
2001	33	42	18
2005	33	36	22
2010	36	29	23

*Liberal/Social Democratic Party Alliance 1983–87, Liberal Democrats from 1992

social sciences employed in the public sector, in welfare professions (education, social work or medicine), or in intellectual private sector occupations such as journalism. The nature and sources of the radicalism of this section of the middle class are discussed below. For the present, the crucial point is that the present-day middle class is just as anxious to change the world as the working class. The changes that these classes desire are not diametrically opposed, but neither are they identical. Indeed, their aspirations have less in common than initial appearances may suggest.

Both favour meritocracy, but in rather different senses. For the middle class merit = qualifications. They expect returns on their investments in education and training. They still feel this way even though it is no longer as obvious as in previous years that extended education requires the deferment of gratifications. This is because earlier school-leavers are unlikely nowadays to move rapidly into well-paid jobs (see Roberts and Parsell, 1991). In the working class merit is equated with effort, skill and the number of hours worked. It is measured in terms of the value that people produce, the output, rather than the quality of the input. From within the working class, inflated middle class salaries do not appear justified on grounds of merit.

The working and middle classes have equally good, albeit different, reasons, for responding favourably to, and also for opposing, proposals to replace the vagaries of the market with planning. The middle class could then become the planners, the distributors; the type of 'new class' that was created by state socialism. This empowering of the middle class would not have to be at the expense of the work situation and market advantages that are available in a market economy. The appeal of planning to the working class has always been rather different: removing the threat of redundancy, lay-offs and short-time, and enabling resources to be distributed in accordance with merit and need. By the end of the twentieth century both classes had good reasons to conclude that the inevitable compromises made planning no more attractive than the market.

The new middle class is certainly not anti-collectivist. Many of them work in the public sector. They use, and obtain good value from, state services such as health and education. And the new middle class are 'joiners'. These are the so-called chattering classes who ensure that their voices are heard, and they are well-represented. They have professional associations, and they are now more likely than manual employees to be members of trade unions. This has now been the case for over 20 years. The middle class has marched into trade unions as its job security has been undermined, and as career opportunities have narrowed (see Redman et al, 1997), and because so many work for the employer where trade union membership is most common – the government.

The middle class supplies most of the members, and certainly most of the activists, in all types of non-profit, voluntary organizations – those that work for charitable causes, and those that exist for the members' interests whether these lie in sport, the arts, maintaining the character of a neighbourhood, or reducing crime. Nowadays the middle class also supplies most of the activists, and even more so the elected representatives, in all the main political parties. In this sense the Labour Party has been taken from the working class. Politicians in all parties now have very similar backgrounds – university, then directly into political jobs (see chapter 9) or employment in management or the professions. Politics has become another middle class career, often a long-term career, and sometimes the individual's only career. The activists may not be middle class representatives in either a technical or a subjective sense, but middle class dominance means that middle class issues and pre-occupations, and definitions of problems, have good chances of reaching government agendas.

The advantages that collectivism offered to the working class have been sidelined. For the working class, collective organization has been a safeguard against individual victimization. Collective agreements have ensured that everyone's rewards, and the contributions required, have been agreed, or at least understood, by all. Middle class collectivism is rather different. It is a means of pursuing specific causes, often of creating or maintaining opportunities for personal enterprise and socio-economic advance, and another source of career opportunities.

The working class has traditionally favoured state guarantees to meet everyone's basic needs, meaning, in practice, income maintenance during retirement, unemployment and sickness, plus assistance with onerous life events – basically births, child-care and death. Adequate housing has been another part of this agenda. Then, the working class has favoured other services, specifically health and education, being removed from the market and managed in response to need and/or merit. None of this clashes with middle class aspirations. The middle class will endorse the entire agenda. However, their motives are more likely to be altruistic than self-interested. They are unlikely to envisage that they themselves will ever depend wholly on the state retirement pension, for example. And members of the middle class are likely to take it for granted that those who want to do so will be able to top-up or opt-out of the 'basic' state provisions, thereby defeating the original working class objective of having all educational and health care resources allocated according to need or merit, nothing else, and state social security guaranteeing a standard of living close to that of other citizens.

There is also the question of how state services are to be financed. In recent years there has been cross-party and, apparently, cross-class agreement that income taxes must not be raised and, if possible, should be lowered. This consensus did not always exist. Until the 1950s people on below-average earnings did not pay income tax. They had everything to gain and nothing to lose when demanding state services funded through taxes on incomes. Subsequently, as incomes rose, virtually all employees were drawn into the income tax-paying bracket, and all tax-payers have shared a concern over the standard rate of income tax. Those with the highest incomes have the most to gain from tax reductions, or avoiding increased taxes on earnings, but this latter option has come to be regarded as contrary to all class interests. It is also noteworthy that the possibility of raising tax thresholds so that below-average earners are once again excluded, and making taxation on higher incomes much more steeply progressive, does not feature on any mainstream political agendas.

Everyone seems to want better state services and lower taxes. There are votes to be won by offering both. Hence the advent of what Sylvia Walby (1999) describes as the 'regulatory state', a form of government that has been pioneered by the European Union. Here the state does not provide, but requires businesses and citizens to do so. For example, businesses can be required to pay a minimum wage. This costs governments nothing. Citizens could be obliged to save towards their retirement in private (non-state) funds. They could also be required to insure their housing costs (mortgage repayments) against the risks of unemployment and chronic illness. The principle could be extended to health care and education. Collectivism is thereby subtly recast in line with middle class interests.

During the last 30 years the new middle class has taken-up a raft of new radical issues which had no place on the old working class radical agenda. The new issues have nothing to do (ostensibly at any rate) with specifically middle class interests. They are about peace, race equality, sex equality, gay rights, fair treatment for asylum seekers, animal welfare and the environment. Support for all these causes is much broader-based, but nearly all the activists in these 'new social movements' are middle class. As explained earlier, they tend to be from a particular section of the middle class: the highly educated, in arts or social sciences. They are usually from middle class families rather than upwardly mobile. Their parents often held or hold similar radical views. The activists are most likely to work in the public sector, in welfare, or in intellectual professions. Of course, not everyone with some or even all of these characteristics becomes a radical activist. There usually has to be a trigger; an 'event' or personally significant experience (Searle-Chatterjee, 1999). However, the same social profile has been discovered again and again no matter which radical movements have been examined (Cotgrove, 1982; Mattausch, 1989a, 1989b; Parkin, 1968; Ridig et al, 1991). There has been intense, and so far unresolved, debate, as to how this radicalism is to be explained. Does it indicate the spread of post-materialist values in post-scarcity societies? (Inglehart, 1977, 1997). Or are the causes expressing the interests of a middle class faction that works neither in the market economy nor in science or technology? (Cotgrove and Duff, 1980, 1981). Or are the activists radical despite, rather than because of, their class situations? (Heath and Savage, 1995). Do those concerned choose their education and occupations on the basis of their radical values rather than develop the values through their educational and occupational experience? (Bagguley, 1995). To what extent is it all just the intelligentsia playing its traditional role of supplying agendas for all social and political movements? (Bagguley, 1992).

The points that can be made unequivocally are as follows. First, it is easy to understand why quite substantial sections of the middle class (the social radicals) were turned-off rather than attracted to the Conservative Party by Thatcherism in the 1980s (Savage et al, 1992). Second, there is nothing in the middle class's radicalism, collectivism, support for the welfare state, support for meritocracy or socio-economic planning that requires any sacrifice of its own interests vis-a-vis the working class. To put this another way, there is little or nothing on offer for the workers. It can be argued that the working class benefits from sex and race equality, peace, environmental improvement and so on, but these have never been working class priorities. Third, there is nothing to challenge the economic system and the position of the upper class within it. Fourth, it is middle class pre-occupations and causes that now shape the agendas of all the main political parties and the governments that they form.

Summary

We have seen that the new middle class has expanded strongly since the mid-twentieth century. During this growth, the middle class has become more diverse in ethnic and gender composition, and it is equally mixed in terms of its members' social class origins. During the twenty-first century the middle class is likely to remain just as mixed, if not more mixed, in terms of gender and ethnicity, but it will definitely become increasingly self-recruiting. It is only at this stage that any characteristic forms of consciousness and politics are likely to solidify. Perhaps the most important point to grasp about the new middle class is that it is still in formation.

The expansion of middle class career opportunities has exacerbated rather than eased the pressures on the middle classes at work. There is now more competition to get in, then to get on. Middle class payrolls have become more expensive to employers whether public or private sector. So the middle class has been deeply affected by cost-cutting and delayering. Promotions now have to be earned. Linear career tracks have snapped. Yet despite all this, chances of career success have not diminished and, if anything, the rewards today are better than ever.

We have seen that there are divisions within the middle class – by levels, between managers and professionals, those in the public and private sectors, and by lifestyle. But we have also seen that these divisions often pale into insignificance when set against the split between the entire middle class on the one hand and the working class on the other. Divisions within the middle class will affect, but will not necessarily impede the development of, a characteristic consciousness and political proclivities.

It is already possible to identify typical middle class pre-occupations – to maintain a 'service' relationship with their employers and opportunities for career progress, and that merit (signalled, above all else, by qualifications) should be properly rewarded. Middle class pre-occupations are not diametrically opposed to, but they are different from, working class interests. The contemporary middle class is not particularly conservative. Some sections are extremely radical. What characterizes all sections is their ability to make their voices heard. Middle class causes, and personnel, have been obliterating other voices. While the working class has shrunk and become disorganized, the trends in the middle class are exactly the reverse.

The Upper Class

7

Introduction

This chapter is not primarily about the aristocracy. They feature because they are part of the present-day upper class, and their importance extends far beyond attracting tourists and offering quaint reminders of olde England. Yet the aristocracy is not the core of the present-day upper class. Wealth is at the core – serious wealth that can be put to productive use and which can expand itself (see Box 7.1).

The first section deals with the creation of Britain's present-day upper class which occurred through a fusion between aristocratic land-owners and the nineteenth century's nouveaux riches – the leading industrialists, traders and bankers.

The next section analyses how ownership and control have subsequently been depersonalized during the growth of large, limited liability companies, the development of City (of London) intermediaries between private investors and the ultimate destinations of their investments, and the more recent merger of British-based wealth into a trans-national upper or capitalist class.

The following two sections deal with arguments which assert either that a separate upper class no longer exists because wealth has been democratized, or that the owners of wealth have been rendered innocuous by a separation of ownership and control. Both arguments are shown to be plain wrong.

The final two sections outline some distinctive features of Britain's upper class: the inclusion of aristocrats; how the class's integration has been cemented by its use of elite educational institutions, inter-marriage, and a set of exclusive social practices; the upper class's confidence and assertiveness; the extraordinary economic power and political influence that the upper class exercises; and why, although essential in a capitalist economy, the existence of an upper class is inherently and never-endingly controversial.

The old and new upper classes

Britain's upper class has been repeatedly reconstituted. Some of the crucial changes occurred ages ago, while the older middle class, with businessmen and

---

Box 7.1   The rich

There are no USA $ trillionaires. The assets of the world's wealthiest are measured in $billions (1000 millions = a billion, 1000 billions = a trillion). In 2009 the richest person in the world was Bill Gates, the American founder of Microsoft, who was estimated to be worth $40 billion. He was followed closely by another American, Warren Buffet, a professional investor, nicknamed the Sage of Omaha, worth $37 billion.

The richest person in Britain was Lakshmi Mittal, the Indian steel magnate, worth $19 billion. The richest Briton was the Duke of Westminster ($11 billion). Roman Abramovich, the owner of Chelsea football club, whose main residence was in Russia, had estimated assets worth $9 billion. He was among a number of wealthy Russians based mainly or partly in London. Only six out of the 20 richest people in Britain were born in Britain. The country, London in particular, has special attractions for the seriously wealthy. It has more super-rich people than any other European city.

In 2009 nearly all the world's richest people saw their assets reduced in value substantially by the collapse of prices on the world's stock markets (which subsequently recovered). The very rich could lose billions (on paper) without this impacting on their lifestyles. The seriously wealthy really do live in a different world than the rest, 99.9%, of the global population.

In Britain today there are three main ways of becoming seriously rich.

■   Entrepreneurship: the very rich may not have been born poor, but most have been creators as well as controllers of capital.

■   Inheritance.

■   A management or professional career leading to the acquisition of serious wealth.

---

independent professionals at its core (see chapter 6), was still being formed. Other crucial changes, specifically the globalization of capital, and thereby the formation of a unitary global upper class into which British wealth has been partly merged, have occurred more recently.

The aristocracy and the present-day upper class

The aristocracy was the core of Britain's old, pre-industrial upper class. Aristocrats owned land which gave them economic power. They were the economically dominant class in the era when agriculture was the mainstay of the economy. They also had titles which gave them seats in parliament, in the House of Lords, which gave them political power. Everyone knew who was in the aristocracy, and also their precise ranks: the monarch was at the head, followed by dukes, marquesses, earls, viscounts, barons, baronets and knights (whose orders were ranked). The boundary beneath this old upper class was never crystal clear. The gentry and 'society' families were either lesser land-owners or people who could claim kinship, sometimes close, sometimes distant, with someone who was definitely 'in'. Such links always ended within the titled aristocracy. Connections were absolutely crucial to many families' status, but they always needed to be complemented by a genteel way of life in which 'sordid' occupations, as in trade and manufacturing, played no direct part.

By the nineteenth century Britain had industrialists, merchants and bankers whose combined wealth exceeded the aristocracy's, and industry and trade had become the cornerstones of the economy. Britain was not alone in this respect. Throughout Europe the old upper classes were having to yield power. The British way was rather special. Aristocrats were not guillotined. They were not even stripped of their wealth, or their titles, or their seats in parliament. Rather, they became merged with the leading members of the new business classes. Industrialists bought land and were awarded titles. Land-owners dug coal-mines, invested in industry, and especially in 'the City' – the financial institutions which were, and still are, based in the City of London. Old and new money sent its sons to public (independent) schools. It is amazing how little has changed since then. Thus the present-day upper class has retained the status, and many of the privileges, of its predecessor. Hereditary lords retained their right to sit and vote in parliament (in the House of Lords) beyond the end of the twentieth century. Britain still has its traditional honours system. Throughout the nineteenth century and, indeed, up to this present-day, there have been people for whom the big social class issue is whether folk who are just very wealthy, the nouveaux riches, should defer to members of old titled families. This question is unlikely to go away completely even if the monarchy is abolished. It can still take generations for families to cement themselves in upper class networks. There are few members of Britain's ethnic minorities in the upper class. Discrimination apart, to be accepted socially, people need to have been to the right schools and universities, to have close connections with other upper class families, and to share their lifestyle. Caution over admission to its inner-circles has been one of the upper class's strategies for survival. However the distinction between old and new money is the really burning class issue of our present time only for the minute proportion of the population that is either titled or very wealthy.

The modern upper class, like any other modern class, is defined by its work and market situations. These are very distinctive. The distinctive work situation is employing other people, usually not directly and personally nowadays, but indirectly and impersonally. The distinctive market situation is having one's life-chances depend not on the sale of one's labour power and associated skills and knowledge, but the returns on one's capital investments. One would expect such distinctive work and market situations to give rise to equally distinctive forms of consciousness and political proclivities, and there is abundant evidence of such a consciousness and proclivities.

Identifying the upper class

It is pointless to try to identify members of the upper class routinely in survey research. They do not all have noble titles. So there is no point in including an upper class in class schemes that are intended for use in this type of investigation. 'How much are you worth?' is not a useful survey question. Many people do not know. Another problem is that the assets of the very wealthy are often held in trusts, so even an honest answer to the above question could result in mis-classification. It is possible to conduct surveys which do establish how much individuals are worth, but this takes pages of questions. It is not as straight-forward as, 'What is your occupation?'

People can be asked whether they own the businesses where they work, and how large the businesses are, but most 'capitalists' thereby identified are either managers with significant shareholdings (though very small as proportions of the companies' total worth) or proprietors of small-to-medium-sized enterprises (Marshall et al, 1988). The very wealthy, the core members of the upper class, are submerged. Even with huge samples, the numbers of very wealthy respondents would be too small to analyse, even if they could be easily identified. The upper class needs to be studied in other ways. Inheritance and other tax data, and share registers, are useful sources of information. Published information about com-pany directors, supplemented by whatever can be learnt about their backgrounds from *Who's Who* and similar publications, and from interviews and question-naires, are also useful (see Scott, 1997; Scott and Griff, 1984). We do in fact know a great deal about Britain's upper class, albeit from investigations using rather dif-ferent research methods than those routinely employed in studying other classes.

Most of the active members of the upper class (those who sit on company boards, and in the House of Lords) are males. This is a male dominated class even though there are more or less just as many wealthy women as wealthy men. Traditional gender divisions are more entrenched within the upper class than in any other section of the population. Ownership of wealth is usually spread around within families, partly as a way of reducing tax liabilities, but it is also in the families' interest to pool their wealth when converting it into power, and the family 'representatives' who exercise this power are nearly all men. Titles still pass to the eldest son. Females may be wealthy individuals in their own right, but convention dictates that males control the wealth. The upper class is skilled at marginalizing women from their own property. Needless to say, women play important roles within and for the upper class. They sit on the boards of charities, and on other local and national committees. They orches-trate the upper class's social occasions. It is quite rare, even today, for women to chair the boards of companies in which their families' wealth is invested, or to seek seats in parliament.

The upper class has an unrivalled record of inter-generational stability. Many families have retained their positions since pre-industrial times (Scott, 1982). Considering its small size (less than one per cent of the population) the upper class has a remarkable level of inter-generational continuity. Roughly a third of Britain's 300 wealthiest individuals have titles (Rojek, 2000). It is still the case that inheritance is a common way in which individuals become seri-ously wealthy, though those concerned may add substantially to the relatively modest assets that they inherit. As we have seen (Box 7.1), the very wealthiest individuals are worth thousands of millions (that is, billions) of dollars (and pounds also). There is no way in which such sums can be saved, even from top managers' salaries.

The upper class is, in fact, Britain's best example of a well-formed class, both as a demographic entity, and in terms of its level of internal social organization which enables the class to act effectively in accordance with its interests. However, the upper class is not, and never has been, a closed group. It has recruited new blood constantly. Some people become seriously wealthy by developing what started off as micro-enterprises. Others acquire such wealth as a result of (very) successful middle class careers. Nowadays there are others who become extremely wealthy by lottery (literally).

Empowerment

The position and power of the modern upper class derive ultimately from ownership and control over productive resources. The members of the upper class set their own, and, directly or indirectly, everyone else's terms and conditions of employment. They decide which businesses will expand and which will close, and whose jobs will remain and whose will end. Yet the upper class are not reviled people. This is because their own hands usually stay clean: their power is exercised through intermediaries – the middle class of managers and professional people.

The power of the upper class is consolidated and enhanced through its ability to act as a class, through its members' relationships with one another which arise basically from the structure of their ownership and control of productive resources. There is no official or unofficial class governing body, but there are several bodies that operate in lieu (see below). And in recent times the upper class has been able to tilt the balance of power in its favour to an even greater extent than formerly.

The upper class has been able to control how new technology has been developed and used. This technology enhances owners' ability to exercise surveillance over their organizations, their direct employees, and other people who are contracted to act on their behalf. The owners of capital have also driven globalization. Capital moves more easily across national boundaries than any other resource. There are institutions and procedures which can transfer capital almost instantly and effortlessly. There are agents of the upper class, trans-national companies and financial institutions, that are able to act globally. Globalization is not so obviously in the interests of any other class.

All present-day governments need to listen to the requirements of capital. The upper classes have guaranteed access to influential politicians in virtually all countries. They can sponsor political parties and politicians who they favour, just as they can choose to invest in countries where their property is secure and will work productively for them.

In Britain the upper class retains its connections with, and the prestige that is still attached to, the aristocracy. The upper class can command the attention and attendance of other celebrities, as can the upper classes in other countries, but the British upper class has additional, traditional cultural resources at its disposal. These relationships, with the very wealthy at their core, comprise what is sometimes called 'the establishment' or 'the old boy network'. The relationships protect and consolidate the upper class. This class is not in decline. It has never been as confident and as powerful as it is today.

The depersonalization of ownership and control

Most members of the upper class are rarely seen in public acting out their roles as owners and controllers of wealth. Rupert Murdock and Richard Branson are exceptions. This slice of business life is usually publicized only in the financial pages of newspapers, and the reporting usually attributes actions and events to institutions and markets rather than individuals or a class of real people. Names are sometimes named, but the upper class's high profile appearances on the public stage are typically at celebrity events, and when meeting government ministers, possibly to discuss investment plans. The upper class often appears to be doing the rest of us a favour, sometimes by its members' mere presence. John Scott (1997) has argued that the ownership and control of productive assets have been thoroughly depersonalized, which is the principal reason why many people today doubt the existence of a powerful upper class.

In detail, how industry is owned and controlled, and the manner in which ownership rights are exercised, and how these have changed over time, are complex tales, but the main features and trends are very simple.

Personal ownership and control

In the early days of industrial capitalism most enterprises were small. This applied to metal factories, cotton mills, shipping companies and banks, though there were exceptions, like the merchant companies which were chartered by the crown and were granted rights not just to trade, but also, in effect, to rule the expanding British Empire. However, in most British-based companies there was a personal owner, a Mr Gradgrind, who everyone in the firm knew because Mr Gradgrind was at the works every day. He ran everything. Workers knew who the boss was. He hired, supervised and fired them. Workers also knew what was happening to the profits from their work. They could see how the Gradgrind family lived.

Managers

When successful companies grew beyond a certain size it became impossible for a single owner to run everything. In addition to office staff who helped with the bookkeeping, it became necessary to employ professionals and managers to supervise the technology, to develop and maintain appropriate accounting systems, and to actually run the works. This is the private sector origin of the new middle class that now accounts for around two-fifths of the workforce. Everyone still knew that the factory belonged to Mr Gradgrind, but the boss who hired, supervised and sacked them would usually be a salaried manager. He was one of 'them', and often the target for all the workers' ill-feelings. Most of Mr Gradgrind's own public appearances could be as a benefactor – opening a civic park on land that he had donated, maybe a civic theatre, and hosting the works' christmas party, for instance. As his daily presence was no longer necessary, Mr Gradgrind could live further away, maybe in a mock stately home built in the surrounding countryside.

Joint-stock companies

For companies to grow beyond another certain size, there needed to be more than one investor. Even persons with sufficient wealth to own a giant company would probably prefer to spread their risks. Joint-stock, limited liability companies make this possible. Here ownership is split between numerous stockholders – dozens, hundreds or even thousands. Each risks no more than his or her personal investment. So no-one need risk their entire fortune in just one business. People may purchase shares in dozens, even hundreds, of enterprises. Once this happens, owners become faceless. Workers may not, probably do not, know precisely who they are working for. The owners become a depersonalized body of shareholders.

Intermediaries

Since the Second World War matters have become much more complicated. We have entered an ongoing era of mergers, takeovers and demergers. Few joint-stock companies have been unaffected. Sometimes a stronger business absorbs a weaker firm. Sometimes two strong firms merge for mutual advantage. An acquiring company may absorb its acquisition. Or the acquired firm may be left intact, with the purchasing company acting as the corporate owner. Some acquisitions may be within the same industry, or a company may decide to diversify, in which case it becomes a conglomerate. A subsidiary firm itself may acquire a third company. It may purchase the entire business or just a proportion of the shares. Other shares may be held by yet another company. Large firms are constantly acquiring bits of others and selling parts of themselves.

The largest companies today operate internationally, with sites in more than one country. They may buy existing companies located in different countries to where the parents are based. Some giant multi-nationals have turnovers in excess of the governments' budgets in some of the world's smaller states. This can give the companies extraordinary power. They can switch production to countries with the cheapest or most compliant labour. They can switch their profits to the countries with the lowest taxes on such earnings. And it can be difficult to identify exactly who is commanding, and benefiting from, this power.

Another type of indirect ownership is via financial intermediaries – the City (of London) firms, which themselves are likely to have branches throughout the world, that handle investments for banks, countries, pension funds, companies and individuals. Around 60 per cent of the shares quoted on the London Stock Exchange are now held by financial institutions, usually on behalf of clients. Using the City in this way makes sense. The people who work there specialize in making investments to obtain the required returns. Why do it yourself when expert (and very well-rewarded) professional help is available?

Most investments are speculative; they are made in the hope of making a short-term financial gain. Globally, every single day, around $25 trillion is invested on financial markets. Only around one per cent of this total is new investment (or disinvestment). Ninety-nine per cent of these capital flows are searching for marginally better financial returns, probably through short-term capital gains. This also applies in currency markets. Every day $1.3 trillion is spent purchasing currencies. Two-thirds of these purchases are held for less than seven days (Robinson and Harris, 2000). The prices of all commodities where most sales and purchases are speculative (in this case shares in companies and currencies) are liable to fluctuate sharply, upwards or downwards, in response to rumour or what is termed 'investor confidence'.

The upshot of all the business that is conducted by intermediaries is that many people today have no idea who they work for. Exactly whose money is a merchant bank investing? Consumers rarely know who owns the firms from which they purchase goods and services. It was different in the past. Everyone knew that the clogs were made at Mr Gradgrind's factory.

Some people do know exactly who owns what. City personnel and financial journalists need to know, certainly within the business sectors in which they specialize. It is their job to know who owns what, who is buying and who is selling. This applies even more so to the active members of the upper class. The information is not secret, but it has become a specialist body of knowledge, a bit like nuclear physics. People work for, and consumers buy from, impersonal firms. Decisions on investment which create and abolish jobs are taken (so it appears) by impersonal organizations, or even by blind market forces.

For present purposes there is no need to name names, but the crucial point is that at the end of the chains of subsidiaries and parent companies, merchant banks and private equity, hedge and investment funds, there are always private individuals who own the wealth. A few adopt high profiles. Personal ownership and control are not entirely things of the past. But most wealthy individuals do not expose themselves in this way. Decisions appear to be taken by, and in the interests of, impersonal businesses.

Business can appear to be in everyone's interest. Government assistance to business can appear to benefit all concerned. So it does not seem to be extremely wealthy individuals who request governments, and tax-payers, to subsidize their investments. There was a time when no-one would have thought it possible that workers (who pay taxes) could be persuaded to pay for their own jobs. This is exactly what happens when governments 'bail out' failing businesses whether these are shipyards, car manufacturers or banks.

Globalization and capital

During the twentieth century the City of London became far and away England's premier financial centre, and then the entire UK's main centre when Scotland's leading banks widened their operations. The Royal Bank of Scotland acquired the NatWest, while the Bank of Scotland took over the Halifax, which became HBOS, which itself was absorbed into Lloyds/TSB in 2008. Earlier on, independent banks based in English regions (District and National Provincial, for example), that had raised capital within and serviced businesses and private customers in their regions, were merged into the main London-based banks. This was at the time when companies that had been owned and run by individuals and families with roots in particular cities and regions were becoming joint-stock companies, quoted on the London Stock Exchange. In this way financial and industrial capital became fused together, and the entire upper class's wealth was mixed in the same national 'pot'. Then, by the end of the twentieth century, along with the assets of the rich in other countries, UK capital was being internationalized, thus making its owners and controllers part of a global capitalist class.

Trans-national companies

One key process has been the formation and growth of trans-national businesses, which are different creatures than businesses with bases in specific countries, from which they are controlled and regulated, but which also operate overseas. Global or trans-national businesses raise capital and hire staff at all levels, including top executives, from all over the world. They are global, cosmopolitan corporate citizens. They manufacture wherever is most cost-effective (wage costs and compliant labour are likely to be among the considerations). They are able to arrange their internal financial affairs so that profits are taken (though not necessarily made) in countries where corporate taxes are low. They are able to site headquarters and to bank assets in countries where disclosure requirements are modest (and therefore secrecy can be maintained), and where governments apply light-touch regulation. These businesses operate largely beyond the control of national governments though, of course, businesses have to respect national laws within all the countries where they operate.

Financial globalization

This has been the second key globalizing process. It is the outcome of a series of developments. Free movement of capital (and labour, goods and services) was a foundation principle of the European Union (in the Treaty of Rome, 1957). Today information technology allows money to be transferred instantly from any point to point not just within Europe, but throughout the entire world. This has made it possible for traders in any country to be in real-time contact with markets in all other major economies.

However, a crucial development in Britain was the deregulation of the City of London (and financial services more generally) in the 1980s. The 'big bang' occurred in 1986 when a series of regulations were scrapped. These included fixed commissions and the distinction between stockjobbers and stockbrokers, opening London trading to foreign-based banks and other financial services, allowing formerly distinct banks and other kinds of financial institutions to cross into each other's territory (banks and building societies, for example), and deregulating banks' ability to create credit. This made London a more attractive trading centre than New York, albeit only temporarily, because New York soon introduced similar 'reforms'. However, an outcome was a growing share of all global financial transactions being channelled through London, and thus 'the City' expanded physically beyond its traditional 'square mile'. It spread onto the Isle of Dogs with spectacular office developments such as Canary Wharf. The competitive regimes in London and New York led to the creation of new financial products (so-called derivatives, for example), and new private equity businesses and hedge funds were created. Tokyo deregulated in 2001 and consolidated its position in the trio of global financial centres, attracting money from, and moving money to, all parts of the world.

The deregulation that eventually proved 'toxic' was the ability to create credit. This fuelled a bubble in primary asset prices (mainly company shares and housing). Like all bubbles, this one eventually burst: defaults in the sub-prime mortgage market in the USA in 2007 spread a credit crunch throughout the international banking system through which risks had been spread via derivatives, thus triggering the global recession that began in 2008.

By then another outcome of deregulation had been the escalation to spectacular levels (some say obscene levels) of financial rewards in certain city occupations. City banking used to be a dull, secure, decently paid (but never very well paid) occupation. What happened? City firms make money by charging clients commission when assets or transactions are managed. Commission rates can be low in percentage terms but the sums mount up when transactions and assets are measured in millions of dollars or pounds. Banks and other City firms also invest their own funds (with money that may be borrowed from other financial institutions) in search of capital gains (possible for all when credit is inflating asset prices). Nevertheless, it is skilled work, not really a casino. Traders need to really know the markets in which they operate. Successful staff can move between employers who need to pay the 'going rate', and this applies when governments wish to incorporate financial expertise into their civil services.

The key point for present purposes is another outcome – capital has become global. The owners of capital, of course, remain citizens of particular countries and their lives can still be led locally. They are not necessarily cosmopolitan,

---

Box 7.2   Executives of the global capitalist class

The main executives of global capital (the top echelons of an emergent global middle class) are the following:

- Top executives in trans-national companies and financial institutions.
- Key politicians and civil servants who insert their countries into the global economy via a discourse of national competitiveness.
- Professional and technocratic elites that create benchmarking systems (such as World Best Practices) to measure the performance of national businesses against global yardsticks, and thereby impose intense discipline on national workforces. These elites also perform essential ideological work in persuading the global population that business is good for humanity. This work includes transforming 'limits to growth' into 'sustainable development', and 'conservation' into 'environmental challenges'.
- Elites in the supra-national organizations that govern the global economy (the World Bank, International Monetary Fund, World Trade Organization, the European Union etc). Just as national economies can operate only within 'rules of law', so the global economy needs a set of rules and mechanisms to enforce them. This is where there are intense debates among the executives of global capitalism. Exactly how much regulation should there be, and what should be the rules? The implosion of the international financial system in 2008 demonstrated the need for a new global financial 'architecture'.

See Robinson and Harris, 2000; Sklair, 2000, 2001.

---

global citizens. It is their wealth that is pooled, not the ultimate owners themselves. This is the basis, but only the basis, for the formation of a global capitalist class. The class needs to be organized so that it can act collectively, in its class interests. Box 7.2 explains how this is being accomplished.

All capitalists now?

The above sections have referred to an upper class comprising less than one per cent of the UK population – extremely wealthy individuals, some titled, some politically active, a larger number well-known in business networks, but many living as rich but otherwise obscure private citizens – who share an ability to live comfortably on their investments, and whose life-chances hinge primarily on how they deploy their wealth. We need to consider an alternative view: that the idea of wealth and power being so concentrated is hopelessly outdated. For example: 'It is simply not possible today to draw a clear distinction between a class of "capitalists" who own all the country's productive resources, and a class of "workers" who own nothing, for most workers have a direct or indirect financial stake in capitalist enterprises, and most companies are owned directly or indirectly by millions of workers' (Saunders and Harris, 1994, p1). So do we all benefit nowadays from our ability to exploit the best investment opportunities that are available in any part of the world, or have fund managers make such investments on our behalf?

Saunders and Harris notwithstanding, there are few British sociologists who dispute the existence of a separate upper class, but, outside sociology, most people either deny that one exists or have grossly mistaken ideas about its character. Political leaders rarely argue in class terms. The media (mostly in upper class ownership) are inoffensive. We have been told for decade after decade that wealth and power have been democratized. Everyone knows that there are some extremely wealthy individuals, but we are told that we should be grateful to them for generating such wealth and keeping it in Britain. The preservation of noble titles is presented as rather quaint and probably useful to us all since the aristocracy and their stately homes attract tourists who are good for the economy, and therefore for all of us.

Over the years a number of serious arguments have in fact been put forward denying the existence of a separate powerful and wealthy upper class. We can start with Saunders and Harris's claim that all, or most of us, are capitalists now.

The spread of wealth

It is certainly true that in Britain wealth is now spread around much more widely than a century ago, and that far more than one per cent of the population own shares in companies. Personal share-owning rose substantially in the 1980s and 90s when a series of nationalized industries were privatized, and shares were offered for sale to their employees and the general public. Roughly a fifth of the adult population bought shares. When building societies converted themselves into banks, shares were issued to most of their existing members, the savers and borrowers, millions of people in total. Of course, some immediately sold their shares and took a pure windfall, a quick capital gain, but many held on. The government-authorized ISA (individual savings account) has encouraged more widespread share ownership. The net effect was that at the end of the 1990s 17 per cent of all adults held shares.

Other forms of wealth are even more widespread. As the population has become more prosperous, more people have saved regularly. Sometimes their savings are in banks and building societies, but it has become increasingly common for savings to be placed in 'unit trusts' where purchasers buy units in trust funds that are invested in many companies thereby enabling small investors to spread their risks.

However, a more significant development from the point of view of democratizing wealth is that over a half of all employees are now in occupational pension schemes. A smaller number have personal pension funds. The sums accumulated in these ways can be considerable. For example, a person with lifetime earnings averaging £27,000 a year (typical male earnings in 2009), whose personal and employer contributions to a pension fund amounted to 15 per cent of his or her income, would have £162,000 invested over a 40 year working life, by the end of which there would have been considerable capital appreciation because most of the funds would be invested in company shares. Obviously, the sums vary depending on the levels of individuals' earnings and contributions, but over a half of the population invest substantial sums in pension funds, or have such sums invested on their behalf, and their financial circumstances in retirement, which can last for many years nowadays, depend on the performance of these investments.

The types of assets that are in fact held most widely are goods with a market value, mainly houses and motor cars, though some people also own art and antiques, and the furniture in people's homes has some value.

When all forms of wealth are taken into account, we see that, over time, wealth has indeed become distributed much more widely and equally through-out the population. So in 1911 the most wealthy one per cent of the popula-tion held 69 per cent of all personally held wealth, whereas by 2003 it was just 21 per cent – a truly massive drop. Some of the redistribution has been within the top end of the wealth scale. So the proportion of personally held assets held by the top 10 per cent decreased less steeply, from 92 per cent in 1911 to 53 per cent in 2003 (Office for National Statistics). Clearly, there is some truth in the view that wealth has been spread around and is no longer confined to a small capitalist class, though even in 2003 10 per cent of the population still commanded just over a half of all personally-held wealth. Even after all the redistribution – the spread of home and car ownership, ISAs, privatizations and building society conversions – wealth is still heavily concentrated. We are certainly not all capitalists now. In 2003 the least wealthy half of the popula-tion owned just seven per cent of all personally held wealth. Around 25 per cent of adults do not own the dwellings in which they live. Nearly a half of all employees do not have significant occupational pensions. In fact a half of the population has near-zero assets. Many are in debt when account is taken of outstanding mortgages, bank overdrafts, hire purchase commitments, loans on credit cards, store cards and all the rest. It is only roughly a half of the popula-tion that has any significant share in the country's wealth.

Wealth, investments and life-chances

Fifty per cent or thereabouts of the population with investments in productive assets, either directly or on their behalf, supports the Saunders and Harris view that capitalists are no longer a tiny class. But the fact that many workers have some assets, and that many capitalists also work (see below), does not neces-sarily prove that there is no longer a glaring class division between them.

First, we need to separate assets that people acquire for their own use (houses and cars, for example), and assets that are held primarily to make a gain or derive an income. Works of art and antiques, and vintage or just 'classic' cars, may be purchased as investments, but this is not how most people regard their home furnishings and motor vehicles. Home-owners can make capital gains, but this is not their main reason for buying their dwellings. We should note, however (see below), that the attractions of home-ownership include the acquisition of an asset which may, eventually, become wealth that cascades down the generations. Most cars depreciate, whereas most houses at least retain their original real value.

Second, there is a difference between, on the one hand, savings which transfer spending power from the time when the money was earned to some later point in life, like retirement, and, on the other hand, assets whose primary use is capital accumulation and/or the generation of a flow of income that need never be exhausted. People who become quite wealthy in terms of the sums invested on their behalf in pension funds do not expect, and cannot realistically hope, to keep most of this wealth intact throughout retirement. It is only the extremely wealthy who can expect to die without having liquidated most of their capital. We must note, however (again, see below), that the size of the pensions that roughly a half of the working population will receive, depends primarily on the performance of stock exchange investments. It is not only the very wealthy who now have a vested interest in growth rates, and rates of return on, productive assets.

Third, and perhaps most crucially, the crunch question in respect of class membership is what a person's life-chances depend upon. For most people, the types of housing that they can afford, and the amounts that they are able to save towards retirement, depend on their incomes from employment. We should note that as more and more wealth cascades down the generations, more and more people's types of housing, and the sums that they can afford to keep as investments, will depend on how much they inherit as well as how much they earn. This will widen rather than narrow class differences within the employed population (those outside the upper class), and strengthen inter-generational continuity within these employee classes, though it may well blur the class division between the very wealthy and the rest.

Similarly, whether people have been able to benefit from privatizations, building society conversions, and ISAs, has depended primarily on their earned incomes. In most cases these investments have not become principal determinants of their life-chances: the investors continue to depend basically on how much they are able to earn.

The proportion of the population with sufficient wealth to make it unnecessary for them to work for someone else, or for themselves in the conventional sense, and who are able to allow their capital to grow rather than deplete it during their lifetimes, is still less than one per cent. The life-chances of this section of the population depend on their ability to employ others to work for them. Other people's (the vast majority's) life-chances depend on the kinds of employment that they can obtain. Despite the spread of wealth, this remains a clear class relationship and division. It is, in fact, the clearest of all class divisions, and it still splits the population into a tiny minority on the one side, and the great mass of the people on the other.

Consciousness and politics

The spread of wealth may not have turned 50 per cent of the population into capitalists, but it may still affect their consciousness and politics. Their stock exchange investments may not be the main factor in the life-chances of most of the 17 per cent of the population who are direct share-owners, but these investments could make a disproportionate impression on the consciousness of many of those concerned. Nearly a half of the middle class has such investments. They account for most of the 17 per cent. The privatizations and building society conversions have not bred a generation of working class Sids but they have given the middle class another ground for perceiving their own interests as basically similar to those of people above. Owning shares, however small the investment, may encourage people to read share prices regularly, and to pay attention to the standard stock exchange item on the broadcast news. A rising stock market possibly makes them feel good, just like rising house prices (provided people have already bought their dwellings).

Peter Saunders and Colin Harris (1994) have speculated that the extent to which share-owning had been widened may have won the 1992 general election for the Conservatives. Their argument is plausible. In 1992 Labour was threatening to restore many of the privatized businesses into some form of public ownership or control. The Saunders and Harris argument is that share-owners may have voted Conservative in order to protect their investments, while few people would have voted Labour through a desire to re-nationalize. The 1992 election was closely fought. It is just possible that this particular issue made the crucial difference. It is unlikely that any party that is perceived as anti-business will poll well among people who are direct share-owners.

While it is true that home-ownership does not make those concerned into capitalists, it may well affect their perceptions of their positions in society. The renovations and customizing, which make it clear which properties on council estates have been privatized, must be saying something about the occupants' feelings. We know that the transition from being a tenant to being a home-owner rarely changes people's class identities or politics in the short-term. Occupational class tends to determine types of housing, social consciousness and politics. Housing is rarely the crucial independent variable (see Forrest and Murie, 1987; Forrest et al, 1990; Saunders, 1990; Wait, 1996). But this will not prevent home-ownership making some long-term difference to how the residents view themselves vis-a-vis others. Dwellings are different from most other assets. They are bought for use but are like substantial stock exchange portfolios in that people have realistic chances of leaving these assets to their descendants. This does not always happen. People may need to sell their dwellings in order to provide income during retirement, especially if they need residential care. No wealth automatically cascades down, and increases in value, from generation to generation. However, the risk that assets might be dissipated may make those concerned all the keener to hold on, and to support policies and politicians who seek to assist people to retain their possessions. It may make people hostile to the very principle of inheritance tax. Members of other classes have been given, or have given themselves, sound material reasons for supporting policies which also enable the upper class to hang on to its assets.

Ownership and control

The managerial revolution

As an alternative to contending that a wealthy class no longer exists because wealth is now spread around more equally than in the past, it has been claimed that the wealthy can no longer harm anyone because private wealth no longer confers power. This is very long-standing argument. It is partly about politics – the widening of the franchise beyond the propertied classes – but it is mainly about who runs privately-owned businesses. Here the argument dates back to the time when joint-stock, limited liability status was becoming the norm for large enterprises. Researchers counted the number of companies where the share of the largest stockholder dipped beneath 50 per cent. These companies, which quickly became the majority, were deemed to have fallen into management control (Berle and Means, 1932).

The argument is straight-forward. It observes that in most joint-stock companies the share-owners are too numerous and too dispersed for them to act as a governing cabal. Also, most owners spread their risks by investing in numerous companies. It would not be possible for them to take the time and trouble to try to become experts in the affairs of them all. Rational investors, it is argued, will leave the management of the companies that they own in the hands of the real experts – professionals with specialist expertise and managers who really know the nuts-and-bolts of the businesses.

The second part of the argument alleges that salaried managers will not run businesses in exactly the same way as the owners. To be sure, investors have to be given satisfactory returns on their investments – sufficient to persuade them to leave their money in the businesses. Beyond this, however, the managers have no need to worry, or so it is said. They do not need to generate the highest possible returns on capital. They are likely to be as concerned to satisfy other 'stakeholders', like the workforces whose co-operation they require. And, of course, the managers will want to enhance their own terms and conditions of employment. In addition to all other considerations, it is argued that professional managers will operate companies within the requirements of the law, and will be responsive to the wishes and policies of the government of the day, unlike owners, such as the petit bourgeoisie (see chapter 5), who characteristically complain and do everything possible to sidestep bureaucracy.

In the 1930s managerialism was an exciting development. James Burnham's *The Managerial Revolution* was first published in 1941. All his major predictions proved wrong. Burnham believed that managers would become a new ruling class, politically dominant, that they would eventually relieve share-owners of their assets, and that fascist Germany and the Soviet Union were prototype manager-run societies. Fortunately for Burnham's reputation, he is best remembered, and became famous, for the phrase in his book's title.

The separation of ownership and control thesis was a sociological orthodoxy by the 1950s. Ralf Dahrendorf (1959) argued that functionalism (then the most influential sociological theory, especially in North America) under-stated the amount of class conflict, but that the main class division was no longer between owners and workers, as Marx had suggested, but between those in authority and those in subordinate positions. Managers were believed to have taken over as the dominant class.

The Labour Party (when it was old Labour) was profoundly influenced by the managerial philosophy. The vehicle that it adopted for taking the means of production into common ownership was the nationalized industry run by a board of management. Alternatives such as workers' and local community control were rejected. The nationalized industries were to be shining examples of efficiency, run by professional managers, appointed for their competence rather than their connections, and unencumbered by the need to pay dividends to share-owners.

By the 1950s a revisionist wing in the Labour Party had decided that ownership had become irrelevant (Crosland, 1956). This idea was less controversial in the social democratic parties of continental Europe than in the British Labour Party at that time. The aim of the so-called 'social market economies' is to use private enterprise to generate the wealth to fund public services, and to pursue whatever other social and economic objectives might be agreed by the 'social partners' – employers and trade unions, acting in collaboration with government. Britain never really embraced the social market, or corporatism as it was being called in Britain by the 1970s. And by then the original idea that the rise of managers had disempowered owners was in tatters.

Owner-power rediscovered

Since the 1970s researchers have been studying exactly who runs joint-stock companies. One result of these studies is that the proportion of a company's shares that needs to be in a single set of hands in order to act as a controlling interest has been revised downwards radically. It has been discovered that a major shareholder with less than 10 per cent of a company's stock can occupy a dominant position if, as is typically the case, most smaller shareholders 'sleep' while the others vote in different ways, or accept the advice of the leading shareholder, on controversial issues.

It has also been discovered that in most companies there is in fact a controlling interest. Sometimes the controlling stock belongs to just one individual. Sometimes it belongs to members of the same family. Sometimes it belongs to a corporate investor or financial institution. Sometimes a 'constellation of interests' act in unison thereby establishing a dominant position (Scott, 1997).

Another discovery is that some shareholders are highly active. It is true that the majority neither attend company meetings nor submit postal votes, but some are active, always including the dominant interest. Those who are active act in the interests of shareholders in general, which is why so many are prepared to 'sleep'. Owners, or their representatives, usually occupy key positions on company boards, such as chairperson (Francis, 1980; Scott, 1997).

We know that a single person, a dominant shareholder, can control all strategic decisions even in a large company that operates globally. NewsCorp (Rupert Murdock's business) is a holding company that in 2007 had 1445 subsidiaries on five continents. It has interests in television, cable, satellite, books and newspapers. By occupying key positions at 'nodes' in the web of businesses, the practices of this entire empire can be coordinated. As well as being able to exploit the opportunities that are normally available to trans-nationals (taking profits where taxes are low, and basing operations where regulation is light) it is possible to use a media empire to exert political leverage via editorial policies. Such leverage is very likely to be used to try to influence media legislation (see Arsenault and Castells, 2008).

Studies of business decision-making have shown that who *takes* decisions can be irrelevant. Salaried managers may decide which new machines to install, which products to develop, and which staff to hire and fire, but they do so in a context where they know that they will be judged by the implications for profitability and the market value of a company's shares. In this sense, decisions are already *made* before managers settle the technical details and put them into effect. Boards of directors, on which owners invariably play a dominant role, or have someone else play such a role on their behalf, fix the parameters within which salaried managers operate (Herman, 1981). Company law in Britain requires boards of directors to act in share-owners' interests, and no-one else's. Managers are rewarded if their performances produce dividends (literally) and they are penalized for failure. An American study found that company profitability (or rather the lack of this) was the best predictor of management dismissals (James and Soref, 1981).

Company boards usually ensure that top managers' interests are aligned with those of the shareholders. A commonly-used device is the stock option: the right to purchase a given number of shares up to a specified date at a pre-fixed price. This gives managers a powerful incentive to run a business so as to ensure that the market price of the shares advances well-beyond what their own purchases will cost. Their salaries, bonuses and stock options can make top managers into extremely wealthy individuals. The costs to existing shareholders are minute. The total value of a company's shares is hardly diluted, and the astronomical salaries and bonuses paid to a few key managers are a minor cost when set against total turnover and profits. Owners would be foolish not to ensure that any managers with real power know whose side they are on.

When one company owns another, the managers of the parent company usually act as if they were personal owners. The evidence suggests that they enjoy this role-play. Pressure on the subsidiaries' managers to deliver are magnified (Windolf, 1998). All the managers stand to gain, but the group that benefits most is the shareholders.

Management buy-outs are rarely what the phrase suggests. Most of the capital to purchase a company is invariably from outside investors. The managers who are part of the buy-out consortium will be required to invest substantial savings of their own, and may well be given additional stock options. It is a splendid vehicle for ensuring that a business is run in the interests of its (mostly absentee) owners (Campbell et al, 1992).

Owners and managers in the class structure

Managers have not been revolutionaries. They run businesses more effectively on the owners' behalf than would the latter if left entirely to themselves. The relationship between the upper class and the middle class is crucial in the contemporary class structure. The upper class needs managers and professionals. Large modern corporations could not be run without them. The businesses need expertise that the owners themselves could rarely supply. The owners also need managers and professionals to control other classes of employees.

Up to now the middle class has offered more than enough willing accomplices. They want to be committed to their organizations and professions. They want careers, and a condition for long-range ascent is accepting a service relationship with the upper class, though few may see their roles in exactly these terms. The rewards for managers and professionals can be considerable: they range up to assimilation into the ranks of the seriously wealthy. There is no fence across the boundary between the upper class and the middle class.

Yet as we saw in chapter 6, there is considerable discontent within the present-day middle class. If this was ever transformed into economic radicalism, the class structure really would be threatened.

British capitalism

Every capitalist country has an upper class within which privately-owned wealth is concentrated. However, there are inter-country differences even in this era of globalization, and some specifics of the British upper class are noteworthy.

Aristocrats included

We have already noted that Britain's modern upper class was formed by a nineteenth century merger of the old upper class, the aristocracy, and the emergent business-based upper class. One result has been that the modern upper class has retained much of the status that was attached to the aristocracy. Another is that Britain never experienced an industrial cultural revolution, and a gentlemanly ethic was maintained in the higher echelons of businesses, which, according to one school of thought, has been a persistent millstone for the British economy (see Weiner, 1981).

In some ways the aristocracy is an irrelevance, a distraction. They are not the core, and they are not essential for the maintenance of a modern upper class. However, aristocratic connections add some 'real class' to Britain's uppers, and they give the entire upper class a circuit of social events where they can all meet people who they need to know. Its visible lifestyle gives the upper class a benign public image while setting them in a world apart. It is a world in which the start of grouse, partridge and pheasant shooting, but no longer stag and fox hunting, are significant dates, and likewise the Derby, the Grand National, Royal Ascot, the Cheltenham Gold Cup, Wimbledon, Hurlingham, Henley, Cowes, the Eton-Harrow cricket match, the Oxford-Cambridge boat race, Chelsea Flower Show, Queen Charlotte's and the rest of the London and county balls. Now it is true that it is unnecessary to be either rich or titled to attend some of these events, but invitations are required to be in the right places, like the royal enclosures. There are other events and places where the seriously wealthy can meet each other without intrusion – conferences of the Institute of Directors, the Confederation of British Industry, London clubs, the Lord Mayor's Banquet, and city lunches to which top politicians are invited (and they attend). There are some leisure activities which exclude all but the very rich – those who can afford to buy ocean racing vessels and racing horses, fly first class, stay in five-star hotels, and spend vacations at exclusive resorts and maybe on privately-owned islands. The aristocratic circuit adds to the number, and adds gloss to the calendar. Britain is a rather good place to be upper class. This will be among the attractions to rich foreigners, alongside the favourable tax regime for those able to live and work in Britain while claiming non-domiciled status, plus access to London City institutions (see Sassen, 1991).

At this point it is necessary to avoid creating an impression that the present-day uppers are a spendthrift leisure class. There are some men, and rather more upper class women, whose lives revolve around social occasions, but the core members of today's upper class have work as their central life interest. Nowadays they do not abstain from labour. Rather, they have embraced the work ethic. They have full diaries which may include business breakfasts in addition to lunches and dinners. They are not idle rich. Indeed, a typical lifestyle problem is 'finding the time'. They do not attend most of the events in the upper class social calendar. It is more a matter of being able to attend if and when they wish, or, more likely, when doing so will be good for business (see Rojek, 2000).

Most wealthy individuals are inconspicuous. You may not have heard of Anar Agarwal, John Fredriksen or Hans Rausing, but they are all among the top 10 billionaires living in Britain. Would you know them in the street? Richard Branson is one of the few seriously rich Britons with a high public profile, but in reality his life is basically work-centred (see Rojek, 2000). He is said to need eight hours sleep but works for virtually all the rest. Sometimes he may snatch naps during the day when en route between meetings. He is well-known for dressing casually and has no expensive gastronomic tastes. For Branson, and in this he appears typical of the modern upper class, work is his main source of fun and excitement. He enjoys the excitement of potentially rewarding but risky ventures, as in air and rail transport. Branson also indulges in intense bursts of leisure activity. Here, once again, he appears to be typical of the present-day upper class. Most of Branson's leisure is not high profile. He has a Caribbean island and a mansion in Oxfordshire as well as a home in London, but without doubt he is best-known for his attempts on trans-Atlantic water-borne records and long-distance hot air ballooning. These are extremely expensive, and therefore exclusive, leisure activities. For Branson, they are brief interruptions in his normal way of life, just like Cowes and suchlike are for most of the seriously rich who attend.

A well-integrated upper class

Investments by very wealthy individuals criss-cross as they move through the city and into various companies. So directorships also criss-cross. Multiple directorships are the norm among active members of the upper class and their representatives from financial institutions. Most joint-stock companies appear to be related to most others, either directly or indirectly, through this interlocking system of directorships (Whitley, 1973; Scott, 1997). This lays the foundation for an unusually well-integrated British upper class. John Scott (1991) estimates that there are just 43,500 active members of the British upper class. They comprise only 0.1 per cent of the population. Such a small number of people can be well-integrated. Everybody may not know everyone else, but everyone's networks interlock, and the entire class is bound in an exclusive system of interpersonal relationships. Nowadays the British wealthy are integrated into a global capitalist class. Directorships in UK companies interlock, and so do directorships in trans-nationals, and the number of these interlocks is increasing over time (see Kentor and Yong Suk Jang, 2008). The upper class is well-integrated, and its active representatives are powerful. They have strategic control over the economy. All businesses compete, including finance houses, but competition itself can be a source of bonds, and mergers and demergers mean that one can never be certain who one's partners and competitors will be tomorrow.

The social integration of the upper class continues to be cemented through its use of Britain's elite system of public (independent) schools such as Harrow, Eton and Winchester, and these schools' links with Oxford and Cambridge universities. Independent schools educate seven per cent of secondary age pupils but provide about a half of all Oxbridge undergraduates. During an elite education young people are introduced to the social events that help to integrate the upper class. They rub shoulders with one another and also with individuals who will become senior civil servants, judges and army officers. The upper class has personal relationships with key members of key professions, and with politicians, many of whom (in all the main parties), have Oxbridge backgrounds. These relationships are further strengthened by the upper class's tendency to inter-marry, and by the class's distinctive lifestyle (see above), which is possible only if one is rich and properly connected. The British upper class is certainly not disorganized. It is extremely well-organized; by itself, rather than by the state. An effect is to create a body of opinion that is known to, and which can be absorbed by, all insiders. So when members of the upper class deal with government personnel, they are most likely to be speaking for their entire class. This is 'the establishment' to which outsiders can find it so difficult to gain admission, especially if they are not male, white and from the right sort of background.

Assertiveness

Britain's upper class has rarely hesitated before making its views known, and making it clear that it expects its views to be heeded, and since the closing decades of the twentieth century this assertiveness has strengthened.

This characteristic of Britain's upper class will owe something to the confidence that accrues after centuries of unbroken privilege. It is also a consequence of Britain having been the first industrial nation whose original mercantile and industrial creeds were laissez-faire. This has made free markets, in which property-owners alone decide how to deploy their assets, appear to be an almost natural order of things. Assertiveness is also a product of Britain having developed only a weak version of social democracy. Even organized labour, at the zenith of its power, subscribed to much of the laissez-faire creed (free collective bargaining, for example).

The confidence of the upper class is also rooted in the closed world that its members inhabit, insulated from challenges to their opinions. They are schooled, work and spend their leisure separately from other citizens. They have very little contact with the working class, even the workers who they (indirectly) employ, their customers, or even small shareholders. It is only occasionally that small shareholders self-organize and force themselves to the attention of the press and company boards, as in the case of 'Cedric the pig', the chair of British Gas in the mid-1990s, who was berated at an annual meeting for his astronomic compensation package before winning the vote (with the support of institutional shareholders). He was followed a decade later by 'Fred the shred', Fred Goodwin, chief executive of the failed Royal Bank of Scotland, who retired with a £700,000 a year pension in 2008, subsequently reduced voluntarily (but under intense public and media pressure) to a mere £350,000. The media are mostly in upper class ownership. The upper class are rarely vilified. Newspaper owners are accustomed to seeing their views in print (though usually without their names attached). They may not dictate to, but they do not expect to be contradicted by, their editors. Politicians usually listen respectfully to actual or potential investors. The higher-rank members of the middle class can be relied on to be compliant and trustworthy. Members of the upper class can exercise extraordinary power within the businesses in which they are major investors. Closed worlds tend to breed closed minds. Hence the apparent arrogance of the upper class when, as occasionally happens, they are exposed to a wider body of contrary opinion.

Occasionally the upper class experiences (usually tepid) scolding. Gordon Brown, when he was Chancellor of the Exchequer in the New Labour governments (from 1997 to 2007), distanced himself from the City by refusing to wear evening dress at its functions, but he had become compliant by the time when he was installed as prime minister in 2007. During 2000, while still Chancellor, he went on a rant about the admissions practices of the top universities, provoked when Oxford turned down a state school applicant with A-grades who subsequently accepted a Harvard scholarship. Oxbridge then continued in its customary ways. During the 1980s, 90s and 2000s company directors were repeatedly invited by government ministers to exercise salary restraint, to set a good example, but they continued to add huge increases to their already huge salaries. In 2008, 2009 and 2010 city bonuses were still being paid by banks that had been saved from ruin only by injections of billions of pounds from public funds. Most hereditaries have been expelled from the House of Lords but the upper class can be confident that it will be adequately represented in a reformed second chamber. None of the proposed reforms of parliament or the (London) City attack the base of the upper class, its wealth, and its ability to deploy this wealth in its own interests. Tough government targets the working class – the unemployed, petty offenders, and single parents who draw state benefits and live in council houses: groups who are unable to bite back.

It has become acceptable for members of the upper class to sponsor/fund/ bribe politicians and their parties. It is no secret that the funders expect access and business-friendly policies. If it's business, then, so it appears, it must be OK. The very wealthy expect political and public acquiescence when they keep their personal fortunes in offshore bases, or in trusts, or in other places where they avoid European levels of taxation.

Class struggle continues

The upper class's problem is that its mere naming makes it vulnerable. The upper class prefers to be described as business, and would prefer class itself to be regarded as a thing of the past, a hark back to the days when the upper class had the aristocracy at its core.

Merely demonstrating the continued existence of an upper class, which is really quite simple, is easily mistaken for critique. So let's be clear. Capitalism requires a capitalist (upper) class. 'Everyone a capitalist' is not a viable option. Markets work in the ways that they are supposed to work, and businesses become innovatory and enterprising, only when there is a separate class of owners. It is plausible to argue that capitalism has proved to be the best of all known economic systems for all classes of people in terms of the standards of living that it delivers, and the quality of life, measured by that most sensitive of all indicators – how long people live (Saunders, 1995b). To vote for capitalism is to vote for the maintenance of an upper class.

Yet the position of the upper class can never be fully secure. Its very existence clashes with core values that have always been nurtured within the working classes (and the middle classes) that the system produces. The existence of an upper class offends both working and middle class notions of meritocracy. The key issue here is not hereditary titles but privately-held wealth – the asset that is most easily passed from generation to generation. The upper class's ways of doing things also offend the working class's preference for matters to be subject to collective agreement, its yearning for the security of a planned economy, and the desire to limit the scope of the market by guaranteeing certain basic social rights, and gearing certain services – particularly health and education – entirely to need or merit.

Summary

Britain's upper class has demonstrated a remarkable capacity to survive and thrive. This chapter has explained how Britain's modern upper class was formed in the nineteenth century through a fusion between the aristocracy and new money. The mixture has worked. We have seen that privately-owned wealth, and the accompanying power, remain heavily concentrated, and that the position of the upper class has been strengthened, and its wealth has increased, during the transition from personal to impersonal ownership and control of major businesses.

While some forms of wealth have indeed become more widely distributed than in the past, the class whose life-chances depend essentially on deploying its wealth effectively still amounts to no more than one per cent of the population, and these owners continue to exercise strategic control over the businesses in which their wealth is invested. Globalization has enhanced their ability to avoid control by national governments.

We have also seen that Britain's upper class has some distinctive features, apart from its close links with the aristocracy. It is well-integrated into a single national network, strengthened by its use of elite schools and universities, inter-marriage, an exclusive social circuit, and the ease with which private wealth can be transmitted down the generations. The upper class controls most of the media and is able to command the respectful attention of leading politicians. Despite its mere existence negating values nurtured in all other social classes, the upper class in this new millennium appears able to convince all who matter that they have no better alternative than to co-operate on terms acceptable to the uppers.

Social Mobility

8

Introduction

A great deal of evidence about social mobility has been introduced in previous chapters. In examining each of the main classes we have noted the members' typical origins, and the likelihood of people born into the class ending-up somewhere else. Here we draw together all the social mobility evidence. There are dangers in doing this. The statistics cascade. So it is important to keep an eye on the main questions that we are trying to answer.

The first section of this chapter explains why mobility is an important topic in class analysis. We are all interested in whether we live in a fair society, commonly understood to mean a 'meritocratic' society where individuals' achievements depend on their own talents and efforts rather than their social origins. Second, and equally important for sociology, we are interested in whether the classes into which we divide the population are demographic entities, meaning whether they have intra- and inter-generationally stable cores, and otherwise whether their members share characteristic life-chances, that is, chances of reaching or routes to ending-up in specific positions.

The next section deals with absolute mobility flows: for example, the chances of people born into the working class reaching the middle class, and vice-versa. Exactly how much mobility is there and have the rates changed over time? We shall see that throughout the twentieth century and up to now there has been more upward than downward mobility in Britain, and that the trend over time has been for upward mobility to increase while downward mobility has diminished. These trends have been due entirely to the changing shape of the class structure, and there are major implications for the composition of all the main social classes. We should note that it could be a grave mistake to assume that these trends will continue during the twenty-first century.

The following sections deal with gender and ethnic divisions. Do gender and ethnicity have independent effects on people's life-chances? We shall see that the answers are more complex than the questions. It is only among individuals born into the middle class that males have been the advantaged sex in terms of life-chances. As regards ethnicity, there are variations between, and gender differences within, all ethnic groups, but amidst the complexities two findings deserve highlighting: the 'ethnic penalty' which we have already encountered (see chapter 3); and Black Africans, and Black Caribbeans even more so, plus Pakistanis and Bangladeshis, tending to remain clustered towards the base of the class structure while other ethnic minorities (Indians and Chinese) experience collective upward mobility.

The final section of the chapter deals with relative rates of mobility. Here we are trying to measure the openness or fluidity of the class structure, trends over time, and differences between countries. The startling finding from the mass of evidence on mobility between occupational classes is how little if any variation there has been over time, and how similar the rates of fluidity are in different modern societies. However, we shall see that evidence from studies that divide the population into income bands rather than occupational classes indicates a rather different situation. Nevertheless, all the analyses agree that there is considerable inter-generational continuity in class positions, and the chapter concludes by considering possible explanations of this continuity – inherited ability, reproduction theory, and rational action theory. We see that, at present, none of the theories is able to marshal evidence to make itself wholly convincing.

A point to bear in mind throughout is that mobility is rather difficult to measure. The statistics are plentiful and precise, but they are all surrounded by margins of error. Measuring mobility involves comparing parents' and their children's class positions. A problem is that the positions do not remain static. A teacher or hairdresser today may have a similar class location to a generation ago, but the location is unlikely to be precisely the same. Also, individuals change occupations and may change their class positions during their adult labour market careers. Their positions at one point in time may be roughly, but not necessarily precisely, the main positions that they occupy throughout their adult lives. Finally, it is necessary to wait until a birth cohort has reached occupational maturity before its mobility rates can be calculated. Any equalization of outcomes at one stage, during primary schooling for example, may be cancelled out at later stages.

Why study mobility?

A fair society?

Everyone is interested in social mobility. Within and outside sociology, people's initial interest is most likely to be in whether we are an equal opportunity society. Meritocratic values are powerful and widespread. Early in its history, the Labour Party abandoned egalitarianism in favour of meritocratic ambitions (Parkin, 1971). There is no difference between Old and New Labour, or the present-day Conservatives, the Liberal Democrats or any of the other political parties in this respect. Inequalities are deemed justifiable only when they reflect merit, though all parties appear to forget the upper class when proclaiming their belief in meritocracy. Sociologists have generally shared the more prevalent belief that inequalities should be merited by the individuals concerned. Showing that people's achievements are often due to their social origins rather than their own merits is commonly regarded as sufficient proof that we live in an unjust world. If inequalities are not based on individual merit, then more or less everyone seems to believe that they cannot be justified. Of course, this begs the question (which we shall return to later) as to how merit should be measured. However, it is not difficult to demonstrate that people who are born into different social classes have very different, very unequal, life-chances. The inequalities are so huge that people are often amazed when they first see the data. Within sociology a prevalent feeling has always been, and remains, that life-chance inequalities are so wide that they cannot possibly reflect neither more nor less than merit alone.

It is very easy to demonstrate that the children of middle class parents are more likely – between three and four times more likely – to remain in the middle class than those born into the working class are to reach a middle class destination. Social mobility tables which describe the destinations of groups born into different social classes are easy to construct, to read and to understand. Matters become complicated only when we ask questions such as whether life-chances have become more or less equal over time. Here it becomes necessary somehow to take into account changes in the proportions of occupations in different classes, and maybe differential class fertility rates and changes in these. Similar complications arise when trying to compare social mobility in different societies. We can never compare like with like. If a society changes very quickly – if the farm population contracts, or the middle class expands rapidly, for example – there is more or less bound to be more movement than in a more stable society. There are ways of subtracting mobility that is inevitable because of structural changes (in the proportions of occupations in different classes) and differential fertility rates, and being left with a measure of social fluidity. It is possible to make calculations comparing the fluidity of a society at different points in time, and the rates in different countries. These figures are important. But it is always equally important to bear in mind that such statistics have little relevance to the experiential worlds in which most people live. The simple figures, describing the proportion of working class children who are upwardly mobile, for example, bear a closer resemblance to the experiential worlds that lay people inhabit.

Classes as demographic entities

It is also important, in sociology at any rate, to realize that establishing how far from, or how close we are, to an equal opportunity society is not the only reason why class analysis needs to engage with social mobility. Another reason is to establish the extent to which occupation-based classes are demographic entities. The assumption here is that the members of a class are more likely to associate with one another than with outsiders, and to develop a characteristic form of consciousness and political proclivities, when most members stay within the same class for their entire working lives, and also when there is substantial inter-generational continuity, or when members have common mobility experiences in starting out from or in reaching specific class positions.

Everyone knows from personal experience or acquaintances that we are not a caste society where everyone remains within the groups into which they are born. But neither are we anywhere near to the other extreme, ideal-typical case of a society where everyone spends a part, and the same proportion, of his or her life, in each of the different classes. We are somewhere between these extremes, and we need to establish exactly where we are located, bearing in mind that some classes are always likely to be more stable than others.

We should note here that although demographically stable classes may be especially likely to develop distinctive class cultures, social mobility is not necessarily incompatible with this development. Specific mobility experiences may be characteristic among people who are born into a class, or who reach a particular class destination, in which case the experience is likely to become part of the characteristic consciousness of the group in question. Hence the importance of identifying major mobility flows and channels. Whether a class is a demographic entity does not necessarily depend on persons who are born into it tending to remain. It can also be considered a demographic entity if persons starting from a specific class position have characteristic life-chances, that is, chances of mobility and immobility that set them apart from other classes, or if adults in a specific class position have shared common experiences in reaching this destination.

It is very, very simple to demonstrate that people with working and middle class origins do indeed have very different life-chances, and that those for whom these are their adult class destinations have common experiences in reaching these positions. Actually, it is much easier to demonstrate all this for men than for women because until recently there was far more research into male than female social mobility. Social mobility research used to assume (sometimes tacitly and sometimes explicitly) that, in studying class structures and processes, females and their employment could be safely ignored (see chapter 2). Hence social mobility research used male-only samples. This is no longer how mobility research is practised, but studies of inter-generational mobility and immobility continue to ignore mothers' occupations when specifying respondents' social origins. Daughters' occupational class positions are compared with those of their fathers, even though it can be argued that mother-to-daughter links are the proper comparisons when measuring female social mobility. Information about respondents' mothers' occupations has simply not been collected in most of the main surveys used to examine social mobility.

Absolute mobility

There have been just two social mobility surveys in Britain; in 1949 (Glass, 1954) and in 1972 (Goldthorpe et al, 1987). Each of these surveys used a newly designed class scheme; the Hall-Jones scheme and the Goldthorpe scheme respectively. Both surveys used male-only samples. Subsequently social mobility has been studied using data sets gathered for other or additional purposes. It is necessary to have a large, nationally representative sample, and data about respondents' and their parents' occupations coded into a common class scheme. The UK birth cohort studies of samples born in 1946, 1958 and 1970 meet these requirements, and comparing their findings enables us to assess trends over time. However, the most useful data sets on which Table 8.1 (then subsequent tables) are based, are from the British Election Studies. We have time series from all general elections since 1964. The respondents are both male and female. The samples are representative of all adult age groups, and this allows us to compare the mobility experiences of people born at different times stretching back to the nineteenth century.

Table 8.1 (and some that follow) is based on the pooled samples from all the British Election Studies between 1964 and 1997. The pooling is necessary to produce sufficient numbers with specific class origins and destinations. Table 8.1 is for males only (data on females will follow), and only those males who were aged 35 or over at the time of the surveys, the reason being that younger respondents were less likely to have reached occupational maturity, that is, to be in their ultimate class positions.

We should note again that it is possible to measure a cohort's social mobility only after it has reached occupational maturity. Mobility rates among young people in school today will not be known for 20 or more years. Politicians are always on safe ground when claiming that their education and other policies will increase social mobility. The politicians have long left office before it is possible to tell whether their measures worked.

Table 8.1 Male outflow mobility (in percentages)

Sons' occupational class	Fathers' occupational class					
	Higher middle class	Lower middle class	Lower non-manual	Self-employed	Skilled working class	Non-skilled working class
Higher middle class	46	30	27	15	12	9
Lower middle class	23	29	21	13	12	9
Lower non-manual	5	10	12	7	7	5
Self-employed	11	10	9	29	8	7
Skilled working class	8	12	19	20	38	32
Non-skilled working class	6	9	13	17	23	38
N (of cases) =	447	535	381	1103	2626	2204

Based on data from Heath and Payne, 1999

In studying social mobility sociologists distinguish between intra- and inter-generational mobility. Studying intra-generational mobility involves comparing the class positions of the same persons at different points in time, like first jobs and current occupations. Inter-generational mobility compares the class positions of parents and children, as in Table 8.1. Another distinction is between absolute and relative rates of social mobility. At this point we are dealing with absolute mobility rates.

Table 8.1 is an outflow mobility table. It shows the percentages of sons whose fathers were in different social classes (the sons' social origins) who reached different class destinations. We can see that 69 per cent of those who were born into the upper middle class and 59 per cent of those born into the lower middle class had remained in one or the other of the two middle class groups. In contrast, just 24 per cent from the skilled working class and 18 per cent from the non-skilled working class had risen into the middle classes. Seventy per cent of sons who were born into the non-skilled working class had become working class adults, as had 61 per cent of the sons who were born into the skilled working class. In comparison, just 14 per cent from the upper middle class and 21 per cent from the lower middle class had descended into the working class. Thus we can see that there was substantial inter-generational continuity from fathers to sons in both the middle and working classes. Rates of inter-generational continuity were lower in the intermediate classes. Among lower non-manual sons, only 12 per cent held similar occupations: 48 per cent had risen into the middle class, 32 per cent had moved into the working class, and the remaining nine per cent had become self-employed. There had been a higher rate of inter-generational continuity in the self-employed class, though not as high as in the working and middle classes. Twenty-nine per cent of the sons of self-employed fathers had become self-employed, 28 per cent had moved into the middle class, 37 per cent into the working class, and seven per cent into lower non-manual occupations.

Table 8.2 simplifies the class breakdown in Table 8.1 and compares rates of inter-generational continuity in the middle and working classes among different

Table 8.2 Percentages of sons remaining in same social class as father

Social Class	Birth cohort						
	Pre–1900	1900–09	1910–19	1920–29	1930–39	1940–49	1950–59
Middle class	51	49	61	69	67	62	73
Working class	76	75	73	67	60	53	50

Source: Aldridge, 2001

birth cohorts. We can see that the trend over time during the twentieth century was for higher proportions of sons with middle class fathers to retain their class positions. Inter-generational continuity rose from around 50 per cent for those born before 1910 to 73 per cent among those born after 1950. This change was not due to the class structure becoming more rigid. We shall see below, when examining relative mobility rates, that this was not the case. The explanation of the rising rate of inter-generational continuity in the middle class is that during the twentieth century the middle class was growing in size, which in itself increased the likelihood of those born into the middle class remaining in this class. Table 8.2 also shows that inter-generational continuity in the working class declined while continuity in the middle class was rising. This was due to the working class shrinking in size. Up to 1920 around three-quarters of sons born into the working class were remaining in that class. Among those born after 1950 it was just 50 per cent: the other 50 per cent had risen, at least into the intermediate classes.

Good chances of ascent

It can be seen in Tables 8.1 and 8.2 that children who started life in the working class in early and mid-twentieth century Britain always enjoyed significant chances of ascent. It is true that three-quarters of those born into the working class at the beginning of the century remained in the working class, but this means that a quarter were climbing: around one child in every two working class families, assuming an average of two children per family. By the 1950s a half of working class children were rising out of that class: typically one of the two children in a two-child family. Most working class adults who became parents in the second half of the twentieth century would have seen one of their children ascend at least into the intermediate classes. So despite the very wide inequalities in life-chances which are apparent in Table 8.1, for males (and we will see below for females also) who have started life in the working class, upward mobility has been a quite common experience, nothing exceptional. Those who have remained immobile will have seen others getting ahead: people who they knew at school, in their neighbourhoods, and sometimes from their own families. Cross-class family links and friendships will mitigate against any tendency for people to see other classes as enemies.

Some plain facts about mobility realities and possibilities are often misunderstood even within sociology. Among the respondents in Goldthorpe's 1972 survey, 27 per cent were in middle class occupations. So if there had been equal life-chances for individuals from all social origins, 27 per cent from every starting point would have reached, or remained in, the middle class. In practice 59 per cent of those who started life in the middle class had remained there, against just 16 per cent of those from working class backgrounds who had reached this destination. If there had been equal life-chances another 11 per cent of working class children would have ascended. It is often not appreciated, even within sociology, how small a proportion of the working class stands to gain from equalizing life-chances. Most of the working class adults in the Goldthorpe study would have remained excluded from the middle class even in an equal life-chance society because there was simply insufficient room at the top. In a sense, among the generation that Goldthorpe studied in 1972, the middle class stood to lose more than the working class stood to gain from equalizing opportunities. Most of the men with middle class origins who had maintained their positions (59 per cent) would have descended in an equal life-chance society (in which just 27 per cent would have remained in the middle class). From this evidence, we should expect stronger opposition from those who stand to lose, than support from those who stand to gain, towards measures that would equalize life-chances. The 2010 general election was fought partly on rival appeals to 'aspirational Britain' (see, for example, Panel on Fair Access to the Professions, 2009). The appeals overestimated the numbers who stood to gain if it had been possible to unleash and satisfy higher aspirations among working class young people, and underestimated the threat that this would pose to the middle classes.

Risks of demotion

Those who start at the bottom can only rise. For the working class, social mobility will appear attractive. Start at the top and the only possible move is down. At this level social mobility is a threat. We have seen that there are wide inequalities in life-chances in Britain, but, despite this, working class parents have reasonably good chances of seeing their children ascend. These statements are not contradictory, though they may appear so at first. One is based on relative, and the other on absolute mobility rates. Both statements are true. Likewise the facts that, on the one hand, risks of demotion for those who start at the top are much lower than they would be in an equal life-chance society, yet are still sufficient to give the middle class realistic grounds for worry.

Among the respondents in Goldthorpe's 1972 survey, 59 per cent of those who began life in the middle class had remained there; far more than the 27 per cent who would have done so in the ideal-typical equal life-chance situation. But another way of looking at these same figures is to say that roughly 40 per cent had not maintained their positions, and 15 per cent had dropped right down into the working class. These statistics mean that it was odds-on, during the second half of the twentieth century, and probably in the first half as well, that the typical middle class family with two children (or two sons, at any rate) would see at least one of them descend. From a primary school class of 30 composed wholly of middle class pupils, around 12 would not have maintained their positions. People who start life in the middle class know full well that not everyone holds on, just as those who start in the working class know from personal experience that not everyone remains.

Social mobility looks most attractive, indeed it only looks attractive, when we contemplate the upward variety. Most working class parents are keen for their children to get on, if at all possible. Downward mobility is entirely different.

Does anyone aspire towards or hope for it? When it happens in objective terms, people often go to great lengths to convince themselves and others that they have not really slipped. They will regard their current positions as temporary, or use class markers (type of housing or who your friends are rather than occupation) that make it appear that they have maintained rank (Roberts et al, 1977). Or they will focus on how they have maintained or even improved upon their parents' standard of living (not usually difficult in a society in which living standards have been improving over time). But of course, some people achieve such outstanding success in business or the professions that it is near-impossible for their children to equal, let alone exceed, their achievements. It can be a mixed blessing to be the child of highly advantaged parents.

Downward mobility from the middle class is sufficiently common to be perceived as a very real threat. Hence the concern of middle class parents to reduce the risks – to do almost anything that might achieve this (see Devine, 2004; Walkerdine et al, 2001). Middle class parents are keen for their children to attend schools with good academic records. At any sign of failure they are likely to provide private coaching, or even opt for full private education. The children are under enormous pressure to succeed. Middle class parents constantly seek assurances that their own children are doing well. Entering higher education used to give such assurance. At one time passing the 11-plus did likewise. Nowadays the parents expect their children to be in the higher streams or sets in their primary and secondary schools, to achieve high scores in the national tests at age 11, to pass GCSEs and A-levels with high grades, then to gain places at high-ranked universities.

Internal and external recruitment

The larger a class, the more likely are those born into it to remain, and the higher the proportion of its adult members who will be inbred. These statements do not require evidence. They are simply mathematical truisms. If a class accounted for 65 per cent of the population, then, in an ideal-typical situation of equal life-chances, and if the society remained stable over time, 65 per cent of those born into the class would remain, and 65 per cent from all other classes would reach this destination. Continuing with the same example, 65 per cent of the adult members of the 65 per cent class would be immobile, internal recruits, and 35 per cent would be drawn in from elsewhere. If the class contracted to just 40 per cent of the population, and stabilized at that level, then only 40 per cent of those born into the class would remain, and 40 per cent from all other origins, would reach the destination. Just 40 per cent of the class's adult members would be lifelong, and 60 per cent would be intergenerationally mobile, all assuming, once again, equal life-chances.

The decline from around 65 per cent to around 40 per cent is what in fact happened to Britain's male working class in the course of the twentieth century. Britain was not a country of equal life-chances, as amply demonstrated in mobility tables, but at any constant rate of social fluidity the point holds that the smaller a class becomes, the less likely are those born into it to remain. Throughout the early twentieth century the working class was usually the life-long position of people born into the class, not due mainly to unequal life-chances, but simply because for most of the century the working class accounted for most of the population.

Now the working class was contracting throughout most of the twentieth century and by its end the class comprised just 40 per cent or thereabouts of the male workforce, and a slightly smaller proportion of women (see below). The effect of the long-term contraction of the working class was that each successive cohort of working class children had better chances of ascending than its predecessor (as shown in Table 8.2). This was not due to any equalization of life-chances: it was due simply to the changing shape of the class structure. Three-quarters of sons born into the working class pre-1920 remained in that class, whereas by the 1950s it was just 50 per cent. Today it will be even fewer because the working class has become even smaller than in the 1950s, but the precise figures will become available only when recent birth cohorts reach occupational maturity.

Working class parents who have told their children that the latter have better opportunities to get on than their parents enjoyed have not been deluding themselves or anyone else; they have been reflecting accurately their own experience. Throughout the twentieth century it will have made increasing sense for working class parents who wanted their children to experience better lives than their own to concentrate upon assisting the children to become upwardly mobile rather than engaging in political struggles to gain a better deal for the working class in its entirety. There are other implications of the rise in the absolute rate of upward mobility from the working class. The present-day equivalents of earlier generations of working class trade union and Labour Party leaders are not leaving school at age 16 and joining the manual workforce but are continuing in education then entering middle class jobs. The diminishing working class will have been progressively stripped of its more talented and/or more ambitious members. Trends in absolute rates of social mobility that are consequences of the working class's contraction will have contributed to its disorganization. Economic trends and government policies (especially policies towards trade unions in the 1980s) were undoubtedly the main factors in the disorganization of the working class towards the close of the twentieth century (see chapter 4), but longer-term trends in the shape of the class structure, with their implications for absolute rates of mobility, will have contributed. Higher proportions of working class children have been moving upwards. The immobile will have found it more difficult to blame society rather than themselves for their lack of ascent (they will have seen so many childhood acquaintances getting ahead). More of those remaining in the working class will have family links with other classes. The upwardly mobile may well be the very persons who, had they remained working class, would have played leadership roles in working class organizations. Moreover, as the middle class grows in size, the downwardly mobile comprise a growing proportion of working class adults (see Noble, 2000).

A class that is large but in numerical decline will normally be overwhelmingly self-recruiting. It has no need of new blood. This applied to the working class throughout the twentieth century, as can be seen in Table 8.3. This is an inflow mobility table. It gives the social class origins of males aged 35 and over who were in different social classes at the time of all the election surveys from 1964 to 1997. The raw figures are the same as in Table 8.1, but in Table 8.3 the percentages are calculated for destination groups rather than origin groups. As many as 82 per cent of males who were in both the skilled and the non-skilled working classes had working class social origins. In this sense, throughout the twentieth century the working class was demographically well-formed, and will remain so well into the twenty-first century. In the second half of the twentieth century the working class was not only supplying fourth-fifths of working class adults, but the majority of members of all other occupational classes except the upper middle class where it was just 44 per cent.

The middle class in the twentieth century was entirely different. Throughout the second half of the twentieth century, and probably before then, most of its members were upwardly mobile – 68 per cent of upper middle class males and 74 per cent of the lower middle class males in Table 8.3. This is what happens when an initially small class grows consistently over a period of decades, as the middle class did in Britain, accounting for less than 20 per cent of the males in cohorts born before 1910, but over 40 per cent of those born after 1950. In the second half of the twentieth century the middle class contained more males with working class than with middle class social origins.

When members of Britain's present-day middle class look at each other they do not see a group with uniformly, or even mainly, privileged origins. This

Table 8.3 Male inflow mobility (in percentages)

Fathers' occupational class	Children's occupational class					
	Higher middle class	Lower middle class	Lower non-manual	Self-employed	Skilled working class	Non-skilled working class
Higher middle class	18	10	4	6	2	2
Lower middle class	14	16	11	7	3	3
Lower non-manual	9	8	9	4	3	3
Self-employed	14	14	15	38	10	11
Skilled working class	27	32	37	26	48	34
Non-skilled working class	17	20	22	19	34	48
N (of cases)=	1146	992	492	820	2094	1754

Based on data from Heath and Payne, 1999

is despite most middle class sons remaining middle class, and the very wide inequalities of life-chances that operate in the middle class's favour. If the middle class regards the class structure as open, and if they believe that they live in a society where anyone from any background can get on if they have the ability and make the effort, this is not solely because they find these ideas comforting: they accord with the middle class's own experiences. Most of them have been upwardly mobile. It is true that if we take people at the peak of prestigious professions – high court judges and the civil service elite, for example – we find fewer individuals with working class origins than in the middle class as a whole. For example, at present 70 per cent of judges, 68 per cent of barristers, and 54 per cent of chief executives of the top stock exchange listed companies were educated at independent schools (which educate just seven per cent of the secondary school age group) (Panel on Fair Access to the Professions, 2009; Sutton Trust, 2009). Even so, the fact remains that what is now a broad band of middle class occupations, accounting for around two-fifths of the workforce in Britain, is populated by people with varied origins.

This will change slowly in the twenty-first century, assuming, as seems likely, that the growth of the middle class has either ended or is continuing but at a slower rate. The larger the middle class becomes, the larger will be the proportion of these positions filled by people born into the class. All discussions about the contemporary middle class must allow for the fact that it is still being formed. The manner in which its demography will change in the twenty-first century (we can predict confidently because the developments are 'in the pipeline') will favour the formation of a distinctive lifestyle, consciousness and politics. Remember, however, that the larger the middle class, the larger will be the proportion of working class children who reach middle class destinations: 16 per cent of the working class respondents in Goldthorpe's 1972 survey, but 36 per cent of all the males from working class homes in the 1958 birth cohort. It may seem paradoxical at first, but it really can be true that the chances of working class children ascending can rise, while the upwardly mobile comprise a declining proportion of all middle class adults, and while risks of demotion from the middle class subside. This is not just a hypothetical possibility: it is what is actually happening in Britain.

Gender

Social class profiles and mobility flows

Chapter 3 explained, first, that the proportion of adult women in the workforce, and the proportion of the workforce that is female, have both risen over time. Second, it explained that despite equal pay and opportunity laws there is still a strong tendency for men and women to enter different occupations, and overall women's jobs are still inferior to men's, most visibly in their pay being lower per hour and in total. That said, today there is little difference between men's and women's distributions between middle class, intermediate and working class occupations. Here we can look more closely at the similarities and differences, using the available evidence that permits systematic comparison of men's and women's experiences of social mobility and immobility. What difference, if any, does gender make?

Chapter 2 explained that how women should be located in the class structure (in sociological analysis) has been hotly contested, and there is some dispute as to whether the Goldthorpe class scheme (and all other class schemes for that matter) are suitable for classifying women's jobs. There are also uncertainties about how part-time employees and housewives should be treated. We also noted in chapter 2 that at present there seems to be no single answer to these questions that is right for all cases. Here it will be best to place these controversies to one side, to continue to use the class scheme that has been adopted, to place women on the basis of their own jobs, ignoring the part-time/full-time split and periods spent out of the labour market, and to examine where women from the same starting points end up compared with men.

All work on female social mobility up to now has used their fathers' occupations to indicate the women's starting points. If women are to be classed by their own occupations, it might appear more reasonable to use their mothers' occupations, or at least to take these into account, in identifying females' social origins. However, all the available data uses fathers' occupations as the baseline, so here we have no option but to follow this practice.

Up to now the main differences between men's and women's mobility flows have been due to men and women tending to do different kinds of jobs. Up to and including cohorts born in the 1950s, there were always higher proportions of male than female workers in middle class jobs, self-employed, and in working class jobs. There were more women, far more women as a proportion of all female employees, in lower non-manual occupations. This is the reason why a more common destination for women than for men from all social class backgrounds (measured by their fathers' occupations) has been lower non-manual work. However, women from upper middle class backgrounds have been more likely to enter middle class than lower non-manual occupations, while women from working class backgrounds have been more likely to enter working class than lower non-manual jobs (see Table 8.4). Despite this, throughout the twentieth century women from middle class homes were more likely to be downwardly mobile (in terms of their own occupations) than males from middle class backgrounds. Conversely, women from working class backgrounds were more likely than their brothers to be upwardly mobile, albeit only, in most cases, into the intermediate, lower non-manual grades (see Table 8.5).

There has been little difference between the social origins of males and females who end up in the same occupational classes (see Table 8.6). Among women we see exactly the same picture as for men: the working class has been overwhelmingly self-recruiting, while middle class positions have been filled mainly by upwardly mobile persons from lower classes. Males' and females' outflow mobility patterns should also be converging given that the distribution of men and women between different occupations is much more similar today than throughout the twentieth century.

Table 8.4 Female outflow mobility (in percentages)

Daughters' occupational class	Fathers' occupational class					
	Higher middle class	Lower middle class	Lower non-manual	Self-employed	Skilled working class	Non-skilled working class
Higher middle class	14	6	9	5	3	2
Lower middle class	32	32	23	17	13	10
Lower non-manual	35	41	42	34	35	29
Self-employed	9	5	5	10	4	3
Skilled working class	3	4	4	7	10	11
Non-skilled working class	7	13	17	28	35	46
N (of cases) =	314	373	271	722	1712	1413

Based on data from Heath and Payne, 1999

Table 8.5 Percentages of daughters remaining in same social class as father

Social Class	Birth cohort						
	Pre–1900	1900–09	1910–19	1920–29	1930–39	1940–49	1950–59
Middle class	33	40	37	40	42	43	50
Working class	68	64	56	57	44	41	30

Based on data from Heath and Payne, 1999

Intra-generational mobility

We study inter-generational mobility by comparing parents and their children (as above). Intra-generational mobility can occur between any two points in the same person's life, but in practice the period focused on is usually the person's working life. An individual who is upwardly or downwardly mobile inter-generationally may make the entire rise or descent in childhood and youth, while in education. Alternatively, part or all of the movement may be after the individual's working life has started. A person who is immobile inter-generationally may hold the same type of job throughout his or her working life, or recover after initially starting employment at a lower level than his or her parents.

Table 8.6 Female inflow mobility (in percentages)

Fathers' occupational class	Children's occupational class					
	Higher middle class	Lower middle class	Lower non-manual	Self-employed	Skilled working class	Non-skilled working class
Higher middle class	22	13	7	12	2	1
Lower middle class	11	15	9	8	4	3
Lower non-manual	12	8	7	6	3	3
Self-employed	18	16	15	30	12	13
Skilled working class	24	29	37	28	42	38
Non-skilled working class	14	18	25	17	38	41
N (of cases) =	203	768	1631	243	412	1568

Based on data from Heath and Payne, 1999

There is a great deal of intra-career movement, and no decline over time in the volume. In his 1972 survey John Goldthorpe tested the 'counterbalance' or 'tightening bond' thesis which suggests that, when it occurs, nowadays mobility is more likely than in the past to happen as a result of, and while the subject is still in, education. This thesis is plausible. We now spend much longer in education than a century ago. It seems likely that those destined to rise and fall will be more likely to do so on the basis of their educational performances rather than their achievements, or lack of them, when in the labour market. In practice, however, there appears to be just as much intra-career mobility as ever, usually short-range, and along a limited number of main routes.

People who start their working lives as traditional apprentices become skilled workers. Others who are not formally trained may become informally recognized as skilled. Some manual workers are promoted to supervisory and even management posts. Some make this step on the basis of qualifications earned through part-time study. Another common career move is from lower-level office and sales jobs into the middle class proper. Another is from the lower to the higher grades within the middle class. A further type of movement is from all other kinds of occupations into self-employment.

Intra-generational mobility is being discussed here (in the section of this chapter which deals with gender) because, up to now at any rate, all these career movements have been most common among men. Women's working lives have followed a rather different typical career pattern. While men have normally built continuous, full-time, labour market careers lasting from full-time education until retirement, women have normally taken career breaks following child-birth. Women returners have often opted for part-time hours, and their career breaks have often been followed by occupational demotion (Martin and Roberts, 1984). On returning to their office jobs or to their professions, women have often been relocated outside the main career streams. Many have stepped downwards, in effect starting again. There have been many cases of quite substantial demotion – from office jobs to supermarket check-outs, cleaning and suchlike.

However, in recent times there has been some convergence in men's and women's typical career patterns. More women (mainly women in management and professional occupations) are now pursuing continuous full-time careers. This trend is discussed further, below. Meanwhile, more men's careers have been terminated prematurely. This is a consequence of post-Fordist flexibility and the rise in levels of unemployment. Company downsizing and site closures, and technological change, have seen people who once believed that they were in stable jobs and career grades, become surplus to requirements. Sometimes all their skills and experience have become redundant. Spells of unemployment have become more common since the 1970s. What was once the female career pattern – a discontinuous working life with risks of demotion at each break – has spread among men. Men over age 50 have often settled for retired status, and some have managed to qualify for incapacity benefit rather than remain in the labour market where they know that the only jobs that they are likely to be offered will be inferior to their earlier positions. Some supermarket chains have realized that it is now possible to hire quality staff from the pool of unemployed over-50 year olds.

Gender convergence, class divergence

Men's career preferences (though not their actual opportunities) seem much as ever, whereas women themselves have changed. Recent school-leaving cohorts have been the first young women in modern times most of whose mothers worked for the greater part of their own adult lives, and during their daughters' (and sons') childhoods. These mothers (and the fathers) have encouraged their daughters to aim for decent jobs – not to be left in the typing pools or at the supermarket check-outs. The girls' teachers (a mainly female occupation) have encouraged female pupils to be ambitious. Recent cohorts of female teenage school-leavers have regarded their own future occupational careers as just as important as boys regard theirs (Roberts and Chadwick, 1991).

Girls nowadays are certainly doing better at school than their predecessors. There have been some remarkable improvements – in their GCSE performances, the numbers taking and passing three or more A-levels and the grades they obtain, and in the numbers going to university (more females than males nowadays unlike in the 1960s when two-thirds of university students were men). Girls now out-perform boys at all levels in education. By 2009 40 per cent of 18/19 year old girls were entering higher education compared with just 32 per cent of boys (Higher Education Funding Council for England, 2010).

Boys' performances have not deteriorated: in fact they have improved. Both boys and girls today are doing better than formerly. There are more grounds for applauding girls' achievements than deploring male under-achievement. Qualified female school-leavers now aim for career jobs, though just like boys, many have to accept jobs that do not match their preferences. More well-qualified female recruits have been studying towards, and obtaining, post-entry professional and other vocational qualifications (Crompton and Sanderson 1986). Provided they remain childless, young women's career prospects remain more or less in line with males', at least until their mid-20s (Bynner et al, 1997). What happens then? Well, women have been postponing marriage and parenthood. When they become parents, more and more women have been taking maternity leave rather than terminating their employment. More of these women have been returning to work on a full-time basis and remaining in the career streams. Hence the forecast that the future will be female with more and more women shattering former glass ceilings. The numbers of women MPs, and members of the government, rose sharply following the 1997 general election. The number of women MPs rose further following the 2010 election, but the first Conservative-Liberal Democrat cabinet contained fewer women than its Labour predecessor (see chapter 9).

If women really are to experience more career success this can only be at the expense of men. There will be more pressure on males' career prospects. Times really have changed, but not equally so, or in exactly the same way, for men and women in all social classes. More women with children aged under five are working full-time, but most of these women are highly-qualified and are in middle class occupations. They are 30 times more likely to work full-time than mothers whose former or current occupations are non-skilled (Kay, 1996). The middle class women tend to have partners in similar occupations. They are in households with two middle class salaries which enable them to pay for quality child-care. Needless to say, some of the women become single parents (usually a temporary situation) but the fathers of the children are usually able, and obliged, to make contributions to their upkeep. Other mothers (particularly working class mothers) are still returning to work on a part-time basis and accepting the occupational downgrading that can be involved. Working class women's child-care arrangements are most likely to involve family and neighbours. These women's male partners are more vulnerable than formerly to occupational change. There has been a serious decline in the number of effective male breadwinners in the working class. It is not the men themselves who have changed so much as their employment opportunities. Working class fathers who become non-resident may simply be unable to remain reliable supporters of their children. Many of the women prefer to be independent of men whose own earning capacities are vulnerable.

Gender convergence at the top of the class structure has been accompanied by wider class inequalities within both sexes. There is more distance in lifestyle and living standards between the top and the bottom, but as much blurring as ever in the middle.

Ethnic differences

We saw in chapter 2 that there are large differences in the occupational class profiles of Britain's ethnic minorities. Indian and Chinese men are over-represented
in the middle class, while Black Caribbean, Pakistani and Bangladeshi
men, and Pakistani and Bangladeshi women are under-represented. Pakistani,
Bangladeshi and Black African men and women, and Black Caribbean women,
are over-represented in the working class.

The performances in education of children from the different ethnic groups
suggest that the over-achievement of Indians and Chinese is likely to be
consolidated or even extended. Pupils from these ethnic groups out-perform all
others in GCSE examinations (see Table 8.7). However, we must not assume
that the differences in achievement presented in Table 8.7 will remain stable over
time. We know that there have been changes since the 1980s when Pakistani,
Bangladeshi and Black pupils were all seriously under-performing compared
with whites. By 2006 only Black Caribbean pupils were still seriously behind:
the others had caught up with whites or were close behind. Needless to say, we
cannot be certain that the ethnic minorities' educational achievements will be
as well-rewarded in the labour market as those of whites. We saw in chapter 2
that, up to now, all the ethnic minorities have endured an 'ethnic penalty'.

All the ethnic minority groups are more likely than whites to remain in
full-time education beyond age 16, 17, and 18 (see Table 8.8), and they are
all over-represented in higher education. Ominously, there are high levels of
unemployment among those ethnic minority youth who do quit education
before age 19.

A likely future scenario is that all the minorities will gradually (or more
rapidly) become proportionately or over-represented (vis-a-vis whites) in middle
class occupations, while the remainder, especially the Blacks, Pakistani and

Table 8.7 Percentages of Year 11 young people gaining
five or more GCSEs grades A-C, 2006

Ethnic Group	Percentage
White	58
Indian	72
Pakistani	52
Bangladeshi	57
Other Asian (including Chinese)	77
Black African	55
Black Caribbean	44

Source: Department for Children, Schools and Families

Table 8.8   Positions of 19 year olds in 2007 (in percentages)

Position	White	Black	Indian	Pakistani and Bangladeshi
Full-time education	40	63	83	59
Government supported training	7	–	–	–
Full-time job	36	23	8	15
Part-time job	7	–	3	9
Unemployed	6	10	–	9
Other	4	–	–	7

Source: National Youth Cohort Survey

Bangladeshis, could be over-represented at the very base of the class structure – unemployed, intermittently employed, and in low income households.

Relative mobility

We now turn to the more complicated issues mentioned at the beginning of this chapter: those that involve measuring relative mobility and fluidity, and making comparisons across time and place.

The constant flux?

We have the mathematics and computer power to take account of structurally induced mobility – the volume that is inevitable as a result of changes over time in the shape of a class structure, and class differentials in fertility rates – and similarly to take account of differences in the shapes of the class structures in different countries (see Box 8.1, p 199). We are then left with measurements of social fluidity which can be used to compare the openness of different societies, or the same society at different points in time. These comparisons require nationally representative samples from all the times and places to be compared, and the relevant information has to be coded using the same class scheme. All this has in fact been done by several groups of researchers using the Goldthorpe, and other class schemes. The orthodox view among the sociologists responsible for this research has been, and remains, that there have been no *major* changes in industrial or post-industrial Britain, and there have been no *major* differences among the modern industrial societies, in their rates of social fluidity (Marshall et al, 1997). There are big differences in absolute rates because of differences in the shapes of the class structures, and the particular times, ways and the pace at which these have changed. There are in fact some differences in fluidity – the rates are not totally identical – but

Box 8.1   Measuring social mobility

Rates of absolute social mobility are easily calculated and expressed. We can see in Table 8.1 that 46% of sons born into the top class (the upper middle class) stayed there, and that as many as 69% remained in one of the two middle class groups. Just 14% descended into the working class. This 14% is an absolute mobility rate. Likewise 18% of those born into the non-skilled working class were upwardly mobile into one of the two middle class groups while 70% remained in one of the working class groups.

A relative mobility rate can be calculated using odds ratios. The 'odds' are the chances of someone born into a specific class reaching a specific destination. An odds ratio compares the odds of persons from different origins reaching a given destination. In Table 8.1 we can see that the relative odds (chances) of someone born into the top class staying there against someone born at the bottom reaching that class were 46–9. We can do the reverse calculation: the chances of someone born at the bottom staying there against the chances of someone starting life at the top descending that far. Here the odds are 38–6. If we multiply these figures we get an odds ratio of 32.4. This figure is unaffected by movements that would have been necessary due to changes over time in the proportions of males in different occupational classes, whereas absolute mobility rates are affected by these changes.

If origins and destinations were completely unrelated, that is, if there was a state of 'perfect' social mobility or fluidity, the answer to the above calculation would be 1.0. The higher the number, the stronger the tendency for people to stick in the classes into which they are born. The problem with odds ratios is that 32.4 is a meaningless number, in that it is unrelated to anything that can be observed. It becomes meaningful (apart from being able to see that it is greater than 1.0) only when we compare it with similar calculations at different points in time in the same country, or at the same point in time in different countries. We can then say which country has the most fluid class structure, and whether in one country the class structure has become more open or more rigid. We can also calculate relative mobility rates between adjacent classes, not just top-to-bottom, and compare fluidity at different levels in the class structure.

There is an alternative procedure that can be used. This is called log-linear modelling. This involves constructing models (this is done by computer) of what the numbers in the different cells in a mobility matrix (as in Table 8.1) would be on certain assumptions, like no connection between fathers' and sons' class positions. The goodness of fit between different models and the actual data is then measured: the lower the number, the better the fit. Again, the number itself is meaningless unless it can be compared with the performances of different models, or the same model at a different time, or in a different place.

the differences are fairly minor and rather difficult to explain. The orthodox view is summarized aptly in the title of Robert Erikson and John Goldthorpe's (1992) book on the subject, *The Constant Flux*. A series of recent reviews of the relevant evidence from England, Scotland and Ireland has confirmed this orthodox view (see Breen and Goldthorpe, 2001; Goldthorpe and Mills, 2008; Iannelli and Paterson, 2006). Prandy and Bottero's (2000) research, using a version of the Cambridge class scale (see chapter 2) adapted to the historical circumstances, traces mobility rates since the end of the eighteenth century, and finds that there was less change during the nineteenth century than had previously been assumed: that pre-industrial Britain was more fluid, and the industrial revolution did less to increase openness, than virtually everyone had previously supposed. This latter finding, if correct, extends the 'constant flux' historically,

Constant fluidity is not a completely solid and unanimously agreed conclusion. As explained in Box 8.1 (p 199), there are alternative ways in which relative mobility can be measured. Some social mobility researchers do not regard the issue as completely settled. They point out that nearly all the historical evidence is about male mobility; that there may have been changes over time, and inter-country differences, in female mobility, especially in view of the trend towards women spending more time in the labour market. They also argue that the measurements of fluidity are rather blunt, and typically involve grouping together individuals born over periods of 30 or even more years, which will conceal shorter-term fluctuations in mobility rates. Researchers who have looked in detail at the history of social mobility in Britain and Ireland (Payne, 1999; Prandy and Bottero, 2000) have concluded that fluidity did increase (temporarily) in the last three decades of the nineteenth century when the examination system was being introduced, and large private businesses, with new middle class jobs, were being formed (see chapter 6). Some researchers have detected an increase in fluidity in Britain during the closing decades of the twentieth century (Heath and Payne, 1999; Payne and Roberts, 2002). Odds ratios became lower, though 'constant fluidity' has continued to be the log-linear model that best fits the data (see Box 8.1, p 199).

One generally agreed qualification to the constant flux thesis is that there have been, and remain, slightly higher rates of social fluidity in the most equal western countries, namely, the Scandinavian countries. It is plausible to argue that under conditions of greater equality of condition, advantaged groups will feel less need, and in any case will be less able to mobilize resources to ensure that their advantages are transmitted to their children. However, there is no clear evidence that these are the processes that are responsible for the slightly higher rates of social fluidity in the Scandinavian countries, or, even if the processes are as stated, that reducing inequalities would trigger these same processes elsewhere.

The main challenge to the constant flux orthodoxy has come from researchers who have adopted an entirely different approach to measuring social mobility. Instead of positioning people in occupational classes, they divide the population into income quartiles. This kind of analysis requires data from nationally representative samples on subjects' incomes, and also their parents' household incomes when the subjects were children. Subjects and parents are divided into income quartiles, and the proportion of subjects in different quartiles than their parents is measured. There is no need to separate absolute from relative mobility, or otherwise to take into account the significance of changes in the shape of the class structure (the proportion of people in different classes), or the distance between the top and bottom. All the necessary evidence is available from Britain's 1958 and 1970 birth cohort studies, and the analysis shows a clear decline in social mobility between these two birth cohorts. Comparable data from cohorts born since 1970, available mainly from the British Household Panel Survey, suggests that the social mobility rate has subsequently remained reasonably steady. This approach to the measurement of social mobility not only contests the constant flux by showing significant historical change, but also in finding large differences in the rates of social mobility in different countries. Mobility in the USA and Britain is shown to be lower than in Germany, which is turn is behind the Scandinavian countries (see Blanden et al, 2005; Blanden and Machin, 2007). The one point of agreement between the occupational class and the income quartile researchers is that the Scandinavian countries are the most fluid (see also Organization for Economic Cooperation and Development, 2010).

The explanation of the post-1958 cohort decline in social mobility in Britain that is favoured by its discoverers is the increased sensitivity of post-16 participation in education to parental income. Stay-on rates were higher in the 1970 than in the 1958 birth cohort, and the steepest rise was in the higher income groups. Subsequently, however, stay-on rates have risen among middle and lower income groups but without the social mobility rate recovering. Nevertheless, the researchers favour economic measures to support extended education for young people from low income homes as a way of increasing social mobility.

However, it is necessary to point out (as we shall see below) that all previous attempts to increase social fluidity through educational reform have not been successful. In any case, there is an alternative explanation of the decline in mobility between income quartiles between the 1958 and 1970 British birth cohorts. Economic inequalities in Britain were widening, which would have made it more difficult for people to change their income quartiles while remaining within the same occupational classes. This would account for the apparent contradiction between the social mobility evidence from income quartiles and occupational classes. It will also explain the much higher mobility in the relatively equal Scandinavian countries that is indicated when using income quartiles.

The limitations of educational reform

Educational reform has widened the opportunities of working class children and boosted their educational attainments. It has created and sustained one of the great illusions of modern times – of society becoming progressively fairer while consistently failing to deliver a more open society. How has this been possible?

First, the expansion of educational opportunities has accompanied the change in the shape of the class structure that has already been described and discussed at length – the long-term upgrading. So, to an extent, the enlarged opportunities for able working class children to qualify for good jobs have simply enabled the additional room at the top to be filled by suitably qualified people (Halsey et al, 1980).

Second, the middle class has managed to take at least equal advantage of every expansion of educational opportunities. Changes have been introduced under the slogan of a fairer deal for the less privileged, and the privileged have instantly seized them. So when publicly-funded scholarship places were created in secondary schools and universities at the beginning of the twentieth century, these were not restricted to poor children. One of the consequences of the 1944 Education Act was that middle class children who would formerly have received a paid-for grammar school education subsequently qualified for free places (see Halsey et al, 1980). The effect of the abolition of fees, and the introduction of mandatory (means-tested) maintenance grants for university students in 1949, was not a new influx of working class entrants, but more state support for the existing students. When former further education colleges were upgraded to Polytechnics in the 1960s it was not the former, largely working class, students who experienced educational upgrading. Rather, the composition of the student bodies changed to resemble the profiles in the existing universities (Whitburn et al, 1976).

Figure 8.1 describes how the proportions of young people from non-manual and manual families entering higher education changed during the 1990s. The graphs show that there were all-round increases in participation, while the class gap remained virtually unchanged. Figure 8.1 also reveals the size of the class gap in educational achievement – huge. Nowadays over 70 per cent of upper middle class children make it into higher education compared with less than 20 per cent in the working class.

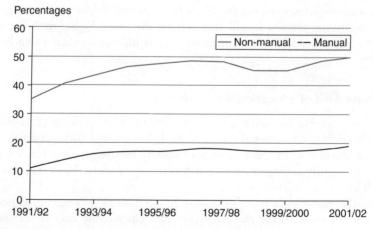

Percentages

Figure 8.1 Participation rates in higher education: by social class
Source: Department for Education and Skills

Third, the expansion of educational opportunities has accompanied, but pushed well-ahead of occupational upgrading. Hence the all-round devaluation of qualifications. It is necessary nowadays to achieve higher standards in education than in the past in order to qualify for any type of job. Careers such as the law and banking which were once open to 16 year olds were first re-targeted at those with A-levels, and more recently at higher education graduates. So as more working class children have reached given levels they have found the achievements counting for less. It was once a labour market advantage to have simply attended a secondary school. This changed when secondary education became universal. Subsequently it has been the qualifications earned in the schools that count. The same has now happened in higher education. Attending university is insufficient. Employers want to know your class of degree. As all-round enrolments and attainments at any level have risen, the class gap at that level has necessarily narrowed, but the attainments have counted for less and the old differentials have resurfaced at subsequent educational levels (Heath and Clifford, 1996).

Fourth, it is not only education and qualifications that determine the types of jobs that individuals obtain, and how their careers progress subsequently. At all levels of qualification, social class origins have always made a difference to immediate job prospects. And entrants from middle class backgrounds have always been more likely to achieve promotions than those from the working class. Why should this be? The answers lie in social and cultural capital (see Box 8.2). These are evident in young people's ambitions. The higher their social origins, the more determined they are to gain full value from their qualifications. Connections are also useful – knowing people who will put in a word at the right time. Then there is the matter of having the right kind of accent, tastes and dress sense to be regarded as the right type of person. Jackson (2001, 2007, 2009) has shown from her analysis of job adverts that non-meritocratic selection criteria (social skills and personality) are used routinely by employers.

In terms of the social mechanics of what happened during the successive waves of educational reform, we have no difficulty in explaining the constant flux. Unresolved controversies arise only when we seek higher-level explanations as to why things worked out this way. There are several higher-level explanations on offer. All have some plausible features, but are insufficient to be wholly convincing.

Intelligence

This is an argument that never goes away because up to now it has been impossible to obtain the crucial evidence to either defeat or prove it. Even so, it is one of those issues on which the protagonists are prepared to take firm stands. So it is important, first of all, to get the argument right. No-one claims that innate (genetically determined) ability is the sole determinant of what people achieve in education, employment or anywhere else. Everyone accepts that abilities relevant to success in all spheres of life, including intelligence tests themselves, are

---

Box 8.2 Social and cultural capital

Economic capital can be passed-down the generations, drawn on when needed, and, when able to do so, individuals can add to their investments. Social and cultural capital are comparable in all these respects.

Social capital consists of social relationships. Kinship relationships are given, but others are made. One can invest by building-up a circle of friends, and by offering them assistance, when possible. People can draw on their social capital when they need to do so – for assistance in finding a job, for instance.

Cultural capital consists of the skills, knowledge, beliefs and values that we acquire in our particular social milieux. Some skills and knowledge are certificated, but others, like a particular accent, can also be useful. Cultural capital is built-up gradually. We all have it. The crucial differences are not so much in the amounts, but the types, and how valuable they prove to be. The stocks that individuals acquire depend on their families, their schooling, the neighbourhoods where they live and who their friends are. When they start work individuals continue to add to their cultural capital. People can add deliberately to their cultural capital: for example, by enrolling in education or training.

How pupils fare at primary school (how easily they adapt to the classroom regime, and learn school subjects) depends partly on the cultural capital that they take into school with them. At all subsequent life stages, and in all spheres of life, the cultural capital that individuals bring to the situations affects their opportunities.

---

influenced by nurture (the effects on our development of the environments in which we are reared and live), and that matters such as being in the right place at the right time (pure chance), and connections, can be extremely important.

What has to be explained for present purposes is not exactly how each and every one of us obtains our particular jobs, but rates of social mobility and immobility that remain stable over periods of historical time, though not necessarily for ever, and innate ability is, in fact, as plausible as any other explanation. The argument is that, first, people with middle class jobs are generally brighter than those with working class jobs. Second, it is argued that there is a genetic base to all or most of the abilities that people develop (as with height and weight). So bright parents tend to have bright children but there is always a tendency for offspring to regress towards the mean, meaning that bright parents tend to have children who are rather less bright than themselves, and vice-versa for the below-average. Of course, there are extreme cases, as in everything else that is governed by genetics. So some parents with above-average ability produce extremely gifted children. Parents with below-average ability may also do this, but such cases will be even more exceptional.

Peter Saunders (1995) has shown that, in Britain, and presumably in other modern societies since they are similar in their rates of fluidity, the volume of mobility and the distances that people typically move are almost exactly what one would predict from the distribution of measured intelligence (IQ scores) among children from different social class backgrounds. He has also shown, using evidence from the 1958 birth cohort study in which the sample's abilities were measured while they were at school, that IQ proves to be the best single predictor of their adult destinations. The second best predictor is a childhood measure of motivation (Bond and Saunders, 1999; Saunders, 1997). On the basis of this evidence, Saunders lambasts what he calls the SAD hypothesis which claims that it is primarily social advantages and disadvantages that determine who gets on.

This is an argument about which many people have feelings as well as opinions. Hackles are easily stirred. The objections are well-known (see Lampard, 1996; Marshall and Swift, 1996; Breen and Goldthorpe, 1999). First, and crucially, it is impossible to measure raw ability (though genetic measurement may one day solve this problem). Performances in intelligence tests, the construction of these tests, and what we mean by ability, are all socially contaminated. There are ideological and political dimensions to these arguments which stem from the firm and widespread hold of meritocratic values in modern societies. If achievements are due to individuals' abilities, then, one can appear to be arguing, the resultant inequalities are merited and therefore justifiable, though one might query why having inherited certain talents should be regarded as particularly meritorious (as do Marshall et al, 1997). It must also be said that sociologists have a professional/ideological stake in rejecting explanations of anything which threaten to remove the topic from their own competence. Saunders is scathing towards sociologists, such as Goldthorpe, who simply refuse to take the ability/ intelligence hypothesis seriously, and who conduct massive, expensive studies without even attempting to measure their subjects' abilities.

Reproduction theory

This has its origins in the neo-Marxist theory-building that captured much of sociology in the 1970s. The core arguments are: different classes tend to develop their own cultures; politically and economically dominant classes have their cultures adopted in education; therefore their children are at an advantage, but the children's success appears to be due to their superior ability in a socially impartial contest; class inequalities are thereby legitimized and the class structure is reproduced in a double sense – class relationships themselves endure, and class positions are transmitted from parents to children (Bourdieu and Passeron, 1977). Everyone has always realized that the real world is not quite this simple. For a start, there is some mobility. This is explained in terms of structural changes which require some movement to be permitted, and concessions which are necessary to sustain an ideology of equal opportunity.

Mike Savage and Muriel Egerton (1997) have used this theory to interpret the evidence from the 1958 birth cohort – exactly the same evidence that Saunders uses to argue the importance of individual ability. Savage and Egerton treat the volume of mobility that occurs as a product of structural requirements, especially the expansion of the middle class. They prefer to treat individual ability as an explanation of exactly who rises, or remains, rather than as an explanation of the volume of movement. Their analysis produces some interesting results. These show, of course, that it is not only ability (IQ) and educational qualifications that account for individuals' eventual destinations. People from working class backgrounds have a greater need for raw ability and qualifications in order to reach the middle class than middle class children need in order to stay there. The able working class child may or may not get on, whereas the equally able and qualified middle class child very rarely slips. Ability and qualifications are rather more important in determining girls' labour market achievements than boys'. Among boys, other kinds of social and cultural capital seem to carry rather more weight than among girls.

Critics argue that socio-cultural reproduction theories place far too much stress on cultural capital, and pay too little attention to economic resources, and also to the different kinds and levels of cognitive ability that, if not inherited, are nurtured in different families (see Barone et al, 2006; Sullivan, 2001).

Rational action theory

This is John Goldthorpe's (1996) preferred explanation of the constant flux. He discounts innate ability as a possible explanation. Goldthorpe has always taken the view that inequalities in life-chances are simply too wide for individual ability to be a credible explanation, though Saunders (1995) has shown that this is not in fact the case. The rational action explanation does not require us to postulate entirely different class cultures. Indeed, it assumes that everyone will prefer a middle class to a working class position, and will want their own children to reach the former if possible. So if ability is not the answer, why do not more working class children ascend? Goldthorpe's explanation is that mobility outcomes, and the constant flux, are the result of rational actors calculating the relative costs and benefits of trying to reach different destinations, and the crucial point here is that these relative costs and benefits will vary in value depending on the actors' starting points. A couple of illustrations will clarify the argument. Supporting a child through higher education will be a greater burden on a working class family, relative to its resources, than for a middle class family. A working class child who achieves an intermediate class position is likely to be regarded as successful, whereas a middle class family will view this as failure and might well do everything possible to secure a better outcome.

The theory does not require us to imagine that all families use electronic calculators to estimate the costs and likely returns from investing in their children's education, any more than economic theory asks us to believe that all consumers make themselves aware of the price of a good at all the accessible outlets prior to every purchase. The assumption in economics is simply that there will be a tendency for consumers to choose the cheapest, all other things being equal, and the cheapest will therefore, eventually, become the market leader. Likewise, the rational action theory makes behaviour comprehensible at the individual level but it is explaining group norms and tendencies rather than attributing to everyone all the rational thought processes that are specified.

A criticism of this entire body of sociological theory and research is that it proceeds on the assumption that any outcome other than perfect mobility, and likewise any inequalities in outcomes between males and females, and ethnic groups, shows that something is amiss in current social arrangements. However, Swift (2004) argues that some mechanisms that produce unequal outcomes are surely non-objectionable. What if some groups are brighter (whether as a result of nature or nurture)? Is it reprehensible if parents use the resources at their disposal (whatever these might be) for their children's benefit?

What has mobility research achieved?

The big achievement of mobility research has been to show how the volume and directions of absolute mobility depend on the shape of the class structure and how this changes over time. Another, still incomplete success, is the startling discovery of the constant flux (assuming that the finding is in fact correct) – how little variation there has been over time, and between modern societies, in rates of social fluidity or relative mobility. This sociological success is incomplete because, at present, we cannot offer an agreed explanation.

What cannot be explained cannot be changed – not deliberatively at any rate. Policy-makers do not seem to have got the message. Every modern society still has batteries of measures that are supposed to improve the life-chances of the disadvantaged. There has been a never-ending stream of such measures since the end of the nineteenth century and the stream shows no sign of drying up. The policy-makers do not seem to have heard: none of their attempts worked in the past and there are no grounds for expecting different results in the present and future. A rational response would be to stop trying, for the time being at any rate, but we know that in practice this is not going to happen. Reproduction theory may not explain the constant flux but it can explain why all countries try constantly to equalize life-chances, or at least try to appear to be doing so: those with privileges to protect need to be seen to be making all possible efforts to ensure that success is open to all talents. The government-appointed Panel on Fair Access to the Professions that reported in 2009 envisaged a further expansion of employment in the management and professional grades leading to a new surge in upward mobility, thereby restoring the mid-twentieth century situation when the upper levels of the occupational structure were populated mainly by recruits from below. This is simply impossible. The aim misunderstands the basic arithmetic of social mobility. It will be impossible (from a higher baseline) to repeat the mid-twentieth century *rate* of expansion in the professional and management grades, and the shape of the twenty-first century occupational class structure guarantees that most additional jobs at these levels will be filled by internal recruitment.

A harder puzzle is why so many sociologists continue to lend support to measures that are supposed to equalize opportunities. Sociologists should know that the best way to change mobility flows is to change the structure of opportunities itself. We are more likely to reduce unemployment rates among the least-qualified by reducing general unemployment than by providing the least-qualified with yet more education and training.

Summary

It is not a straight-forward matter, but is has been possible for sociology to produce agreed answers to questions about the volume of mobility flows, and the extent to which our society is fluid or closed. Whether it is all fair and meritocratic proves an entirely different matter.

We have seen that there has been a substantial and increasing volume of upward mobility from the working class, and a smaller and diminishing downward flow from the middle class. All this is due to the shape of the class structure, and changes therein over time. Recent trends in mobility will have contributed to the disorganization of the working class. The diverse origins of its members will have helped to keep the middle class disorganized during the twentieth century, but twenty-first century mobility flows favour the development of characteristic middle class lifestyles, forms of consciousness and political dispositions.

The recent convergence in men's and women's social class profiles (their distribution between the middle, intermediate and working classes) is likely to converge their rates and patterns of social mobility.

In the future all Britain's ethnic minorities are likely to be at least proportionately represented in the middle class. Some minorities (Indians and Chinese) will very likely be over-represented. Others – Blacks, Pakistanis and Bangladeshis – look likely to remain over-represented at the base of the class structure.

In this chapter we have encountered one of the most startling discoveries in the whole of sociology: the absence of major variations between modern societies, and over time within these societies, in their degrees of fluidity, though this is now challenged by the rather different findings from research that groups the population into income bands, and the discrepancies between the two sets of findings require an agreed explanation. There are explanations on offer of the stability of relative social mobility (if this finding is accepted) – inherited ability, reproduction theory, and rational action theory – but up to now none have been able to marshal the evidence that would win all-round assent. It is equally startling that this finding, one of sociology's firmer conclusions, has been ignored by virtually all social policy-makers, and by many sociologists, who continue to act as if they expect modest interventions in education or labour markets to bring about a significant redistribution of life-chances between the social classes.

Politics

9

Introduction

This chapter examines how the relationship between class and politics has changed since the mid-twentieth century, alongside the changes that have taken place in the class structure and politics themselves.

First, it is argued that class analysis needs to address medium- and long-term political trends and regularities rather than events that require a political explanation. Recent events include the successes of the Conservative Party led by Margaret Thatcher in the 1980s, the successes of New Labour in the 1990s and 2000s, and the formation of a Conservative-Liberal Democrat coalition government in 2010. We need to separate the ways in which these events were just blips from the ways in which they were part of longer-term trends, and we need to separate their short-term impacts from their enduring consequences.

The chapter then identifies four long-term (since the mid-twentieth century) trends in party politics and voter behaviour in Britain.

- A decline in support for the Labour Party until this trend was interrupted by spikes in the 1997 and 2001 general elections following the party's rebranding as New Labour, after which, in 2005 and 2010, Labour support fell back to its pre-1997 level.
- Steady electoral support for the Conservative Party until this support slumped in the 1990s – a slump that has continued up to and through the general election of 2010.
- A general decline in voter partisanship – a weakening of voter attachments to all the main parties.
- A loosening of the link between class and party choice – a process known as class de-alignment.

The chapter then identifies and discusses over-arching trends in the relationship between political elites and the people.

- How politics has become 'a profession', with elites gaining corporate sponsorship then marketing a 'party brand', the prime target being the floating voter.

■ Popular political activity has moved outside the main parties into new social movements, in networks maintained through the internet complemented by the mobile phone. The chapter notes that the overwhelming majority of the activists in these movements are from a radical section of the new middle class, and that the movements' issues are primarily middle class priorities.

The chapter concludes by explaining how this new politics reflects the new balance of class relationships, and the main class struggles, in twenty-first century Britain.

What sociology can explain

Sociology is best at explaining what Emile Durkheim called social facts – persistent regularities and trends in social behaviour. It is futile to seek a class explanation, or any other sociological explanation, of political events where the most plausible explanations are simply political. These events include Thatcherism (see Box 9.1), New Labour (see Box 9.2), and the coalition Conservative-Liberal Democrat government that was formed in 2010.

In the 1980s there were numerous attempts to explain the success of Thatcherism. Some said that Thatcherism was the outcome, which might have been predicted, of deep-seated changes in the economy and class structure

---

Box 9.1 Thatcherism

Margaret Thatcher was elected to the leadership of the Conservative Party in 1975 by her fellow MPs. This followed the Conservatives' defeats in the two general elections held during 1974. Thatcher's most senior post in the 1970–74 Conservative government had been as Minister of Education. In 1974 she was not widely regarded as a likely successor to the incumbent leader, Edward Heath. However, she challenged Heath for the leadership and built a successful bandwagon of support among parliamentary colleagues.

Thatcher belonged to a 'new right' group within the Conservative Party that wished to break with the post-war consensus and adopt radical policies. Her colleagues doubted whether she could win an election with such an agenda. Had Margaret Thatcher been defeated in her first general election as party leader, she would almost certainly have been replaced, in which case we would never have heard of Thatcherism.

James Callaghan, the Labour prime minister since 1976, had been expected to call a general election in 1978 (after the government had served for four years). Had he done so it is quite possible that Labour would have won. However, Callaghan decided to delay until 1979, hoping that a stronger economy would make re-election certain. In the event, 1978–79 became the 'winter of discontent' with a succession of strikes in public services, and in 1979 Margaret Thatcher led her party to victory.

Thatcher's radical 'monetarist' policies instantly accelerated de-industrialization and set unemployment soaring, and the Conservatives were soon lagging in opinion polls. She was expected to be a one-term prime minister. Then in 1981 and 1982 she had two strokes of luck.

■ The Labour Party split. A 'gang of four' senior Labour politicians founded the Social Democratic Party (which merged with the Liberals to become the Liberal Democrats in 1988. In 1981 the break-away immediately split the Labour vote.

■ In 1982 General Galtieri, the Argentine leader, invaded the Falkland Islands. Margaret Thatcher ordered a task force to retake the territory and became a victorious war leader.

The Conservative's popularity soared. Thatcher led her party to victory with an increased majority in the 1983 election, after which the policies known as Thatcherism were implemented

---

Box 9.2   New Labour

The Labour Party had been expected to win the 1992 general election. In 1990 Margaret Thatcher had been forced to resign by her own cabinet. Her authoritarian style of leadership was resented (by some). More to the point, the Conservatives were floundering in the opinion polls. A 'poll tax', a flat rate 'community charge' that had replaced 'the rates' as a local council tax, was deeply unpopular.

Despite replacing Thatcher with John Major, the Conservatives remained behind in the opinion polls until the week of the 1992 general election. Labour was ahead again in the polls soon after the election. The consensus afterwards was the Labour had run a self-defeating, 'triumphalist' election campaign. If Labour had campaigned more effectively, Neil Kinnock would probably have become prime minister without re-imaging 'old' Labour.

After the 1992 defeat Kinnock resigned and was succeeded by John Smith, a 'safe pair of hands' with a bank manager persona. Smith died prematurely in 1994. If he had lived he would surely have led 'old' Labour to victory in the next general election.

His successor was Tony Blair, one of a group who believed that his party need to be thoroughly modernized. Thus it was 'New' Labour that won the 1997 general election.

(Jessop et al, 1988). Others explained the success of Thatcherism in terms of the project's 'authoritarian populism' – its stances on law and order, immigration, nationalism, and intolerance of homosexuality. Thatcherism was said to harmonize with some deeply-rooted traits in working class culture (Hall, 1988; Hall and Jacques, 1983).

Despite the huge parliamentary majorities, the Conservatives were actually no more popular in the 1980s than on the occasions of their election victories in the 1950s and in 1970. Many of the Thatcher government's policies were distinctly unpopular – economic management, tolerance of high unemployment, and cut-backs in public services. There was no upsurge of an enterprise culture. The policies that appealed to working class voters were not all nationalist and socially authoritarian. Tax-cutting was popular, and likewise the restrictions on trade unions' power, and the sale of council houses to sitting tenants. Even so, only a minority of voters could be described as Thatcherites. Fairly solid and enthusiastic support was confined to limited sections of the electorate, mainly the upper class and the petit bourgeoisie (see Edgell and Duke, 1991). Instead of trying to explain a non-existent popularity, Thatcherism's success really needed, and still needs, to be explained despite its unpopularity in many sections of the population (as recognized at the time by, for example, the contributors to Brown and Sparks, 1989).

The best explanations of the success of Thatcherism in the 1980s are basically political. There was the depth of unpopularity to which the Labour Party sank, and the divisions in its ranks which led to the break-away of the Social Democratic Party in 1981. A Labour government had presided over the 'winter of discontent' (strikes in the public services) in 1978–79. It is possible that Labour could have held onto office had it called the general election six months earlier (before the winter). It is possible that Labour would have won in 1979 if it had been able to maintain a parliamentary pact with the Liberals, or had not the Scottish National Party been making inroads into the Labour vote in Scotland. It is possible that Labour could have regained office in 1983 with more effective leadership. The image projected by Michael Foot, the Labour leader elected following the 1979 defeat, was unattractive to many voters. His famous donkey jacket, and his long-standing links with CND and other left-wing causes, rallied traditional support within the Labour Party itself but invited much ridicule beyond, and played a role in provoking the split in the Labour Party. Soon the Social Democrats were syphoning off additional MPs, party workers, and hundreds of thousands of former Labour voters. The crucial point is that with more skilled leadership in the late-1970s and early-1980s, Labour might have been the main party of government during the latter decade.

We also need to pay due respect to the political skill of Margaret Thatcher herself. In 1979 the policies that became the hallmarks of Thatcherism would not have received majority support if placed before her cabinet or the parliamentary Conservative Party. In her early years in office it appeared quite likely that, before long, Thatcher would be ditched by her own party. As unemployment rose towards two million in 1980–81, the Conservative government's popularity nose-dived. It looked as though Margaret Thatcher was leading her party to certain defeat at the next general election. In the event, the 1983 election was won with an increased majority, and 'wets' were gradually relieved of key government posts. The country then encountered Thatcherism. It is pointless to seek the explanation of her success in deep-seated changes and tendencies in the wider society when there is a much simpler political explanation.

In the late-1990s pundits were seeking the deep-seated sources of the appeal of Blairism and New Labour. Once again, it is best to look first at the simple explanations (see Box 9.2). At the time, Tony Blair was an extremely popular party leader and prime minister. Even so, the share of the vote achieved by Labour in 1997 was lower than in the Labour victories between 1945 and 1966. Labour was assisted by the unpopularity of the Conservatives in the 1990s – the sleaze, the split over Europe, sterling being forced out of the European exchange rate mechanism and the aura of economic incompetence that this created. Also, we need to recognize that with a little more luck or astute election campaigning, Labour under Neil Kinnock might well have won the general election in 1992. John Smith, who replaced Neil Kinnock as Labour leader, might have lived to become prime minister. In either event there would have been no New Labour. Given these circumstances, it is futile to seek a correspondence between the New Labour project and fundamental shifts in the class structure or any other deeply-rooted features of Britain in the 1990s.

The formation of a coalition government between the Conservatives and Liberal Democrats in 2010 was not an outcome of long-term social or even long-term political trends, but a 'wobble', always possible in Britain's 'first past the post', single member constituencies electoral system. New Labour won the 2005 general election comfortably (in terms of seats in parliament) by gaining 36 per cent of the popular vote against the Conservatives' 33 per cent. In 2010 the Conservatives won 36 per cent of the votes while the Labour vote slumped to 29 per cent. The Conservatives' margin of victory was wider than Labour's in 2005, but in 2010 the Conservative vote was distributed between constituencies in a way that did not yield a House of Commons majority. The Liberal Democrats did not achieve an electoral breakthrough in 2010: their share of the vote rose marginally from 22 per cent in 2005 to 23 per cent in 2010. Their major breakthroughs had occurred in 1974 and 1983 (see Table 6.3, p 151). In February 1974 the Liberal share of the vote rose to 19 per cent from eight per cent in 1970. The years following 1970 had been a period of industrial conflict and rocketing price inflation. The popularity of both Labour and the Conservatives (who were in office from 1970–1974) had ebbed. The February 1974 election was fought during a coal-miners strike during which failures in electricity supplies forced industry onto a three-day working week. In 1983 the combined vote of the Liberals and the Social Democratic Party was 25 per cent, the highest ever recorded by the Liberals (and partners, where applicable) since 1945. This boost followed the split in the Labour Party in 1981. The 1983 result was not bettered in 2010 despite impressive performances in televised prime ministerial debates by the Liberal Democrat leader, Nick Clegg.

If class analysis can deliver, its achievements will not be in explaining these and similar political events, but longer-term trends and stabilities.

Trends

Labour party support

Table 6.3 (chapter 6, p 151) presented the proportions of the total vote received by the three main parliamentary political parties – Conservatives, Labour and the Liberal Democrats (and their predecessors) – in every general election from 1945 up to 2010. The Labour figures in Table 6.2 show a clear long-term trend between the 1950s and 1990s. The electoral fortunes of Labour fluctuated from election to election, but the fluctuations were around a long-term trend, which was downwards up to 1997. In every general election between 1945 and 1970 Labour won over 40 per cent of all the votes that were cast. Then, in the six elections between 1974 and 1992, Labour never reached the 40 per cent level of support, and polled as few as 28 per cent of votes cast in 1983. New Labour support bounced back to 43 per cent and 42 per cent of the total vote in 1997 and 2001, but fell back to 36 per cent in 2005 and 29 per cent in 2010. Apart from the New Labour spike, the clear long-term trend has been downwards.

Now the most plausible explanation for this trend is sociological, and involves the changing shape of the class structure. Labour's original electoral base has contracted. Most of its support has always been from the working class, and the working class became smaller from decade to decade up to the 1980s. Furthermore, it has become rarer for manual workers to possess additional characteristics which increase their likelihood of voting Labour. Manual workers have been most likely to vote Labour if they:

- Rent rather than own their own homes.
- Are trade unionists.
- Work in the public sector.

Owner-occupation has risen gradually since the 1950s, and in the 1980s (aided by the sale of council houses) it surged upwards in the class where it had been least common, namely, the working class. After the 1970s trade union membership declined, especially among manual workers. Thatcherism's denationalization programme, and the contracting-out of non-core services from the remaining public sector, transferred swathes of manual jobs into private businesses. All these trends were bad for Labour. The sole favourable long-term trend was the rise in the number of people dependent on state benefits due to the increase in those of pensionable age, the rise in single parenthood, and higher unemployment than from the 1940s up to the 1970s. State welfare dependents have been another group who have been particularly likely to vote Labour, and since the 1970s this has created a danger (for Labour's appeal in other sections of the electorate) of the party becoming too closely associated with welfare dependents.

In 1997 Labour bucked the trend. The party won a landslide election victory with a House of Commons majority of over 160 MPs. However, the percentage of the total vote won by Labour (43 per cent) was not particularly high; in fact it was rather modest, set against the party's performances in the 1950s and 60s. The scale of the landslide victory in 1997 was not due to Labour's exceptional popularity but to the collapse of Conservative support. The Conservatives won just 31 per cent of all votes cast in 1997; the party's worst performance in the twentieth century.

By 1997 the Labour Party had re-invented itself; it had become New Labour with new policies, a new image, and, perhaps most important of all, a new publicity machine. New Labour had leapt into the marketing age. The party was marketed as a brand. Focus groups were used extensively. The target was the floating voter. The party membership and internal committees were bypassed by the owners of the brand (see Wring, 2005). In 2001 New Labour held on to most of the support that it had received in 1997: 43 per cent of all votes in 1997 and 42 per cent in 2001. Then in 2005 Labour held onto office with just 36 per cent of all votes cast, representing support from only around 20 per cent of all the people who could have voted (approximately 40 per cent stayed away from the polls). Thirty-six per cent was the lowest level of support with which any party in Britain had won a general election since 1945. In 2010 the Labour vote slumped to just 29 per cent. Labour's period in office from 1997 to 2010 owed much more to the unpopularity of the Conservatives than to Labour's own exceptional electoral appeal.

Different conclusions were drawn following Labour's bounce back in 1997. One view was that this victory vindicated the party's modernizers who had deliberately sought to distance New Labour from its working class roots, in particular from organized labour (the trade unions), to make the party acceptable to 'business' and private enterprise (relaxed about people becoming filthy rich), and friendly towards the middle classes (no increase in standard or higher rates of income tax). According to this view, class divisions and identities had weakened, and social democratic politics needed a new base. Anthony Giddens (1998, 2000) argued that the success of New Labour was due to the party leadership embracing a 'third way', freeing itself from the old first way versus second way, right versus left politics of industrial society. Third way politics, according to Giddens, address new challenges posed by globalization, new technology, the need to invest in human capital, threats to the environment, claims for rights by women and ethnic minorities, and social policies that aim not to equalize conditions but to give all sections of the population equal opportunities to succeed in life. However, an alternative analysis, based more firmly on studies of voters' attitudes and behaviour, has queried whether its 'new' policies and image played any significant part in New Labour's electoral successes between 1997 and 2005 (Heath et al, 2001). People who live in the 'political village' are always liable to overestimate the role of policies in swinging the support of the 'floating voters' who decide the results of elections, who tend to be less interested in and knowledgeable about politics than committed party stalwarts. Could Labour have won its 1997 landslide without becoming New Labour? Would the Conservatives' unpopularity have been sufficient in itself to deliver victory to Labour? We shall never know, but the rebirth of the party has had consequences.

Conservative party support

From 1945 until 1992 Conservative support was remarkably stable. There were trendless fluctuations, ups and downs from election to election with peak support of 50 per cent in 1955 and a low of 36 per cent in October 1974, but no long-term trend whatsoever.

As noted in chapter 6, this trendlessness is more remarkable than the decline of the Labour vote, given the wider social trends which one might have expected to work in the Conservatives' favour, especially the expansion in the numbers of middle class employees and home-owners. Why did the Conservative Party fail to benefit electorally from these trends? This question was partly answered in chapter 6. As it has grown, the middle class has become better-educated. The types of middle class voters who have increased in number are those least likely to be conservative either socially or politically. This has neutralized the effects of the change in the shape of the class structure which should otherwise have been to the Conservatives' electoral benefit.

Throughout the history of the labour movement, parties of the left have attracted the support of left-wing intellectuals. Karl Marx was among them. The left-leaning section of the middle class has tended to be highly (university) educated, and to work with ideas or people rather than in manufacturing or finance. During the second half of the twentieth century this section of the middle class grew strongly as a result of the expansion of higher education, the growth of employment in public service professions, then, towards the close of the century, the growth of the creative industries whose main capital is intellectual property rights. This section of the middle class tends to be radical on social issues (civil rights and sexual issues, for example), and has supplied most of the activists in the 'new social movements' (see below). These middle class radicals have been less likely to seek state ownership and control of the economy. In Britain their preferred mainstream political party has been Labour, especially when it fought as New Labour, or alternatively, in recent elections, the Liberal Democrats (Roux et al, 2008). Over time, with the numerical decline of the working class, this section of the middle class has contributed a larger share of Labour votes, though never the majority, but for a long time now it has supplied the party with the majority of its activists and elected representatives (see below). The Conservative Party in Britain, and indeed its equivalents in Europe, have been less successful in attracting working class votes. Those disillusioned with the main parties of the left have recently been more likely to turn to what are called 'right-wing populist' parties, in practice parties with nationalist ideologies and anti-immigration policies (see Achterberg, 2006; Oesch, 2008; Svallfors, 2005; Werfhorst and Graaf, 2004).

Another crucial fact is that the expansion in the middle class during the second half of the twentieth century has placed many upwardly mobile, first-generation managers and professionals in the Conservative Party's main electoral base. Many appear to have retained at least vestiges of class identities and political loyalties from their social origins. The Conservative Party has needed to win these new middle class voters. In its early years the Labour Party was unable to rely on the working class vote. This vote needed to be won. The Conservatives were in a similar position vis-a-vis the expanding middle class in the second half of the twentieth century, and in the twenty-first century it remains unclear that the Party will eventually be victorious. Since 1997 (31 per cent) the Conservative Party has succeeded in raising its share of the popular vote to no higher than 36 per cent (in 2010).

The decline of partisanship

Since 1970 voters' loyalties have been more fickle than in the 1940s, 50s and 60s. Between 1945 and 1970 the share of the vote won by the Conservatives did not change by more than four per cent between any two successive general elections, and Labour's share did not vary by more than five per cent. Thereafter there were larger swings: a fall of eight per cent for the Conservatives between 1970 and 1974, a rise of eight per cent between 1974 and 1979, and a drop of 11 per cent between 1992 and 1997. Labour's vote fell by nine per cent between 1979 and 1983, rose by nine per cent between 1992 and 1997, and fell by seven per cent between 2005 and 2010.

Since the 1970s the parties' opinion poll ratings have swung sharply. Governments have plumbed depths of unpopularity between elections, then achieved re-election. Opinion has sometimes swung decisively during election campaigns. Unless the opinion polls were wrong (as many suspect), it appears that in 1992 some voters left home intending to vote Labour, changed their minds before entering the polling booths, then became Labour supporters again by the time that they had returned home (see Box 9.2). In 2010, during the televised prime ministerial debates, Liberal support rose to match that of Labour and the Conservatives, but had fallen back to little more than its 2005 level by polling day.

Earlier on, political scientists had developed theories of political socialization (Butler and Stokes, 1974; Rose and McAllister, 1990). These emphasized how most people formed party loyalties during childhood, usually identifying with their parents' parties. These loyalties developed prior to young people acquiring any detailed knowledge about party policies. Often this knowledge was acquired later, and filtered through pre-formed loyalties. Some young people changed their loyalties during youth. This was especially likely if they were socially mobile. Thereafter, voters became attached to their preferred parties, and were most likely to remain loyal supporters for the rest of their lives. So the main parties had solid bedrocks of reliable support. The parties' electioneering problem was to 'get the vote out'. Their supporters could abstain, but there was usually no danger of them switching to the other side.

These solid bedrocks of support still exist, but in a shrunken state. The Economic and Social Research Council's 16–19 Initiative questioned representative samples (panels) of young people in four parts of Britain on three occasions between 1987 and 1989, and found that just 43 per cent (including the don't knows) gave the same replies on each occasion to the standard, 'How would you vote?' question. Only 28 per cent were firmly attached to either Labour or the Conservative Party (Banks et al, 1992). This sample was aged 16–20 at the time of the research. The proportion with firm party loyalties could expand with age. Or the majority could remain non-partisan. Recent cohorts of young people have been moving into adulthood, and passing the age when they become eligible to vote, without, in most cases, developing any firm party attachments.

There has been a corresponding decline in party memberships. In the 1950s the Conservatives had nearly three million individual members. By 1979 there were just 1.5 million, and a mere 300,000 in 1997 with an average age of 62. Most of Labour's members have always been affiliated via their trade unions. From the 1940s until the 1980s Labour could not match the Conservatives' figures for individual party members. The Labour Party had around a million individual members in the 1950s, and around 300,000, roughly the same as the Conservatives, in the mid-1990s. New Labour then launched repeated recruitment drives, using its party political broadcasts for this purpose. The party's problem has not been in persuading people to sign-up so much as retaining them. The present-day recruit, it appears, is more likely to be a temporary paying supporter than a long-term active member. New Labour's dream in the 1990s of regaining a million members has remained just a distant aspiration.

All the above is consistent with answers given to a standard question in British Election Studies since 1964: 'How strongly do you support the party that you are most likely to vote for?' As can be seen in Figure 9.1, the proportion describing their party attachment as 'very strong' declined from over 40 per cent to less than 10 per cent between 1964 and 2005. The proportion saying 'not strong' rose from 11 per cent to 36 per cent. This has been a general trend affecting all the political parties.

Minor parties

As party support has softened, the share of all votes attracted by the two main parties has declined. The Northern Ireland parties severed their earlier

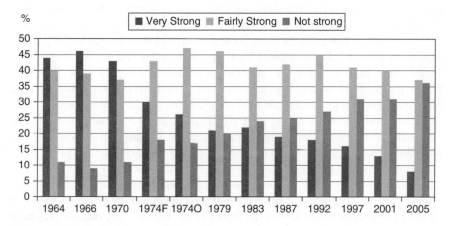

Figure 9.1 Strength of party attachments

connections with the Conservatives and Labour following the re-ignition of 'the troubles' in the late-1960s. The Ulster Unionists restored their earlier formal link with the Conservatives prior to the 2010 election, then won no seats. Actually, Northern Ireland is the one part of the UK where there has been little political change. In every election there are in fact two contests: one for the unionist/protestant vote, and the other for the nationalist/catholic vote, with hardly anyone crossing this divide.

In Scotland, and to a lesser extent in Wales, nationalist parties have grown in strength – sufficiently so to gain a parliament for Scotland and an assembly for Wales, both of which opened in 1999. In England, the Liberal Party, the Social Democrats, then the alliance between the two in the 1983 and 1987 general elections, then the Liberal Democrats after these parties merged in 1988, have achieved a larger share of the vote since the 1970s than the Liberals achieved during the 30 previous years. Indeed, there have been periods in recent times when the Liberal Democrats have been England's second party of local government in terms of council seats held, and the number of council chambers where the party has been in sole or joint control.

The minor parties in England have suffered under the first-past-the-post, single-member constituency, electoral system, especially in national elections. However, these parties have not been disadvantaged in this way in elections to the European Parliament, where the election system is more proportionate, with large, multi-member constituencies. So the LibDems, and also other 'minor' parties – the Greens, the UK Independence Party, and in 2009 the British National Party – have been able to secure seats in the European Parliament. In 2010 the Greens gained their first UK parliamentary seat – a spectacular breakthrough. The winner-takes-all, single member voting system still operating for elections to the Westminster parliament, has proved less disadvantageous for the regional/nationalist parties in Wales and Scotland because their support is concentrated in a limited number of constituencies where they have been able to take seats in parliament reflecting their popularity in the regions where their support is based. Needless to say, support for 'other' parties has been just as fickle in recent times as Conservative and Labour support.

It is possible that all the above are features of a new politics, but it is also possible that politics in the UK is currently in a transitional state. There have been earlier historical periods when the main parties had only narrow bedrocks of reliable, dependable support, and when the combined vote for the two main parties was squeezed (see Box 9.3). This applied early in the twentieth century when Labour was replacing the Liberals as the main alternative to the Conservatives. No-one can be sure, but it is possible that UK politics will firm up once more at some point in the twenty-first century.

Class de-alignment

Amid the above, a major debate since the 1980s has been about an additional alleged trend – class de-alignment. There is no dispute about the basic facts

---

Box 9.3   The two-party system

Between 1900 and 1910 the two main parties, at that time the Liberals and the Conservatives, shared at least 90% of the votes cast in each general election.

Between 1918 and 1923 these parties' combined vote slumped to less than 70% of all votes cast in each general election.

The combined appeal of the two main parties, by then Labour and the Conservatives, recovered and remained above 90% in every general election between 1935 and 1970.

Since then their combined share has exceeded 80% only in 1979.

---

of this matter. From the 1940s up until the 1960s, in every general election in Britain, two-thirds or more of white-collar voters supported the Conservative Party and around two-thirds of manual electors voted Labour. These statistics have never been as high since then. There are different ways of calculating index scores of class voting. An absolute class voting index is calculated by adding together the number of manual workers voting Labour and the number of white-collar workers voting Conservative, then dividing by the total number of voters. The possible range of scores is zero to 100. An Alford index subtracts the percentage of non-manuals voting Labour from the percentage of manuals who vote Labour. The possible range of scores is −100 to +100. With minor fluctuations, both indices have declined since the 1960s: from over 65 per cent to just over 40 per cent in the case of the absolute index, and from just over 40 per cent to under 20 per cent on the Alford index (see Figure 9.2).

Ivor Crewe was among the first to identify class de-alignment (Crewe, 1977, 1986; Sarlvik and Crewe, 1983), and nowadays most political scientists accept that this trend has in fact taken place (see Franklin, 1985). It is said that class alignment occurred when each party was identified with a particular class, when most people had definite class identities, and voted for the parties that represented their classes. The de-alignment thesis claims that some, if not all, of these links have weakened.

Now it is possible to show that if votes for parties other than Labour and the Conservatives are taken out of the picture, and if we make allowances for the general decline in partisanship (party support becoming more fickle), and if we also take into account Labour's unpopularity in all sections of the electorate in the 1980s, and the Conservatives' unpopularity in the 1990s, we see that class alignment is more or less as strong as ever: that there have been fluctuations from election to election but no clear long-term trend (Evans, 1993; Heath et al, 1985, 1991). This is all rather ingenuous, but the manipulation of the evidence is not really convincing. These analysts are taking out of account the very features of voters' attitudes and behaviour that the de-alignment thesis seeks to explain. We have seen that support for 'other' parties has been higher since the 1970s than during the previous 30 years. These other parties have

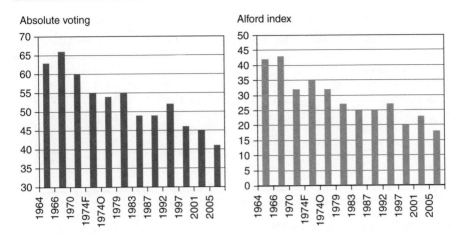

Figure 9.2 Class voting indices

drawn support from all social classes. Since these parties now account for a significant share of the vote in local, national and European elections, their presence really needs to be taken into account when measuring the strength of the class-vote link. After all, The LibDems have become a major force in local government in England, part of the UK coalition government in 2010, and the Scottish National Party became the largest party in its country's parliament in 2008. It is possible that, after what turns out to be a period of transitional politics, the main parties will regain their former dominance, but it is equally possible that the present so-called transitional state is in fact the new politics.

Jan Pakulski and Malcolm Waters (1996) attach considerable importance to class de-alignment in announcing 'the death of class'. They also draw attention to there being few references to class nowadays in parties' policy statements and electioneering. However, as regards political rhetoric, in the past it was usually other parties that were accused of being dependent upon, and seeking to serve the interest of, just one particular class. The leaders of all major parties have always attempted to appeal across class divisions. Also, Peter Achterberg (2006) has analysed party manifestoes since the Second World War in 20 Western countries, and has found that class issues have not diminished, but have been joined by other, socio-cultural issues. In any case, even if class and politics had been totally de-aligned, this would not mean that class was dead; only that it had been de-aligned from politics. That said, class would have become significantly less influential.

However, it is possible to insist that there remains a clear, albeit weakened, relationship between class and voting, and that class is still the best of all single predictors (Robertson, 1984; Weakliem, 1989, and see below). It is worth taking a closer look at how the different classes have voted in particular general elections. There has yet to be a general election in Britain in which at least one of the main parties (Conservatives and Labour) failed to gain at least a half of

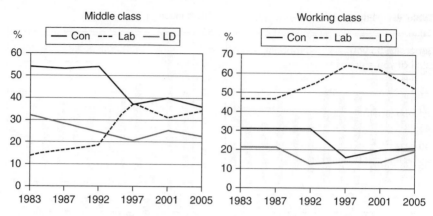

Figure 9.3 Class voting, 1983–2005

all votes cast by its 'own' class, and where the winning party did not receive more than twice the proportion of votes from its 'own' class than from all other parties combined. Labour did poorly in elections between 1983 and 1992 because on each of these occasions it won fewer than half of all the votes cast by manual workers and their families, but even in these elections the working class was considerably more likely to vote Labour than Conservative (see Figure 9.3). The Conservatives did poorly in 1997, 2001 and 2005 because they were supported by no more than 40 per cent of middle class voters. The 1997 and 2005 elections were unusual in that the middle class (just managers and professionals here) was as likely to vote Labour as Conservative. However, in these same elections the working class was far more likely to vote Labour than Conservative, and workers were also much more likely than the middle class to vote Labour (see Figure 9.3). In every general election there has been a clear class-vote relationship even after 40 years of class de-alignment.

The relationships between age and voting, and sex and voting, are extremely weak when compared with the present-day class-vote relationship. Nowadays men and women hardly differ in their party choices. This is novel, because until the 1990s women were the more Conservative sex. Older voters are more Conservative than younger voters, and this has been the case ever since the relevant information began to be collected. We really do become more Conservative, on average, as we grow older. However, the age-relationship is much weaker than the class-vote link.

Ethnicity is very strongly related to voting. Labour wins consistently and overwhelmingly among all the non-white ethnic minorities, and has done so ever since the 1960s (see Table 9.1). It is difficult to say whether it is the Conservatives' policies, people or rhetoric that repels the minorities. There are implications here for both politics and race relations. The ethnic vote has become crucial to Labour's success in constituencies where the minorities are concentrated. This could lead to Labour being highly responsive to minority

Table 9.1 Ethnicity and party support

Generally, do you think of yourself as:	Caribbean %	African %	Indian %	Bangladeshi %	Pakistani %
Labour	70	64	52	39	49
Conservative	2	2	12	4	6
Liberal democrat	2	7	10	11	15

Source: Electoral Commission, 2005

concerns. Alternatively, Labour could take the minorities for granted on the basis that they have nowhere else to go. Local ethnic minority 'take-overs' of the Labour Party in some Labour 'heartlands' could repel some of the party's traditional white working class voters. David Cameron's Conservatives departed from the former practice of concentrating on more friendly sections of the electorate and began giving the party a more diverse character and appeal. There was a substantial increase (though only to 11) in the number of ethnic minority Conservative MPs in 2010. However, a crucial point here is that the minorities are not numerous enough, even in total, for ethnicity to become the main base of UK party politics.

Politics, politicians and the people

Social backgrounds of MPs

There have been changes over time in the types of people who become elected representatives, and how these correspond to both party memberships and the people who vote for the parties' candidates in elections. The most dramatic change in recent years has been the influx of new women MPs, elected as part of the new Labour landslide in 1997. Change usually occurs more gradually, as retiring politicians are replaced by younger representatives.

The Conservative Party changed gradually from the late-nineteenth century onwards, as aristocrats in parliament gave way to people from business and the professions. Nowadays the Conservative Party's elected representatives have a broadly similar class profile to the party's active rank-and-file (whereas lower-level white-collar employees and the working class are much better-represented among Conservative voters). There is a much wider discrepancy nowadays between Labour voters and the types of people who they elect. In terms of education and former occupations, Labour MPs are now more similar to their Conservative opposites than to Labour voters. Today both Labour and Conservative MPs tend to have reached the House of Commons via university, then jobs in the professions, business, management or politics.

Table 9.2 Occupations of MPs elected in 2005 (in percentages)

Occupation	Labour	Conservatives
Profession	40	38
Business	7	38
White-collar	20	2
Politician/political organizer	17	10
Publisher/journalist	7	7
Manual	10	1

Source: Cracknell, 2005

In the Labour Party the trend throughout the twentieth century was for elected representatives with personal experience in working class jobs to give way to people from the professions and other non-manual occupations. In 1906 86 per cent of Labour MPs were from the working class. By 1945 this was down to 38 per cent and by 2005 just 10 per cent. There has been a similar exodus of working class activists from many local Labour Parties and their replacement by people from the non-conservative middle class. Barry Hindess (1971) noted such a trend in Liverpool as early as the 1960s.

Table 9.2 gives the occupational backgrounds of the MPs who were elected in 2005. Roughly two-fifths on both the Conservative and Labour benches were from the professions. The Conservatives had more MPs with 'business' backgrounds (38 per cent against seven per cent) whereas Labour MPs were more likely to have held other white-collar jobs (20 per cent against two per cent), and more had worked in politics (17 per cent against 10 per cent) and in manual occupations (10 per cent against one per cent).

Conservative and Labour MPs differ more sharply in their educational backgrounds (see Table 9.3). More Conservatives have attended independent schools (54 per cent against 15 per cent of Labour MPs and 40 per cent of LibDems in 2010). There has been a slight decline since the mid-twentieth century in the proportion of Labour MPs with independent education and a much steeper decline among Conservatives – 75 per cent in 1951 to 54 per cent in 2010. There have been increases in all parties in the proportions who have been to university (from 65 per cent to 95 per cent among Conservatives from 1951 to 2010, and from 41 per cent to 86 per cent among Labour MPs). Oxford and Cambridge universities were slightly less well-represented in the 2010 House of Commons than in 1951, but even so, as many as 38 per cent of Conservative MPs, 28 per cent of LibDems and 20 per cent of Labour MPs in 2010 had been to Oxbridge. The main route into a career as a Conservative MP is still via private schooling, then Oxford or Cambridge University, then

Table 9.3 Education of MPs elected in 1951, 2005 and 2010

Year	Labour	Conservative	Liberal Democrat
Percentages educated at independent schools			
1951	20	75	
2005	18	60	39
2010	15	54	40
Percentages with university education			
1951	41	65	
2005	64	81	79
2010	86	95	88
Percentages with Oxbridge education			
1951	19	52	
2005	16	43	31
2010	20	38	28

Based on data from Sutton Trust, 2005, 2010

employment in business, a profession or management. Labour MPs have somewhat more diverse backgrounds. Private schooling and Oxbridge backgrounds have always been atypical. The most common route for Labour MPs today is from state education, university (but not Oxbridge), then employment in a profession or some other non-manual occupation. The LibDems are consistently in between the Conservatives and Labour in terms of their MPs' pre-parliamentary backgrounds.

The higher up we look in both parties, the more elevated are the backgrounds of the politicians. A half of the 1945 Labour cabinet was from the working class compared with just five per cent (one person, John Prescott) in 1997 and one person (Alan Johnson) immediately before the 2010 general election. One might argue that the Labour Party has not really changed as dramatically as these figures suggest. The volume of upward mobility from the working class has increased (see chapter 8). Many of the present-day Labour MPs whose own previous jobs were middle class spent their childhoods in working class homes. The kinds of people from working class backgrounds who once left school before age 16, entered manual jobs, became active in trade unions and politics, and eventually became elected politicians, are now staying in education beyond age 16 and becoming university graduates. However, the fact remains that personal experience of being an adult manual worker has become quite rare among Labour parliamentarians. The contrast with the typical Labour voter (still a manual worker) is glaring.

Another trend is that it has become quite common for national politicians to spend almost their entire working lives in politics. In 2005 17 per cent of Labour MPs and 10 per cent of the Conservatives had moved into parliament from other political jobs. This is not a completely new development. The head offices of the main parties always recruited some bright young graduates who went on to become MPs, but in the past there were very few such jobs. Over time, the party headquarters have expanded. Also, elected representatives at national and European levels, and at regional levels in Scotland, Wales and Northern Ireland, have acquired budgets with which they can appoint staff. When parties are in government, it is now normal for ministers to make political appointments to their state-paid staffs. Also, there are now numerous pressure and campaigning groups with paid staff in which starters can gain political experience. A consequence is that politics has become another (middle class) career: one which exhibits, in a very extreme form, features of some other present-day middle class careers – the insecurity and work pressure, for example. The European and Scottish parliaments, and the Welsh Assembly notwithstanding, there has been little change over time in the number of paid positions for elected politicians. There has been a greater increase in the number of unelected career politicians. Some stay backstage by choice, others because they are unable to gain elected office.

The proportion of MPs who are women rose from three per cent in 1979 to 20 per cent in 2005 and 21 per cent in 2010. The big change was in 1997 when the proportion of women among Labour MPs rose from 14 per cent to 24 per cent. There was still a big difference here between the two main parties in 2005 when 28 per cent of Labour MPs were women compared with just nine per cent of Conservative MPs. This difference remained, but narrowed, following the 2010 general election.

Fifteen ethnic minority MPs were elected in 2005 and 26 in 2010, up from six in 1992, but still in 2010 only just over five per cent of all MPs were from ethnic minorities whereas eight per cent of the adult UK population is now from an ethnic minority. Thirteen out of the 26 ethnic minority MPs elected in 2010 were Labour, 11 were Conservatives, and none were LibDems. In 2010 Labour lost its former position as the ethnic minorities' clear champion in terms of elected representatives, but not in terms of the behaviour of voters.

Political campaigning

There has been a major shift over time in the relationship between paid politicians and the people. The political parties used to be composed of active members who were broadly representative, in socio-demographic terms, of the parties' voters. In this sense, the parties represented broad sections of society. Elected representatives gained their positions on the basis of their skill in saying, and putting into effect, what other members willed. Politics no longer works in this way. Nowadays the young adults who remain active in party politics for years and years tend at least to envisage paid careers as elected or unelected politicians. There are fewer active stalwarts who do not expect such careers, and the activists who become elected representatives in all the parties tend to be from similar social backgrounds – university educated, with subsequent career experience either confined to politics, business, management or the professions.

Today's politicians are more of a distinct career group, described by Peter Oborne (2007) as a political class, but even so, they are probably better-informed than ever before about the state of public opinion. All the parties pay for regular opinion surveys and run focus groups to ensure that they remain in touch. The leaders want to know, and they are in fact well-informed about, what all classes of people are thinking. None want to ignore any substantial sections of the population. Party channels are considered less trustworthy. Party leaders often suspect, usually with good reason, that their party activists' opinions are unrepresentative of the electorate. Party conferences are always likely to pass embarrassing resolutions unless they are managed carefully. Election campaigns are now fought through the media. Active members are not as crucial as they once were. Parties that are represented in parliament are able to draw some funds from tax-payers. They continue to need, and to seek, contributions from individual members and supporters, but in practice they rely heavily on corporate sponsorship – from trade unions and business in the case of Labour, and from business alone in other parties. Needless to say, the manner in which grassroots party members are treated, often bypassed, by their party leaders, can only reduce the rank-and-file's incentives to engage in long-term party political activity.

We should note that both Thatcherism and New Labour were initially the projects of small elites, who gained the acquiescence first of parliamentary colleagues, then, on the basis of electoral success, their parties in the country. Europe is a similar elite project. As yet there can be few people outside Brussels who are excited and enthusiastic about a future United States of Europe.

Politicians worry not so much about whether they are in touch (they know what voters are thinking) as whether they are trusted. On this they have cause for concern. In a 2006 survey, 63 per cent of UK voters said that they tended not to trust their local councils, national politicians, the national government, or political parties. This is not a UK-specific phenomenon: it is Euro-wide. Denmark is Europe's most trusting (in politicians) country and Poland is the least trusting. The scandal over MPs' expenses in 2009 was less likely a major cause than a spark that exposed the mistrust between politicians and voters. There is also periodic alarm at low voter turn-outs, especially in local and European elections, though in fact there has been no long-term decline in the proportion of electors who vote. There is constant discussion about possible constitutional reforms. Should there be proportional representation at Westminster and on local councils as well as in the Scottish parliament, the Welsh assembly, all elected bodies in Northern Ireland and the European parliament? Should there be elected regional assemblies in England? What about having elected mayors? The first (Ken Livingstone) was elected in London in 2000. It is doubtful whether any of these reforms will bring parties, politicians and the people closer together. Proportional representation can leave people feeling that, whoever they vote for, the same faces re-appear and fix things among themselves. Moreover, all the above reforms would increase the party machines' control over the individuals offered to the electorate on party lists for election to assemblies and parliament, and as candidates to become city bosses.

New issues and new social movements

Only a tiny proportion of citizens belong to a political party, but many more are politically active, and their numbers are more likely to be growing than shrinking. Any activity can be described as political if it involves mobilizing people in ways that exert pressure on politicians, civil servants, or commercial businesses. There have always been pressure groups which seek to influence public opinion and political parties rather than to replace them in government. So what are described as 'new social movements' have some familiar features. It is more the character of the campaigning groups, and the types of issues that they represent, that are novel. The new issues are said to arise from the interests of no particular classes, or any other specific sections of the population, and are said to actually create collective political actors.

New social movements are likely to have members, committees and officials, but this is not how most activists are involved. Rather than attending meetings, supporters are more likely to communicate via the internet and mobile phone. In this way, huge armies of demonstrators can sometimes be mobilized: the London demonstration against the war in Iraq in 2003, and the protests surrounding the 2009 meeting of the G20 in London, for example. These movements are networks rather than industrial-type organizations. Within the overall network there may be a large number of smaller networks that function independently. The movements often straddle national borders. Meetings of the world's leaders regularly attract protesters from all over the world, often under an 'anti-globalization' banner. Mysteriously, there are no leaders who can be deemed in control or responsible for the behaviour of these movements.

Henrik Bang (2003), a Danish political scientist, has identified two new types of political activists:

- Expert citizens, who tend to be professionals, who may work for or through voluntary associations, and who use their expert knowledge to influence politicians and civil servants.
- Everyday makers who do politics entirely in their own localities and workplaces, typically just for the intrinsic satisfaction, who help to sensitize people to issues, create an awareness of common concerns, and provoke fellow citizens to act (maybe by writing to an MP, signing a petition, or taking part in a boycott or buycott).

Yaojun Li and David Marsh (2008) have analysed the 2001 Home Office Citizenship Survey to identify and estimate the numbers of different kinds of political activists. They claim that in Britain:

- 8.4 per cent of the population are political activists who play an active role in political parties or trade unions.
- 15.0 per cent are expert citizens who act as leaders, and are often office holders, in their areas of interest in political parties, trade unions, professional associations, neighbourhood associations and other voluntary groups.
- 37.3 per cent are everyday makers, involved in some form of civic activity, either formally or informally, but not as expert citizens.

According to these estimates, only 39 per cent of the UK population can be described as wholly non-participant. Previously, political scientists had estimated that around a half of all adults were participating in politics solely by voting in elections, that a quarter were (for practical purposes) completely inactive, and that only the remaining quarter voted and did other things besides (Coxall and Robins, 1998). The 'other things' could include signing petitions, writing to MPs, and attending meetings and demonstrations. Li and Marsh offer a rather higher estimate. Some of the activity is informal, but much is co-ordinated by new social movements, or related to these movements'' issues. New social movements, it is said, raise issues that really capture people's interest, ignite their enthusiasm, and mobilize them into political action.

New social movements campaign for peace, animal welfare, the quality of our food and other environmental causes, gay rights, women's rights, civil rights for all or for particularly vulnerable groups, the right to life, or to abortion. It is claimed that these movements are characteristic of, and are engaged in the most important struggles about the character of, post-industrial societies. The movements are not based on pre-existing socio-demographic groups. Rather, the issues create the groups, which become movements. It is claimed that nowadays it is these movements, rather than the older political parties, that are addressing the basic faults in modern societies, mobilizing the people, and generating visions of alternative futures. In time, some believe, these movements will change the world. The growth of these movements has been likened to the earlier rise of the bourgeoisie, and subsequently the working class (see Galtung, 1986; Meier, 1988; Touraine et al, 1983).

The crucial issue for present purposes is not whether these movements really are destined to change the world, but the ways in which their development, and the extent to which they develop, affect the class-politics relationship. Now it is true that the new social movements do not explicitly appeal to any specific class interests. Rather, all the movements claim to represent 'the people'. In this sense the movements are classless. There is no class rhetoric, except in so far as some activists believe that their opponents are the political-industrial-military-financial establishment. 'Except' is probably the wrong word here, because this type of thinking implies at least an awareness of, and more likely an acute sensitivity to, the division between the upper class and the rest. In contrast, none of the movements see a major division of interest separating the working class from the middle class.

However, a fact of this matter is that the activists in all the new social movements are mainly from the non-conservative middle class. The activists are certainly not representative of 'the people' in general in terms of social backgrounds. They tend to be second generation middle class, university educated, to have above-average incomes, and professional jobs (see Gillham, 2008; Li et al, 2008). In these respects, they bear a canny resemblance to the mainstream 'political class'.

The middle class and the working class do not differ so much in their amounts as in their types of social capital (trusted social relationships). Working class social capital tends to be family and neighbourhood-based, created and sustained through informal relationships. Middle class social capital is also generated through, and facilitates participation in, wider social networks and formal kinds of civic engagement (Li et al, 2005). Some activists are active in several new social movements. While the movements may not seek to promote explicitly middle class interests, they are based on issues which, from the activists' profile, appear to be of greatest concern to the middle classes.

On the basis of their research among young Norwegians and the environmental movement, Ase Standbu and his colleagues have disputed this (see Standbu and Krange, 2003; Standbu and Skogen, 2000). They claim that support for environmental issues is widespread among all sections of Norwegian youth, but that only 2.1 per cent are members of the leading youth environmental action group, and they tend to be 'older' young females from a humanistic section of the middle class. Standbu and his colleagues claim that these activists unintentionally erect cultural barriers that inhibit wider participation. They are said to do this through their androgynous (genderless) style and more general middle class tastes and interests (see chapter 6). However, the fact that working class youth (in Norway) support environmental causes does not necessarily mean that these are the issues that are of greatest concern to them. The rise of these movements, and the insertion of their issues onto political agendas, are in fact political outcomes of the enlargement, and the progressive organization, of middle class opinion. Traditional working class issues – economic management to secure regular work and income, linking rewards to merit (skills, effort and hours worked), settling issues by collective agreement, guarantees of social security for all, and the extraction of crucial services from the market place – are sidelined on new political agendas.

Restructuring class and politics

De-alignment has not diminished the relevance of class theory. Class, and only class, can explain not just de-alignment but all the other long-term trends in the politics-society relationship: trends in support for Labour and the Conservatives, the general decline in partisanship, increased support for minor parties, and the rise of new social movements. All these developments are exactly what should be expected given the way in which the class structure has changed.

The upper class

For the upper class the late-twentieth century was a new dawn. With the collapse of communism, capitalism became a truly global system. Capital was able to globalize itself and harness new technology. Enterprises, their managers and workers, and even countries, have been placed in the position of needing to compete for capital. Capital is no longer throttled by regulation, burdened by taxation or threatened by trade unions. Representatives of the upper class advise one-and-all on how to become business-friendly. Ownership and control have been depersonalized. Investment appears a neutral force which rewards workers, firms and countries that are efficient and competitive. Business is willing to fund all business-friendly, and at least potentially powerful, political parties. Parties that are serious about seeking office need this sponsorship in order to campaign. So they are all business-friendly. The middle class is tempted with the prospect of extremely rewarding careers, for the successful. It is no surprise, therefore, that middle class radicalism is no threat to the capitalist economy. It is truly remarkable how the upper class escapes censure. Site closures that create unemployment, human resource management that creates precarious jobs, huge hikes to already huge directors' salaries: it seems that everything is tolerable if it is good for business.

The middle class

This class has grown in size, and has an expanding, inter-generationally stable core. It has taken over the leadership positions, and comprises the majority of the activists, not only in all significant political parties but also in new social movements. The threat of working class power had receded. Small wonder then that the middle class today is less securely attached to any single party than in previous years. Up to now the main political division within the middle class has been between the socially radical and the rest. The latter have mostly voted Conservative, while the former have voted for other parties, and some are active in new social movements. The Conservatives still benefit from being the traditional middle class party. Unless they have a particular reason to change, middle class adults from middle class Conservative families are most likely to continue to vote Conservative. The challenge for Britain's Conservative Party is to attract the upwardly mobile and socially radical. Up to now they have been more attracted by Labour and other (minor) parties.

The middle class is now too large to be ignored by any political party with pretensions to office. So none threaten middle class incomes with more progressive taxation. Indeed, all the parties seem to agree that the middle class must be provided with tax shelters. History may still tell the middle class that its interests lie with the Conservatives, but New Labour was desperate to prove otherwise.

However, at present none of the parties have answers to characteristic middle class discontents: of those whose career commitment is unrewarded, sometimes unwanted, whose career progress is blocked, or who are not given the opportunities that they feel their qualifications merit. Up to now the middle class's typical responses to its discontents have been non-political, though most who work in the public sector have become trade unionists, and likewise the lower and middling ranks in large, private sector businesses. However, the standard middle class responses to career discontents have been to try even harder, or to withdraw psychologically from work and engage in lifestyle politics, sometimes alongside involvement in new social movements.

The working class

During the last third of the twentieth century the entire working class became, in a sense, an excluded group. Many workers' links with the labour force became precarious or non-existent. They lost the protection of trade unions, in some cases through loss of employment, in others through moving to non-unionized firms, and in others because the unions to which they continued to belong were unable to defend them.

There are remnants of the working classes that were shaped earlier on. There is still an original working class of trade union members, living in rented accommodation, who remain in the Labour Party, and who would support Old Labour if that was still an option. The original working class culture is not completely extinct. Then there are still examples of the new working class that was created in the post-war years – employees in large, unionized firms, with well-paid jobs, who nowadays own their own homes and take regular overseas holidays. But the core of the new millennium working class is simply disorganized. At the end of the twentieth century, a sixth of all households which contained adults of working age had no-one in employment, and a third of all children were being born into poverty. The core members of today's working class are unemployed or in precarious jobs. None of the political parties have much to offer to this new working class.

All sections of the present-day working class know that they have failed to 'get on' while others who were reared in similar circumstances have done better. They do not necessarily blame themselves, but they know that others believe that they are responsible for their own problems, or, at any rate, that they should devise solutions by making themselves employable. They can, of course, hope that their children or grandchildren will benefit from their enhanced opportunities to get on. Politics, it must appear, has nothing more to offer. Even if it was possible to rebuild the old working class coalition, this would represent but a minority of the population. There is not even an agenda around which the working class might be re-mobilized. Key elements of the old working class agenda have ceased to inspire. Public ownership may have improved, but it did not transform, the status of workers. Public services are often poor quality, especially those on which the middle class has never depended. And workers find that they themselves need to pay for these services through taxation. There is no longer a vision of a better future. Hence the weakening of support for working class parties.

No-one can predict the future. This is one thing that we have learnt from nearly two centuries of sociology. The twenty-first century could be shattered by war. At the end of the nineteenth century, very few, if any, social theorists envisaged the new modern societies becoming more violent than their predecessors. Alternatively, the twenty-first century could be shaken by global economic collapse, eliminating everyone's savings and pushing life back to basics. There could be a nuclear, or a slower, ecological disaster. The international indications are that the most likely alternatives to class-based politics are politics based on national, ethnic, religious or regional populations and identities.

It is possible that UK party politics will become based upon two, three, four or more main parties, all acceptable to, and therefore funded by the upper class, run mainly by middle class activists, and with very few elected representatives from any other class. Such parties could compete, possibly with more or less equal success, for the votes of the intermediate and working classes. It will take a long time, generations rather than decades, for the historical legacy of class voting (middle class-Conservative, working class-Labour) to be expunged entirely, but this is the current direction of change.

What is to stop this development? If there are no disasters, and if nationalism is contained, the most likely disturbances will be through the mobilization of one or both of the two main classes, when one or more of the parties (probably in an effort to avert decline) decides that it needs to prioritize its traditional 'heartland' vote, or that it can enlarge its vote by appealing to a particular faction of an additional class. A remobilization of the working class would send the middle class scurrying back to a party that was prepared to put middle class interests first, and up to now most people have looked to the working class as the most likely source of a return to the mid-twentieth century brand of class politics. But the working class is no longer the mass of the people. It is disorganized and becoming more so. Its characteristic pre-occupations and associated values may well be as always, but the means to their realization (nationalization and the development of state services) that once ignited enthusiasm have been tarnished. All the current conditions are wrong for the rebirth of a modernized, but basically old style, working class politics.

In the twenty-first century it is more likely that the middle class will take the initiative, using its collective organizations – professional bodies and trade unions. Remember, the middle class is now more likely to be in trade unions than manual employees. There are widespread, often keenly felt, specifically middle class frustrations and aspirations which could be politicized. Working class politics might then be revived as a defensive response.

This is not a prediction. It is just one of several possible future scenarios. The crucial point is that all of the more likely political scenarios are class-linked in some way or another. Class analysis has been, and still is, the key to understanding the links between the economy, politics and society, how these have changed in the past, and the alternative ways in which they might change in the future.

Bibliography

Abercrombie N. and Turner B. S. (1978), 'The dominant ideology thesis', *British Journal of Sociology*, 29, 149–170.

Abercrombie N. and Warde A. (2000), *Contemporary British Society*, Third Edition, Polity Press, Cambridge.

Abbott P. (1987), 'Women's social class identification: does husband's occupation make a difference?' *Sociology*, 21, 91–103.

Abrams M., Rose R. and Hinden M. (1960), *Must Labour Lose?* Penguin, Harmondsworth.

Achterberg P. (2006), 'Class voting in the new political culture: economic, cultural and environmental voting in 20 Western countries', *International Sociology*, 21, 237–261.

Aldridge S. (2001), *Social Mobility: A Discussion Paper*. www.cabinet.office.gov.uk/innovation/papers/socialmobility.shtml.

Allatt P. and Yeandle S. M. (1991), *Youth Unemployment and the Family: Voices of Disordered Times*, Routledge, London.

Anderson B., Ruhs M., Rogaly B. and Spencer S. (2006), *Fair Enough? Central and East European Migrants in Low-Wage Employment in the UK*, Joseph Rowntree Trust, York.

Aronowitz S. and DiFazio W. (1994), *The Jobless Future: Sci-Tech and the Dogma of Work*, University of Minnesota Press, Minneapolis.

Arsenault A. and Castells M. (2008), 'Switching power: Rupert Murdock and the global business of media politics', *International Sociology*, 23, 488–513.

Arthur M. B., Inkson K. and Pringle J. K. (1999), *The New Careers: Individual Action and Economic Change*, Sage, London.

Ashton D., Felstead A. and Green F. (2000), 'Skills in the British workplace', in Coffield F, ed, *Differing Visions of a Learning Society: Research Findings, Volume 2*, Polity Press, Cambridge, 192–228.

Bagguley P. (1992), 'Social change, the new middle class and the emergence of new social movements: a critical analysis', *Sociological Review*, 40, 26–48.

Bagguley P. (1995), 'Middle class radicalism revisited', in Butler T and Savage M, eds, *Social Change and the Middle Classes*, UCL Press, London.

Bagguley P. and Mann K. (1992), 'Idle thieving bastards? Scholarly representations of the underclass', *Work, Employment and Society*, 6, 113–126.

Bain A. N. J. (1972), *Pilots and Management*, Allen and Unwin, London.

Bain G. S. (1970), *The Growth of White-Collar Trade Unionism*, Clarendon Press, Oxford.

Bang H. (2003), 'A new ruler makes a new citizen: cultural governance and everyday making', in Bang H, ed, *Governance as Social and Political Communication*, Manchester University Press, Manchester, 241–266.

Banks M., Bates I., Breakwell G., Bynner J., Emler N., Jamieson L. and Roberts K. (1992), *Careers and Identities*, Open University Press, Milton Keynes.

Barone C. (2006), 'Cultural capital, ambition and the explanation of inequalities in learning outcomes: a comparative analysis', *Sociology*, 40, 1039–1058.

Bauman Z. (1998a), *Work, Consumerism and the New Poor*, Open University Press, Buckingham.

Bauman Z. (1998b), *Globalization: The Human Consequences*, Polity Press, Cambridge.

Bechoffer F. and Elliott B, eds (1981), *The Petit Bourgeoisie: Studies of the Uneasy Stratum*, Macmillan, London.

Beck U. (1992), *Risk Society: Towards a New Modernity*, Sage, London.

Beck U. (2000), *The Brave New World of Work*, Polity Press, Cambridge.

Beck U. and Beck-Gernsheim E. (2009), 'Global generations and the trap of methodological nationalism for a cosmopolitan turn in the sociology of youth and generation', *European Sociological Review*, 25, 25–36.

Bennett T., Savage M., Silva E., Warde A., Gayo-Cal M. and Wright D. (2009), *Culture, Class, Distinction*, Routledge, London.

Berle A. A. and Means G. C. (1932), *The Modern Corporation and Private Property*, Macmillan, London.

Bernadi F. and Garrido L. (2008), 'Is there a new service proletariat? Post-industrial employment growth and social inequality in Spain', *European Sociological Review*, 24, 299–313.

Beynon H. (1973), *Working for Ford*, Penguin, Harmondsworth.

Beynon H., Grimshaw D., Rubery J. and Ward K. (2002), *Managing Employment Change*, Oxford University Press, Oxford.

Blackburn R. M. (1967), *Union Character and Social Class*, Batsford, London.

Blackburn R. M. (1998), 'A new system of classes: but what are they and do we need them?' *Work, Employment and Society*, 12, 735–741.

Blackburn R. M. and Mann M. (1979), *The Working Class in the Labour Market*, Macmillan, London.

Blanchflower D. G., Deeks A. J., Garrett M. D. and Oswald A. J. (1987), *Entrepreneurship and Self-Employment in Britain*, Department of Economics, University of Surrey, and Centre for Labour Economics, London School of Economics.

Blanden J., Gregg P. and Machin S. (2005), *Intergenerational Mobility in Europe and North America*, Centre for Economic Performance, London School of Economics.

Blanden J. and Machin S. (2007), *Recent Changes in Intergenerational Mobility in Britain*, Sutton Trust, London.

Blokland T. (2004), 'Memory magic: how a working class neighbourhood became an imagined community and class started to matter when it lost its base', in Devine F, Savage M, Scott J. and Crompton R, eds, *Rethinking Class: Culture, Identities and Lifestyle*, Palgrave Macmillan, Basingstoke.

BMRB International Limited (1997), *Prince's Youth Business Trust (PYBT 1 Scheme)*, Research Report 5, Department for Education and Employment, Sheffield.

Bogenhold D. and Stabler U. (1991), 'The decline and rise of self-employment', *Work, Employment and Society*, 5, 223–239.

Bond R. and Saunders P. (1999), 'Routes of success: influences on the occupational attainments of British males', *British Journal of Sociology*, 50, 217–249.

Bonney N. (2007), 'Gender, employment and social class', *Work, Employment and Society*, 21, 143–155.

Bottero W. (2004), 'Class identities and the identity of class', *Sociology*, 38, 985–1003.

Bottero W. (2005), *Stratification: Social Division and Inequality*, Routledge, London.

Bottero W. and Prandy K. (2003), 'Social interaction distance and stratification', *British Journal of Sociology*, 54, 177–197.

Bourdieu P. and Passeron J. D. (1977), *Reproduction in Education, Society and Culture*, Sage, London.

Bradley H. (1996), *Fractured Identities: Changing Patterns of Inequality*, Polity, Cambridge.

Bradley H. and Devadason R. (2008), 'Fractured transitions: young adults' pathways into contemporary labour markets', *Sociology*, 42, 119–136.

Braverman H. (1974), *Labour and Monopoly Capital*, Monthly Review Press, New York.

Breen R. and Goldthorpe J. H. (1999), 'Class inequality and meritocracy: a critique of Saunders and an alternative analysis', *British Journal of Sociology*, 50, 1–27.

Breen R. and Goldthorpe J. H. (2001), 'Class, mobility and merit: the experience of two British birth cohorts', *European Sociological Review*, 17, 81–101.

Breen R. and Whelan C. T. (1995), 'Gender and class mobility: evidence from the Republic of Ireland', *Sociology*, 29, 1–22.

Bridges W. (1995), *Job Shift*, Allen and Unwin, London.

Britten N. and Heath A. (1983), 'Women, men and class analysis', in Garmarnikow E., Morgan D., Purvis J. and Taylorson D, *Gender, Class and Work*, Heinemann, London.

Brown P. and Hesketh A. (2004), *The Mismanagement of Talent: Employability and Jobs in the Knowledge Economy*, Oxford University Press, Oxford.

Brown P. and Scase R. (1994), *Higher Education and Corporate Realities*, UCL Press, London.

Brown P. and Sparks R, eds (1989), *Beyond Thatcherism: Social Policy, Politics and Society*, Open University Press, Milton Keynes.

Brown R. K. and Brannen P. (1970), 'Social relations and social perspectives amongst shipbuilding workers: a preliminary statement', *Sociology*, 4, 71–84 and 197–211.

Buchholz S., Hofacker D., Mills M., Blossfeld H-P., Kurz K. and Hofmeister H. (2009), 'Life courses in the globalization process: the development of social inequalities in modern societies', *European Sociological Review*, 25, 53–71.

Buckingham A. (1999), 'Is there an underclass in Britain?' *British Journal of Sociology*, 50, 49–75.

Burchardt T. (2000), 'Social exclusion: concepts and evidence', in Gordon D. and Townsend P, eds, *Breadline Europe: The Measurement of Poverty*, Policy Press, Bristol, 385–405.

Burchell B. L., Day D., Hudson M., Lapido D., Mankelow R., Nolan J. P., Reed H., Wichert I. C. and Wilkinson F. (1999), *Job Insecurity and Work Intensification*, Joseph Rowntree Foundation, York.

Burnham J. (1941), *The Managerial Revolution*, John Day, New York.

Butler D. and Stokes D. (1974), *Political Change in Britain*, Macmillan, London.

Butler T. and Savage M, eds (1995), *Social Change and the Middle Classes*, UCL Press, London.

Bynner J., Ferri E. and Shepherd P, eds (1997), *Twenty-Something in the 1990s*, Ashgate, Aldershot.

Byrne D. (1995), 'Deindustrialisation and dispossession: an examination of social division in the industrial city', *Sociology*, 29, 95–115.

Cabinet Office (2009), *New Opportunities: Fair Chances for the Future*, Cm 7533, London.

Campbell N. (1999), *The Decline of Employment Among Older People in Britain*, CASE Paper 19, London School of Economics, London.

Campbell S., Bechoffer F. and McCrone D. (1992), 'Who pays the piper? Ownership and control in Scottish based management buyouts', *Sociology*, 26, 59–79.

Cannon I. C. (1967), 'Ideology and occupational community: a study of compositors', Sociology, 1, 165–185.

Carter R. (1985), *Capitalism, Class Conflict and the New Middle Class*, Routledge, London.

Casey R. and Allen C. (2004), 'Social housing managers and the performance ethos: towards a "professional project of the self"', *Work, Employment and Society*, 18, 395–412.

Chan T. W. and Goldthorpe J. H. (2004), 'Is there a status order in contemporary British society? Evidence from the occupational structure of friendship', *European Sociological Review*, 20, 383–401.

Chan T. W. and Goldthorpe J. H. (2007), 'Social stratification and cultural consumption: music and England', *European Sociological Review*, 23, 1–19.

Charles N. (1990), 'Women and class: a problematic relationship', *Sociological Review*, 38, 43–89.

Cloke P., Phillips M. and Thrift N. (1995), 'The new middle class and social constructs of rural living', in Butler T. and Savage M, eds, *Social Change and the Middle Classes*, UCL Press, London.

Coffield F., Borrill C. and Marshall S. (1986), *Growing Up at the Margins*, Open University Press, Milton Keynes.

Conley H. (2002), 'A state of insecurity: temporary work in the public services', *Work, Employment and Society*, 16, 725–737.

Connolly M., Roberts K., Ben-Tovim G. and Torkington P. (1992), *Black Youth in Liverpool*, Giordano Bruno, Culemborg.

Cotgrove S. (1982), *Catastrophe or Cornucopia?* Wiley, Chichester.

Cotgrove S. and Duff A. (1980), 'Environmentalism, middle class radicalism, and politics', *Sociological Review*, 28, 333–351.

Cotgrove S. and Duff A. (1981), 'Environmentalism, values and social change', *British Journal of Sociology*, 32, 92–110.

Coxall B. and Robins L. (1998), *Contemporary British Politics*, Macmillan, Basingstoke.

Cracknell R. (2005), *Social Background of MPs*, Standard Note 1528, House of Commons Library, London.

Craine S. and Coles B. (1995), 'Youth transitions and young people's involvement in crime', *Youth and Policy*, 48, 6–26.

Creighton C. (1996), 'The family wage as a class-rational strategy', *Sociological Review*, 44, 204–224.

Crewe I. (1977), 'Political dealignment in Britain, 1964–1974', *British Journal of Political Science*, 7, 129–190.

Crewe I. (1986), 'On the death and resurrection of class voting: some comments on How Britain Votes', *Political Studies*, 34, 620–638.

Crompton R. (1996a), 'The fragmentation of class analysis', *British Journal of Sociology*, 47, 56–67.

Crompton R. (1996b), 'Gender and class analysis', in Lee D. J. and Turner B. S, eds, *Conflicts About Class*, Longman, London, 115–126.

Crompton R. (1998), *Class and Stratification: An Introduction to Current Debates*, Polity, Cambridge.

Crompton R. and Jones G. (1984), *White-Collar Proletariat*, Macmillan, London.

Crompton R. and Sanderson K. (1986), 'Credentials and careers', *Sociology*, 20, 25–42.

Crompton R. and Scott J. (2000), 'Introduction: the state of class analysis', in Crompton R., Devine F., Savage M. and Scott J, eds, *Renewing Class Analysis*, Blackwell, Oxford.

Crosland A. (1956), *The Future of Socialism*, Cape, London.

Crossick G, ed (1977), *The Lower Middle Class in Britain*, 1870–1914, Croom Helm, London.

Dahrendorf R. (1959), *Class and Class Conflict in an Industrial Society*, Routledge, London.

Dale A., Gilbert G. N. and Arber S. (1985), 'Integrating women into class theory', *Sociology*, 19, 384–409.

Dale J. R. (1962), *The Clerk in Industry*, Liverpool University Press, Liverpool.

Davidson J. O. (1990), 'The road to functional flexibility: white-collar work and employment relations in a privatised public utility', *Sociological Review*, 38, 689–711.

Davidson J. O. (1990), 'The commercialisation of employment relations: the case of the water industry', *Work, Employment and Society*, 4, 531–549.

Davis N. J. and Robinson R. V. (1988), 'Class identifications of men and women in the 1970s and 1980s', *American Sociological Review*, 53, 103–112.

Dennis N., Henriques F. and Slaughter C. (1956), *Coal is our Life*, Eyre and Spottiswoode, London.

Denny C. (1999), 'You're only as insecure as you feel', *Guardian*, 2 November, 27.

Devadason R. (2007), 'Constructing coherence? Young adults' pursuit of meaning through multiple transitions between work, education and unemployment', *Journal of Youth Studies*, 10, 203–221.

Devine F. (1992), *Affluent Workers Revisited? Privatism and the Working Class*, Edinburgh University Press, Edinburgh.

Devine F. (1998), 'Class analysis and the stability of class relations', *Sociology*, 32, 23–42.

Devine F., Britton J., Mellor R. and Halfpenny P. (2000), 'Professional work and professional careers in Manchester's business and financial sector', *Work, Employment and Society*, 14, 521–540.

Devine F. and Savage M. (2000), 'Conclusion: renewing class analysis', in Crompton R., Devine F., Savage M. and Scott J, eds, *Renewing Class Analysis*, Blackwell, Oxford.

Dispatches (2009), 'Too old to work', *Channel 4 TV*, broadcast 9 February.

Doherty M. (2009), 'When the working day is through: the end of work as identity?' *Work, Employment and Society*, 23, 84–101.

Doogan K. (2001), 'Insecurity and long-term employment', *Work, Employment and Society*, 15, 419–441.

Dunkerley M. (1996), *The Jobless Economy?* Polity Press, Cambridge.

Durkheim E. (1893, 1938), *The Division of Labour in Society*, Free Press, Glencoe, Illinois.

Ebbinghaus B. and Visser J. (1999), 'When institutions matter: union growth and decline in Western Europe, 1950–1995', *European Sociological Review*, 15, 135–158.

Edgell S. and Duke V. (1991), *A Measure of Thatcherism*, Harper-Collins, London.

Egerton M. and Savage M. (2000), 'Age stratification and class formation: a longitudinal study of the social mobility of young men and women, 1971–1991', *Work, Employment and Society*, 14, 23–49.

Electoral Commission (2005), *Black and Minority Ethnic Survey*, Electoral Commission, London.

Erikson B. H. (1996), 'Culture, class and connections', *American Journal of Sociology*, 102, 217–251.

Erikson R. and Goldthorpe J. H. (1988), 'Women at class crossroads: a critical note', *Sociology*, 22, 545–553.

Erikson R. and Goldthorpe J. H. (1992), *The Constant Flux: A Study of Class Mobility in Industrial Societies*, Clarendon Press, Oxford.

European Commission (1998), *Job Opportunities in the Information Society*, European Commission, Luxembourg.

European Commission (2007), *European Social Reality*, Special Eurobarometer, Directorate-General Communication, Brussels.

European Commission, Directorate-General for Employment, Industrial Relations and Social Affairs (1999), *Employment in Europe 1998*, Office for Publications of the European Communities, Luxembourg.

European Commission, Directorate-General for Employment, Social Affairs and Equal Opportunities (2009), *Industrial Relations in Europe 2008*, Office for Official Publications of thee European Communities, Luxembourg.

Evans G. (1993), 'The decline of class divisions in Britain?' *British Journal of Sociology*, 44, 449–471.

Evans G. (1996), 'Putting men and women into classes?' *Sociology*, 30, 209–234.

Evans G. (1998), 'On tests of validity and social class: why Prandy and Blackburn are wrong', *Sociology*, 32, 189–202.

Evans G. (2006), *Educational Failure and Working Class White Children in Britain*, Palgrave Macmillan, Basingstoke.

Evans G. and Mills C. (1998), 'Identifying class structure: a latent class analysis of the criterion-related and construct validity of the Goldthorpe class scheme', *European Sociological Review*, 14, 87–106.

Eyal G., Szelenyi I. and Townsley E. (1998), *Making Capitalism Without Capitalists: The New Ruling Elites in Eastern Europe*, Verso Books, New York.

Felstead A., Gallie D. and Green F. (2002), *Work and Skills in Britain, 1986–2001*, Department for Education and Skills, London.

Felstead A., Jewson N. and Walters S. (2005a), *Changing Places of Work*, Macmillan, Basingstoke.

Felstead A., Jewson N. and Walters S. (2005b), 'The shifting locations of work: new statistical evidence on the spaces and places of employment', *Work, Employment and Society*, 19, 415–431.

Ferge Z. (1979), *A Society in the Making: Hungarian Society and Social Policy, 1945–75*, Penguin, Harmondsworth.

Field F. (1989), *Losing Out: The Emergence of Britain's Underclass*. Blackwell, London.

Fieldhouse E. and Hollywood E. (1999), 'Life After Mining: Hidden Unemployment and Changing Patterns of Economic Activity amongst Miners in England and Wales, 1981–1991', *Work, Employment and Society*, 13, 483–502.

Fielding T. (1995), 'Migration and middle class formation in England and Wales, 1981–91', in Butler T. and Savage M, eds, *Social Change and the Middle Classes*, UCL Press, London.

Forrest R. and Murie A. (1987), 'The affluent home owner: labour market position and the shaping of housing histories', *Sociological Review*, 35, 370–403.

Forrest R., Murie A. and Williams P. (1990), *Home Ownership, Differentiation and Fragmentation*, Unwin Hyman, London.

Forrester V. (1999), *The Economic Horror,* Polity Press, Cambridge.

Francis A. (1980), 'Families, firms and finance capital', *Sociology*, 14, 1–27.

Franklin M. (1985), *The Decline of Class Voting in Britain*, Oxford University Press, Oxford.

Fukuyama F. (1992), *The End of History and the Last Man*, Penguin, London.

Fulcher J. and Scott J. (1999), *Sociology,* Oxford University Press, Oxford.

Full Employment UK (1990), *Britain's New Underclass: Challenges for the Employment Services,* Full Employment UK, London.

Gallie D. (1994), 'Are the unemployed an underclass?' *Sociology*, 28, 737–757.

Gallie D. (1996), 'New technology and the class structure: the blue-collar/white-collar divide revisited', *British Journal of Sociology*, 47, 447–473.

Gallie D., Felstead A. and Green F. (2004), 'Changing patterns of task discretion in Britain', *Work, Employment and Society*, 18, 243–266.

Gallie D., Marsh C. and Vogler C, eds (1994), *Social Change and the Experience of Unemployment*, Oxford University Press, Oxford.

Gallie D. and Paugam S. (2003), *Social Precarity and Social Integration*, Directorate-General for Employment, Industrial Relations and Social Affairs, Brussels.

Gallie D. and White M. (1993), *Employee Commitment and the Skills Revolution*, Policy Studies Institute, London.

Gallie D., White M., Cheng Y. and Tomlinson M. (1998), *Restructuring the Employment Relationship*, Clarendon Press, Oxford.

Galtung J. (1986), 'The green movement', *International Sociology*, 1, 75–90.

Genov N. (1999), 'Risks of unemployment: global, regional, national', in Genov N, ed, *Unemployment: Risks and Reactions*, MOST/Friedrich Ebert Stiftung, Paris/Sofia.

Giddens A. (1973), *The Class Structure of the Advanced Societies*, Hutchinson, London.

Giddens A. (1998), *The Third Way: The Renewal of Social Democracy*, Polity Press, Cambridge.

Giddens A. (2000), *The Third Way and its Critics,* Polity Press, Cambridge.

Gillham P. F. (2008), 'Participation in the environmental movement: analysis of the European Union', *International Sociology*, 23, 67–93.

Glass D. V. (1954), *Social Mobility in Britain*, Routledge, London.

Goldthorpe J. H. (1969), 'Social inequality and social integration in Modern Britain', *Advancement of Science*, 26, 190–202.

Goldthorpe J. H. (1979), 'The current inflation: towards a sociological account', in Hirsch F. and Goldthorpe J. H, eds, *The Political Economy of Inflation*, Martin Robertson, London.

Goldthorpe J. H. (1983), 'Women and class analysis', *Sociology*, 17, 465–488.

Goldthorpe J. H, (1996), 'Class analysis and the re-orientation of class theory: the case of persisting differentials in educational attainment', *British Journal of Sociology*, 47, 481–505.

Goldthorpe J. H., Llewellyn C. and Payne C. (1987), *Social Mobility and Class Structure in Modern Britain*, Clarendon Press, Oxford.

Goldthorpe J. H., Lockwood D., Bechoffer F. and Platt J. (1969), *The Affluent Worker in the Class Structure*, Cambridge University Press, London.

Goldthorpe J. H. and Mills C. (2008), 'Trends in intergenerational class mobility in modern Britain: evidence from national surveys, 1972–2005', *National Institute Economic Review*, 205, 83–100.

Goldthorpe J. H. and Payne C. (1986), 'Trends in intergenerational class mobility in England and Wales, 1972–1983', *Sociology*, 20, 1–24.

Goos M. and Manning A. (2003), *Lousy and Lovely Jobs: The Rising Polarization of Work in Britain*, Working Paper, Centre for Economic Performance, London School of Economics, London.

Gorz A. (1999), *Reclaiming Work: Beyond the Wage-Based Society*, Polity Press, Cambridge.

Grainger H. and Crowther M. (2007), *Trade Union Membership 2006*, Department of Trade and Industry, London.

Gregson N. and Lowe M. (1994), *Servicing the Middle Classes*, Routledge, London.

Grimshaw D., Beynon H., Rubery J. and Ward K. (2002), 'The restructuring of career paths in large service sector organizations: "delayering", upskilling and polarisation', *Sociological Review*, 50, 89–116.

Gubbay J. (1997), 'A Marxist critique of Weberian class analyses', *Sociology*, 31, 73–89.

Hakim C. (1996), *Key Issues in Women's Work*, Athlone Press, London.

Halford S. and Savage M. (1995a), 'The bureaucratic career: demise or adaptation?' in Butler T. and Savage M, eds, *Social Change and the Middle Classes*, UCL Press, London.

Halford S. and Savage M. (1995b), 'Restructuring organisations, changing people: gender and restructuring in banking and local government', *Work, Employment and Society*, 9, 97–122.

Hall J. and Jones D. C. (1950), 'The social grading of occupations', *British Journal of Sociology*, 1, 31–55.

Hall S. (1988), *The Hard Road to Renewal*, Verso, London.

Hall S. and Jacques M, eds (1983), *The Politics of Thatcherism*, Lawrence and Wishart, London.

Halsey A. H., Heath A. F. and Ridge J. M. (1980), *Origins and Destinations*, Clarendon Press, Oxford.

Hanlon G. (1998), 'Professionalism as enterprise: service class politics and the redefinition of professionalism', *Sociology*, 32, 43–63.

Hayes B. C. and Jones F. L. (1992a), 'Marriage and political partisanship in Australia', *Sociology*, 26, 81–101.

Hayes B. C. and Jones F. L. (1992b), 'Class identification among Australian couples', *British Journal of Sociology*, 43, 463–483.

Hayes B. C. and Miller R. L. (1993), 'The silenced voice: female social mobility with particular reference to the British Isles', *British Journal of Sociology*, 44, 653–672.

Heath A. and Clifford P. (1996), 'Class inequalities and educational reform in twentieth century Britain', in Lee D. J. and Turner B. S, eds, *Conflicts About Class*, Longman, London.

Heath A., Evans G., Field J. and Witherspoon S. (1991), *Understanding Political Change: The British Voter, 1964–1987*, Pergamon Press, Oxford.

Heath A., Jowell R. and Curtice J. (1985), *How Britain Votes*, Pergamon Press, Oxford.

Heath A., Jowell R. and Curtice J. (2001), *The Rise of New Labour: Party Policies and Voter Choices*, Oxford University Press, Oxford.

Heath A. and Payne C. (1999), *Twentieth Century Trend in Social Mobility in Britain*, Working Paper 70, Centre for Research into Elections and Social Trends, University of Oxford, Oxford.

Heath A. and Savage M. (1995), 'Political alignments within the middle classes, 1972–89', in Butler T. and Savage M, eds, *Social Change and the Middle Classes*, UCL Press, London.

Herman E. S. (1981), *Corporate Control, Corporate Power*, Cambridge University Press, New York.

Higher Education Funding Council for England (2010), *Trends in Young Participation in Higher Education: Core Results for England*, Higher Education Funding Council for England, Bristol.

Hills J., Le Grand J. and Piachaud D, eds (2002) *Understanding Social Exclusion*, Oxford University Press, Oxford.

Hindess B. (1971), *The Decline of Working Class Politics*, MacGibbon and Kee, London.

Hoffman D. E. (2002), *The Oligarchs: Wealth and Power in the New Russia*, Public Affairs Ltd, Oxford.

Hoggart R. (1957), *The Uses of Literacy*, Chatto and Windus, London.

Hutton W. (1995), *The State We're In*, Jonathan Cape, London.

Iannelli C. and Paterson L. (2006), 'Social mobility in Scotland since the middle of the twentieth century', *Sociological review*, 54, 520–545.

Inglehart R. (1977), *The Silent Revolution*, Princeton University Press, New Jersey.

Inglehart R. (1997), *Modernization and Postmodernization: Cultural, Economic and Political Change in 43 Societies*, Princeton University Press, New Jersey.

Inkson K. and Coe T. (1993), *Are Career Ladders Disappearing?* Institute of Management, London.

International Labour Office (1962), *Workers' Self-Management in Yugoslavia*, International Labour Office, Geneva.

Jackson M. (2001), 'Non-meritocratic job requirements and the reproduction of class inequality: an investigation', *Work, Employment and Society*, 15, 619–630.

Jackson M. (2007), 'How far merit selection? Social stratification and the labour market', *British Journal of Sociology*, 58, 367–390.

Jackson M. (2009), 'Disadvantaged through discrimination? The role of employers in social stratification', *British Journal of Sociology*, 60, 669–692.

James D. R. and Soref M. (1981), 'Profit constraints on managerial autonomy', *American Sociological Review*, 46, 1–18.

Jessop B., Bonnett K., Bromley S. and Ling T. (1988), *Thatcherism: A Tale of Two Nations*, Polity Press, Cambridge.

Jones G. (2002), *The Youth Divide: Diverging Paths to Adulthood*, Joseph Rowntree Foundation, York.

Jordan B. and Redley M. (1994), 'Polarisation, underclass and the welfare state', *Work, Employment and Society*, 8, 153–176.

Kay T. (1996), 'Women's work and women's worth: implications of women's changing employment patterns', *Leisure Studies*, 15, 49–64.

Kellard K. and Middleton S. (1998), *Helping Unemployed People into Self-Employment*, Research Report 46, Department for Education and Employment, Sheffield.

Kentor J. and Suk Jang Y. (2004), 'Yes, there is a (growing) transnational business community: a study of global interlocking directorates 1983–98', *International Sociology*, 19, 355–368.

King R. and Nugent N, eds (1979), *Respectable Rebels*, Hodder and Stoughton, London.

Koyama Y. (1995), *Self-Managing Socialist Regime of the 1974 Constitution in Former Yugoslavia*, Faculty of Economics, Nilgata University, Japan.

Lampard R. (1995), 'Parents' occupations and their children's occupational attainments', *Sociology*, 29, 715–728.

Lampard R. (1996), 'Might Britain be a meritocracy?' *Sociology*, 30, 387–393.

Lane D. (1982), *The End of Social Inequality?* Allen and Unwin, London.

Lane D. and O'Dell F. (1978), *The Soviet Industrial Worker*, Martin Robertson, Oxford.

Lash S. and Urry J. (1987), *The End of Organised Capitalism*, Polity Press, Oxford.

Lawler S. (2005), 'Disgusted subjects: the making of middle class identities', *Sociological Review*, 53, 429–446.

Layard R. (2005), *Happiness: Lessons from a New Science*, Allen Lane, London.

Lee D. J. and Turner B. S, eds (1996), *Conflicts About Class*, Longman, London.

Leiulfsrud H. and Woodward A. (1987), 'Women at class crossroads: repudiating conventional theories of family class', *Sociology*, 21, 393–412.

Levitas R. (1998), *The Inclusive Society?: Social Exclusion and New Labour*, Macmillan, Basingstoke.

Levitas R. (2004), 'Let's hear it for Humpty: social exclusion, the third way and social capital', *Cultural Trends*, 13, 41–56.

Lewis O. (1959), *Five Families: Mexican Case Studies in the Culture of Poverty*, Basic Books, New York.

Lewis R. and Maude A. U. E. (1949), *The English Middle Classes*, Phoenix House, London.

Li Y. (2002), '"Falling off the ladder?" Professional and managerial career trajectories and unemployment experiences', *European Sociological Review*, 18, 253–270.

Li Y., Bechhofer F., Stewart R., McCrone D., Anderson M. and Jamieson L. (2002), 'A divided working class? Planning and career perception in the service and working classes', *Work, Employment and Society*, 16, 617–636.

Li Y., Devine F. and Heath A. (2008), *Equality Group Inequalities in Education, Employment and Earnings: A Research Review and Analysis of Trends over Time*, Research Report 10, Equality and Human Rights Commission, Manchester.

Li Y. and Marsh D. (2008), 'New forms of political participation: searching for expert citizens and everyday makers', *British Journal of Political Science*, 38, 247–272.

Li Y., Pickles A. and Savage M. (2005), 'Social capital and social trust in Britain', *European Sociological Review*, 21, 109–123.

Li Y., Savage M. and Warde A. (2008), 'Social mobility and social capital in contemporary Britain', *British Journal of Sociology*, 59, 391–411.

Lindsay C. (2003), 'A century of labour market change: 1900 to 2000', *Labour Market Trends*, March, 133–144.

Lockwood D. (1958), *The Blackcoated Worker*, Allen and Unwin, London.

Lockwood D. (1966), 'Sources of variation in working class images of society', *Sociological Review*, 14, 249–267.

Lupton R., Sigle-Rushton W., Obolenskaya P., Sabates R., Meschi E., Kneale D. and Salter E. (2009), *Growing Up in Social Housing in Britain*, Tenant Service Authority, London.

MacDonald R. (1994), 'Fiddly jobs, undeclared working and the something for nothing society', *Work, Employment and Society*, 8, 507–530.

MacDonald R. (1996), 'Welfare dependency, the enterprise culture and self-employed survival', *Work, Employment and Society*, 10, 431–447.

MacDonald R. and Coffield F. (1991), *Risky Business? Youth and the Enterprise Culture*, Falmer, Lewes.

MacDonald R. and Marsh J. (2005), *Disconnected Youth: Growing Up in Britain's Poor Neighbourhoods*, Palgrave Macmillan, Basingstoke.

MacKenzie R., Stuart M., Forde C., Greenwood I., Gardiner J. and Perrett R. (2006), '"All that is solid?" Class identity and the maintenance of a collective orientation among redundant steelworkers', *Sociology*, 40, 833–852.

Mann K. (1991), *The Making of an English Underclass*, Open University Press, Milton Keynes.

Mann M. (1970), 'The social cohesion of liberal democracy', *American Sociological Review*, 35, 423–439.

Mann M. (1973), *Consciousness and Action in the Western Working Class*, Macmillan, London.

Marks A. and Baldry C. (2009), 'Stuck in the middle with who? The class identity of knowledge workers', *Work, Employment and Society*, 23, 49–65.

Marmot Review (2010), *Fair Society, Healthy Lives*, University College London, London. www.ucl.ac.uk/marmotreview Accessed 11 February 2010.

Marsden D. (1982), *Workless*, Croom Helm, London.

Marsh C. (1988), 'Unemployment in Britain', in Gallie D, ed, *Employment in Britain*, Blackwell, Oxford.

Marshall G., Rose D., Newby H. and Vogler C. (1988), *Social Class in Modern Britain*, Hutchinson, London.

Marshall G. and Swift A. (1996), 'Merit and mobility', *Sociology*, 30, 375–386.

Marshall G., Swift A. and Roberts S. (1997), *Against the Odds?* Clarendon Press, Oxford.

Marshall T. H. (1950), *Citizenship and Social Class and Other Essays*, Cambridge University Press, Cambridge.

Martin B. (1998), 'Knowledge, identity and the middle class: from collective to individualized class formation', *Sociological Review*, 46, 653–686.

Martin J. and Roberts C. (1984), *Women and Employment: A Lifetime Perspective*, HMSO, London.

Marx K. (1962), 'The class struggles in France 1848–1850', in Marx K. and Engels F, *Selected Works, Volume I*, Lawrence and Wishart, London.

Mattausch J. (1989), 'The peace movement', *International Sociology*, 4, 217–225.

Mattausch J. (1989), *A Commitment to Campaign*, Manchester University Press, Manchester.

Matthews M. (1978), *Privilege in the Soviet Union*, Allen and Unwin, London.

McGovern P., Hope-Bailey V. and Stiles P. (1998), 'The managerial career after downsizing: case studies from the leading edge', *Work, Employment and Society*, 12, 457–477.

McKendrick J., Scott G. and Sinclair S. (2007), 'Dismissing disaffection: young people's attitudes towards education, employment and participation in a deprived community', *Journal of Youth Studies*, 10, 139–160.

Meager N. (1992), 'The fall and rise of self-employment (again): a comment on Bogenhold and Stabler', *Work, Employment and Society*, 6, 127–134.

Meier A. (1988), 'The peace movement – some questions concerning its social nature and structure', *International Sociology*, 3, 77–87.

Metcalf H. (1998), *Self-Employment for the Unemployed: The Role of Public Policy*, Research Report 47, Department for Education and Employment, Sheffield.

Mills C. (1994), 'Who dominates whom? Social class, conjugal households and political identification', *Sociological Review*, 42, 639–663.

Mills C. (1995), 'Managerial and professional work histories', in Butler T and Savage M, eds, *Social Change and the Middle Classes*, UCL Press, London.

Milner A. (1999), *Class*, Sage, London.

Morris L. (1992), 'The social segregation of the long-term unemployed in Hartlepool', *Sociological Review*, 40, 344–369.

Morris L. and Irwin S. (1992), 'Employment histories and the concept of the underclass', *Sociology*, 26, 401–420.

Mulholland K. (1998), 'Survivors versus movers and shakers: the reconstitution of management and careers in the privatised utilities', in Thompson P. and Warhurst C, eds, *Workplaces of the Future*, Macmillan, Basingstoke.

Murray C. (1984), *Losing Ground: American Social Policy, 1950–1980*, Basic books, New York.

Murray C. (1990), *The Emerging British Underclass*, Institute of Economic Affairs, London.

Murray C. (1994), *Underclass: The Crisis Deepens*, Institute of Economic Affairs, London.

Nakao K. and Treas J. (1992), *The 1989 Socioeconomic Index of Occupations: Construction from the 1989 Occupational Prestige Scores*, GSS Methodological Report No 74, National Opinion Research Centre, Chicago.

National Equality Panel (2010), *An Anatomy of Economic Inequality in the UK*, Government Equalities Office, London.

Newby H. (1977) *The Deferential Worker*, Allen Lane, London.

Nichols T. and Armstrong P. (1976), *Workers Divided*, Fontana, London.

Nichols T. and Davidson J. O. (1993), 'Privatisation and economism: an investigation among producers in two privatised utilities in Britain', *Sociological Review*, 41, 705–730.

Noble T. (2000), 'The mobility transition: social mobility trends in the first-half of the twenty-first century', *Sociology*, 34, 35–51.

Noon M. and Blyton P. (1997), *The Realities of Work*, Macmillan, Basingstoke.

Oborne P. (2007), *The Triumph of the Political Class*, Simon and Schuster, London.

Oesch D. (2008), 'The changing shape of class voting: an individual-level analysis of party support in Britain, Germany and Switzerland', *European Societies*, 10, 329–355.

Ophem, van J. and Hoog, de K. (1998), 'Differences in leisure behaviour of the poor and the rich in the Netherlands at the beginning of the 1990s', in Kloetze, te J. W, ed, *Family and Leisure in Poland and the Netherlands*, Garant, Leuven-Apeldoorn, 115–132.

Organisation for Economic Cooperation and Development (2010), *Economic Policy Reforms: Going for Growth 2010*, Organisation for Economic Cooperation and Development, Paris.

Pahl R. (1989), 'Is the emperor naked? Some questions on the adequacy of sociological theory', *International Journal of Urban and Regional Research*, 13, 709–720.

Pakulski J. and Waters M. (1996), *The Death of Class*, Sage, London.

Panel on Fair Access to the Professions (2009), *Unleashing Aspiration*, Cabinet Office, London.

Parkin F. (1968), *Middle Class Radicalism*, Manchester University Press, Manchester.

Patterson S. (1965), *Dark Strangers: A Study of West Indians in London*, Penguin, Harmondsworth.

Payne G. (1999), 'Does economic development modify social mobility?', paper presented to *British Sociological Association Conference*, Glasgow.

Payne G. and Grew C. (2005), 'Unpacking "class ambivalence": some conceptual and methodological issues in accessing class cultures', *Sociology*, 39, 893–910.

Payne G. and Roberts J. (2002), 'Opening and closing the gates: recent developments in male social mobility in Britain', *Sociological Research Online*, 6, 4.

Payne J. (1987), 'Does unemployment run in families?' *Sociology*, 21, 199–214.

Payne J. (1989), 'Unemployment and family formation among young men', *Sociology*, 23, 171–191.

Penn R., Rose M. and Rubery J. (1994), *Skill and Occupational Change*, Oxford University Press, Oxford.

Peterson R. A. (1992), 'Understanding audience segmentation: from elite and mass to omnivore and univore', *Poetics*, 21, 243–282.

Peterson R. A. and Kern R. M. (1996), 'Changing highbrow taste: from snob to omnivore', *American Sociological Review*, 61, 900–907.

Phillips T. and Western M. (2004), 'Social change and social identity: postmodernity, reflexive modernisation and the transformation of social identities in Australia', in Devine F., Savage M., Scott J. and Crompton R, eds, *Rethinking Class: Culture, Identities, Lifestyle*, Palgrave Macmillan, Basingstoke, 163–185.

Pollock G. (1997), 'Uncertain futures: young people in and out of employment since 1940', *Work, Employment and Society*, 11, 615–638.

Prandy K. (1965), *Professional Employees*, Faber, London.

Prandy K. (1990), 'The revised Cambridge scale of occupations', *Sociology*, 24, 629–655.

Prandy K. (1998a), 'Deconstructing classes: critical comments on the revised social classification', *Work, Employment and Society*, 12, 743–753.

Prandy K. (1998b), 'Class and continuity in social reproduction: an empirical investigation', *Sociological Review*, 46, 340–364.

Prandy K. and Blackburn R. M. (1997), 'Putting men and women into classes: but is this where they belong?' *Sociology*, 31, 143–152.

Prandy K. and Bottero W. (2000), 'Social reproduction and mobility in Britain and Ireland in the nineteenth and early twentieth centuries', *Sociology*, 34, 265–281.

Prandy K. and Lambert P. (2003), 'Marriage, social distance and social space: an alternative derivation and validation of the Cambridge Scale', *Sociology*, 37, 397–411.

Prowse P. and Turner R. (1996), 'Flexibility and coal', *Work, Employment and Society*, 10, 151–160.

Purcell K., Hogarth T. and Simm C. (1999), *Whose Flexibility?* Joseph Rowntree Foundation, York.

Rannie A. (1985), 'Is small beautiful?' *Sociology*, 19, 213–224.

Randle K. (1996), 'The white coated worker: professional autonomy in a period of change', *Work, Employment and Society*, 10, 737–753.

Reay D. (2004), '"Mostly roughs and toughs": social class, race and representation in inner-city schooling', *Sociology*, 38, 1005–1023.

Redman T., Wilkinson A. and Snape E. (1997), 'Stuck in the middle? Managers in building societies', *Work, Employment and Society*, 11, 101–114.

Reich R. R. (1991), *The Work of Nations: A Blueprint for the Future*, Simon and Schuster, London.

Reid I. (1998), *Class in Britain*, Polity Press, Cambridge.

Reiss Jr, A. J. (1961), *Occupations and Social Status*, Free Press, Glencoe, Illinois.

Rex J. and Moore R. (1967), *Race, Community and Conflict: A Study of Sparkbrook*, Oxford University Press, London.

Rex J. and Tomlinson S. (1979), *Colonial Immigrants in a British City*, Routledge, London.

Riach K. and Loretto W. (2009), 'Identity work and the "unemployed" worker: age, disability and the lived experience of the older unemployed', *Work, Employment and Society*, 23, 102–119.

Ridig W., Bennie L. G. and Franklin M. N. (1991), *Green Party Members: A Profile*, Delta Publications, Glasgow.

Robbins Report (1963), *Higher Education*, HMSO, London.

Roberts B. C., Loveridge R. and Gennard J. (1972), *Reluctant Militants*, Heinemann, London.

Roberts K., Barton A., Buchanan J. and Goldson B. (1997), *Evaluation of a Home Office Initiative to Help Offenders into Employment*, Home Office, London.

Roberts K. and Chadwick C. (1991), *Transitions into the Labour Market: The New Routes of the 1980s,* Youth Cohort Series 16, Research and Development Series 65, Employment Department, Sheffield.

Roberts K., Clark C. S., Cook F. G. and Semeonoff E. (1977), *The Fragmentary Class Structure*, Heinemann, London.

Roberts K. and Parsell G. (1991), 'Young people's sources and levels of income, and patterns of consumption in Britain in the late-1980s', *Youth and Policy*, 35, December, 20–25.

Roberts S. and Marshall G. (1995), 'Intergenerational class processes and the asymmetry hypothesis', *Sociology*, 29, 43–58.

Robertson D. (1984), *Class and the British Electorate*, Blackwell, Oxford.

Robinson W. I. and Harris J. (2000), 'Towards a global ruling class? Globalization and the transnational capitalist class', *Science and Society*, 64, 11–54.

Rojek C. (2000), 'Leisure and the rich today: Veblen's thesis after a century', *Leisure Studies*, 19, 1–15.

Rose D. (1998), 'Once more unto the breach: in defence of class analysis yet again', *Work, Employment and Society*, 12, 755–767.

Rose D. and Harrison E. (2007), 'The European Socio-Economic Classification: a new social class scheme for comparative European research', *European Societies*, 9, 459–490.

Rose D. and O'Reilly K, eds (1997), *Constructing Classes*, ESRC/ONS, Swindon.

Rose R. and McAllister I. (1990), *The Loyalties of Voters*, Sage, London.

Routh G. (1965), *Occupations and Pay in Great Britain*, 1906–1960, Cambridge University Press, London.

Roux, Le B., Rouanet H., Savage M. and Warde A. (2008), 'Class and cultural division in the UK', *Sociology*, 42, 1049–1071.

Runciman W. G. (1990), 'How many classes are there in contemporary British society?' *Sociology*, 24, 377–396.

Rutter M. and Madge N. (1976), *Cycles of Disadvantage*, Heinemann, London.

Sarlvik B. and Crewe I. (1983), *Decade of Dealignment*, Cambridge University Press, Cambridge.

Sassen S. (1991), *The Global City: New York, London, Tokyo,* Princeton University Press, NJ.

Saunders P. (1978), 'Domestic property and social class', *International Journal of Urban and Regional Research*, 2, 233–251.

Saunders P. (1981), 'Beyond housing classes: the sociological significance of private property rights in the means of consumption', *International Journal of Urban and Regional Research*, 5, 202–227.

Saunders P. (1990), *A Nation of Home Owners*, Unwin Hyman, London.

Saunders P. (1995a), 'Might Britain be a meritocracy?' *Sociology*, 29, 23–41.

Saunders P. (1995b), *Capitalism: A Social Audit*, Open University Press, Buckingham.

Saunders P. (1997), 'Social mobility in Britain: an empirical evaluation of two competing explanations', *Sociology*, 31, 261–288.

Saunders P. and Harris C. (1994), *Privatization and Popular Capitalism*, Open University Press, Milton Keynes.

Savage M. (2000), *Class Analysis and Social Transformation*, Open University Press, Buckingham.

Savage M. (2005), 'Working class identities in the 1960s: revisiting the Affluent Worker study', *Sociology*, 39, 929–946.

Savage M., Bagnall G. and Longhurst B. (2001), 'Ordinary, ambivalent and defensive: class identities in the northwest of England', *Sociology*, 35, 875–892.

Savage M., Bagnall G. and Longhurst B. (2004), 'Local habitus and working class culture', in Devine F., Savage M., Scott J. and Crompton R., eds, *Rethinking Class: Culture, Identities and Lifestyle*, Palgrave Macmillan, Basingstoke.

Savage M., Barlow J., Dickens P. and Fielding T. (1992), *Property, Bureaucracy and Culture*, Routledge, London.

Savage M. and Egerton M. (1997), 'Social mobility, individual ability and the inheritance of class inequality', *Sociology*, 31, 645–672.

Sayer A. (2002), 'What are you worth? Why class is an embarrassing subject', *Sociological Research Online*, 7, 3.

Sayer A. (2005), *The Moral Significance of Class*, Cambridge University Press, Cambridge.

Scase R. and Goffee R. (1989), *Reluctant Managers*, Unwin Hyman, London.

Scott J. (1982), *The Upper Classes*, Macmillan, London.

Scott J. (1991), *Who Rules Britain?* Polity Press, Cambridge.

Scott J. (1997), *Corporate Business and Capitalist Classes*, Oxford University Press, Oxford.

Scott J. and Griff C. (1984), *Directors of Industry: The British Corporate Network, 1904–76*, Polity Press, Oxford.

Seabrook J. (1971), *City Close-Up*, Allen lane, London.

Searle-Chatterjee M. (1999), 'Occupations, biography and new social movements', *Sociological Review*, 47, 258–279.

Sennett R. (1998), *The Corrosion of Character: The Personal Consequences of Work in the New Capitalism*, Norton, New York.

Skeggs B. (1997), *Formations of Class and Gender*, Sage, London.

Skeggs B. (2004), *Class, Self, Culture*, Routledge, London.

Sklair L. (2000), 'The transnational capitalist class and the discourse of globalization', http://www.theglobalsite.ac.uk/press/012sklair.htm.

Sklair L. (2001), *The Transnational Capitalist Class*, Blackwell, Oxford.

Smith C. (1987), *Technical Workers: Class, Labour and Trade Unions*, Macmillan, Basingstoke.

Stanworth M. (1984), 'Women at class crossroads: a reply to Goldthorpe', *Sociology*, 18, 159–170.

Stewart S., Prandy K. and Blackburn R. M. (1980), *Social Stratification and Occupations*, Macmillan, London.

Strandbu A. and Krange O. (2003), 'Youth and the environmental movement – symbolic inclusions and exclusions', *Sociological Review,* 51, 177–198.

Strandbu A. and Skogen K. (2000), 'Environmentalism among Norwegian youth: different paths of attitudes and action?' *Journal of Youth Studies,* 3, 189–209.

Sullivan A. (2001), 'Cultural capital and educational achievement', *Sociology,* 35, 893–912.

Sullivan O. and Katz-Gerro T. (2007), 'The omnivore thesis revisited: voracious cultural consumers', *European Sociological Review,* 23, 123–137.

Surridge P. (2007), 'Class belonging: a quantitative exploration of identity and consciousness', *British Journal of Sociology,* 58, 207–226.

Sutton Trust (2005), *The Educational Backgrounds of Members of the House of Commons and the House of Lords,* Sutton Trust, London.

Sutton Trust (2009), *The Educational Backgrounds of Leading Lawyers, Journalists, Vice Chancellors, Politicians, Medics and Chief Executives,* Sutton Trust, London.

Sutton Trust (2010), *The Educational Backgrounds of Members of Parliament in 2010,* Sutton Trust, London.

Svallfors S. (2005), 'Class and conformism: a comparison of four Western countries', *European Societies,* 7, 255–286.

Swift A. (2004), 'Would perfect mobility be perfect?' *European Sociological Review,* 20, 1–11.

Tampubolon G. (2010), 'Social stratification and cultures hierarchy among the omnivores: evidence from the Arts Council England surveys', *Sociological Review,* 58, 1–25.

Taylor I., Evans K. and Fraser P. (1996), *A Tale of Two Cities,* Routledge, London.

Taylor M. P. (1994), *Earnings, Independence or Unemployment?* Working Paper 26, British Household Panel Survey, University of Essex.

Taylor R. (2002), *Britain's World of Work – Myths and Realities,* Economic and Social Research Council, Swindon.

Thiel D. (2007), 'Class in construction: London building workers, dirty work and physical cultures', *British Journal of Sociology,* 58, 227–251.

Thompson P. (1983), *The Nature of Work,* Macmillan, London.

Touraine A., Hegedus Z., Dubet F. and Wievorka M. (1983), *Anti-Nuclear Protest,* Cambridge University Press, Cambridge.

Travis A. (1999), 'Sex in the 90s: the young take a moral stand', *Guardian,* 29 December, 3.

Traxler F. (1996), 'Collective bargaining and industrial change: a case of disorganisation?' *European Sociological Review,* 12, 271–287.

Truss C. J. G. (1993), 'The secretarial ghetto: myth or reality. A study of secretarial work in England, France and Germany', *Work, Employment and Society,* 7, 561–584.

Turnbull P. and Wass V. (1994), 'The greatest game no more – redundant dockers and the demise of dock work', *Work, Employment and Society,* 8, 487–506.

Turner G. (1963), *The Car-Makers,* Eyre and Spottiswoode, London.

Turok I. and Edge N. (1999), *The Jobs Gap in Britain's Cities: Employment Loss and Labour Market Consequences,* Policy Press, York.

Tyler M. and Abbott P. (1998), 'Chocs away: weight watching in the contemporary airline industry', *Sociology,* 32, 433–450.

Watt P. (1996), 'Social Stratification and Housing Mobility', *Sociology,* 30, 533–550.

Walby S. (1999), 'The new regulatory state: the social powers of the European Union', *British Journal of Sociology,* 50, 118–140.

Walkerdine V., Lucey H. and Melody J. (2001), *Growing Up Girl: Psychosocial Explorations of Gender and Class*, Macmillan, Basingstoke.

Walsh T. J. (1990), 'Flexible labour utilisation in the private service sector', *Work, Employment and Society*, 4, 517–530.

Warde A. (1995), 'Cultural change and class differentiation: distinction and taste in the British middle classes, 1968–88', in Roberts K, ed, *Leisure and Social Stratification*, Leisure Studies Association, Publication 53, Eastbourne.

Warde A., Martens L. and Olsen W. (1999), 'Consumption and the problem of variety: cultural omnivorousness, social distinction and dining out', *Sociology*, 33, 105–127.

Warhurst C. and Thompson P. (1998), 'Hands, hearts and minds: changing work and workers at the end of the century', in Thompson P and Warhurst C, eds, *Workplaces of the Future*, Macmillan, Basingstoke.

Watson T. and Harris P. (1999), *The Emergent Manager*, Sage, London.

Weakliem D. (1989), 'Class and party in Britain, 1964–1983', *Sociology*, 23, 285–297.

Webb J. (1999), 'Work and the new public service class?' *Sociology*, 33, 747–766.

Webb J. (2004), 'Organizations, self-identities and the new economy', *Sociology*, 38, 719–738.

Weiner M. J. (1981), *English Culture and the Decline of the Industrial Spirit*, Cambridge University Press, Cambridge.

Werfhorst, Van de H. D. and Graaf, de N. D. (2004), 'The sources of political orientation in post-industrial society: social class and education revisited', *British Journal of Sociology*, 55, 211–235.

Westergaard J. (1992), 'About and beyond the underclass: some notes on the influence of social climate on British sociology', *Sociology*, 26, 575–587.

Westergaard J. (1994), *Who Gets What?* Polity Press, Cambridge.

Westergaard J. and Resler H. (1975), *Class in a Capitalist Society*, Heinemann, London.

Whelan C. T. and Maitre B. (2008), 'Social class variation in risk: a comparative analysis of the dynamics of economic vulnerability', *British Journal of Sociology*, 59, 637–659.

Whitburn J. et al (1976), *People in Polytechnics*, Society for Research into Higher Education, Guildford.

Whitley R. (1973), 'Commonalities and connections among directors of large financial institutions', *Sociological Review*, 21, 613–632.

Whyte W. H. (1957), *The Organization Man*, Anchor Books, New York.

Wilkinson R. and Pickett K. (2009), *The Spirit Level: Why More Equal Societies Almost Always Do Better*, Allen Lane, London.

Wilson W. J. (1987), *The Truly Disadvantaged: The Inner-City, the Underclass and Public Policy*, University of Chicago Press, Chicago.

Windolf P. (1998), 'Elite networks in Germany and Britain', *Sociology*, 32, 321–351.

Witz A. (1992), *Professions and Patriarchy*, Routledge, London.

Wright D. (1994), *Workers Not Wasters*, Edinburgh University Press, Edinburgh.

Wright E. O. (1979), *Class, Crisis and the State*, Verso, London.

Wright E. O. (1985), *Classes*, Verso, London.

Wright E. O. (1994), *Interrogating Inequality*, Verso, New York.

Wright E. O. (1996), *Class Counts*, Cambridge University Press, Cambridge.

Wright E. O. (2000), 'Working class power, capitalist class interests, and class compromise', *American Journal of Sociology*, 105, 957–1002.

Wright-Mills C. (1956), *White-Collar*, Galaxy, New York.

Wring D. (2005), *The Politics and Marketing of the Labour Party,* Palgrave Macmillan, Basingstoke.

Wynne D. (1998), *Leisure, Lifestyle and the New Middle Class,* Routledge, London.

Yanowich M. (1977), *Social and Econo0mi Inequality in the Soviet Union,* Martin Robertson. London.

Young M. and Willmott P. (1957), *Family and Kinship in East London,* Routledge, London.

Zipp J. F. and Plutzer E. (1996), 'Wives and husbands: social class, gender and identification in the US', *Sociology,* 30, 235–252.

Zweig F. (1961), *The Worker in an Affluent Society,* Heinemann, London.

Zweig F. (1976), *The New Acquisitive Society,* Brian Rose, London.

Index

omnivore thesis, 145–146
Ophem, J van, 145, 246
O'Reilly, K, 20, 133, 248
Organisation for Economic Cooperation and Development, 205, 246
organisation man, 142
Oswald, A J, 236
outsourcing, 71, 123
  public services, 93
over-class *see* upper class
over-qualified workers, 62
owner occupation, 214
ownership functions, 23
Oxbridge, 176, 178, 224–225

Pahl, R, 10, 246
Pakulski, J, 221, 246
Panel on Fair Access to the Professions, 187, 191, 207, 246
Parkin, F, 154, 181, 246
Parsell, G, 152, 248
Partisanship, in politics, 217–218
part-time employment, 52, 55
Passeron, J D, 205, 236
Paterson, L, 199, 243
Patterson, S, 97, 246
Paugam, S, 62, 241
Payne, C, 241–242
Payne, G, 12, 67–69, 184, 190, 193–194, 200, 247
Payne, J, 103, 247
pecuniary orientations, 86–87
pendulum migrants, 78
Penn, R, 61, 247
pension funds, 167–168
pension schemes, occupational, 167–168
PEPs, 149
Perrett, R, 245
Peterson, R A, 145, 247
petit bourgeoisie, 121–127, *see also* self-employment
Phillips, M, 238
Phillips, T, 12, 247
Piachaud, D, 243
Pickett, K, 1–2, 251
Pickles, A, 244
planning, middle- and working-class attitudes, 152
Platt, J, 84, 241
Plutzer, E, 41, 252
Poland, 227
Policy Action Teams, 100
political parties, 7
  campaigning, 226–228
  contraction of support, 217–218

funding, 178, 227
membership, 152, 218
minor parties, 218–219
Northern Ireland, 218–219
populist, 95, 216
Scotland, 219
Wales, 218
political socialisation, 217
politicians
  backgrounds, 152, 223, 226
  ethnicity, 223, 226
  gender, 196, 226
  political class, 226–228
politics
  career, 152
  class and, 12–14, 219–223
  effects of share-ownership, 170–171
  party support, 150–151
  working class, 147
Poll Tax, 211
Pollock, G, 53, 247
Portugal, 1
post-Fordism, 54–55, 106, 142, 195
post-industrialism, 54, 229
post-modern thought, 4
posted workers, 56
power model, 83
poverty, 83
Powell C, 98
Prandy, K, 9, 33–34, 36, 117, 199–200, 236, 247, 249
precarious jobs, 56
Prince's Youth Business Trust, 122
Pringle, J K, 235
privatisation of nationalised industries, 72, 93
privatism, new working class, 85, 88
productive resources, control
Prowse, P, 90, 247
public sector employment, 72
Purcell, K, 56, 247
Purvis, J, 236

race, 4, *see also* ethnicity
Rainnie, A, 127, 247
Randle, K, 136, 247
rational action theory, 206–207
Reagan, R, 99
Reay, D, 95, 247
Redley, M, 102, 243
Redman, T, 135, 149, 152, 247
Reed, H, 236
Registrar General's Social Classes, 14, 19–20
regulatory state, 53

voting
  age, 222
  gender, 222
  ethnic groups, 222–223

Wait P, 170, 250
Walby, S, 153, 250
Walkerdine, V, 11, 119, 121, 139, 149, 188, 250
Walsh, T J, 89, 251
Walters, S, 221, 240
Ward, K, 236, 243
Warde, A, 12, 145–146, 236, 244, 248, 251
Warhurst, C, 61, 251
Wass, V, 90, 250
Waters, M, 221, 246
Watson, T, 137, 143, 251
Weakliem, D, 221, 251
wealth, 156
Webb, J, 61, 144, 148, 251
Weber, M, 6–7, 22, 35
Weiner, M J, 174, 251
welfare state, 105
Werfhorst, H D Van de, 216, 251
Westergaard, J, 33, 87, 97, 251
Western, M, 12, 247
Whelan, C T, 25, 41, 236, 251
Whitburn, J, 202, 251
White, M, 61, 134, 241
white-collar workers, 112
  proletariat, 115–116
  trade unions, 116–118
  see also non-manual workers
Whitley, R, 176, 251
Whyte, W H, 142, 251
Wichert, I, 236
Wievorka, M, 250
Wilkinson, A, 247
Wilkinson, F, 236
Wilkinson, R, 1–2, 251
Williams, P, 241
Willmott, P, 83, 252
Wilson, W J, 98, 251
Windolf, P, 173, 251
Witherspoon, S, 242
Witz, A, 131, 251
women
  and class analysis, 38–44
  class assignment, 38–43
  employment, 42

office employment, 69
part-time employment, 55
Woodward, A, 43, 244
work commitment, 53, 61, 103
work intensification, 61, 135
work situation, 22, 123
Workfare, 99, 101
workforce
  age composition, 75–77
  composition, 75–79
  dispersal, 70–75
working class, 80–107, 232–233
  communities, 81
  composition, 75–79
  current trends, 66, 88–97
  decline, 88
  deferential, 83
  demography, 70
  devaluation, 93–95
  disempowerment, 93–95
  embourgeoisement, 93–95
  ethnic composition, 75
  gender, 75
  leisure, 81, 85, 94
  new, 84–88, 89–90
  original, 80–82
  respectable and rough, 81–82, 94
  skill, 81
  us–them mentality, 81, 83
working on the move, 74–75
working time
  ceiling, 91
  lengthening, 61
World Bank, 51, 166
World Trade Organization, 51, 166
Wright, D, 103, 236
Wright, E O, 6, 25, 28–33, 251
Wright-Mills, C, 113, 251
Wring, D, 215, 252
Wynne, D, 145, 252

Yanowich, M, 2, 252
Yeandle, S M, 103, 235
Yong Suk Jang, 176
Young, M, 83, 252
Youth Training Schemes, 122
Yugoslavia, 2

Zipp, J F, 41, 252
Zweig, F, 84, 252